THE
CAUSES
OF
QUARREL

THE
CAUSES
OF
QUARREL

Essays on Peace, War, and Thomas Hobbes

Edited by
Peter Caws

BEACON PRESS
Boston

Beacon Press
25 Beacon Street
Boston, Massachusetts 02108-2800

Beacon Press books
are published under the auspices of
the Unitarian Universalist Association of Congregations.

"An Irish Airman Foresees His Death" by William Butler Yeats is
reprinted with permission of Macmillan Publishing Co. from *The
Poems of W. B. Yeats: A New Edition*, edited by Richard J.
Finneran, © 1919 by Macmillan Publishing Co.; © renewed 1947
by Bertha Georgie Yeats; and by permission of A. P. Watt Limited,
on behalf of Michael B. Yeats and Macmillan (London) Ltd.

96 95 94 93 92 91 90 89   1 2 3 4 5 6 7 8

Text design by Hunter Graphics

Library of Congress Cataloging-in-Publication Data
The Causes of quarrel : essays on peace, war, and Thomas Hobbes /
edited by Peter Caws.
p. cm.
Bibliography: p.
Includes index.
ISBN 0-8070-1410-9
1. Hobbes, Thomas, 1588–1667—Contributions in concepts of peace
and war. 2. Hobbes, Thomas, 1588–1667—Contributions in doctrine of
man. 3. Philosophical anthropology—History—17th century.
4. Peace (Philosophy)—History—17th century. 5. War (Philosophy)—
History—17th century. I. Caws, Peter.
B1248.P4C38 1989
320'.01—dc20   89-42592

Contents

Acknowledgments

The editor gratefully acknowledges the practical and financial help of the Office of the Vice-President for Academic Affairs at the George Washington University, the skilled and conscientious collaboration of the Division of Continuing Education at that university, the generous support of the John Merck Fund, and the invaluable assistance of Karen Greisman.

One

Introduction:
Philosophy and Politics

Peter Caws

Politics is in general indifferent to philosophy, except in cases of open ideological interest (as in communist countries) or in the contingent overlapping of the two domains in persons or groups (as frequently in Western Europe and very occasionally in the United States). We have to look back to an earlier epoch to find in the American experience a closer interaction of the philosophical and political domains. Their association in the eighteenth century was due less to the fact that the founding principles of the Republic were derived at least in part from the thought of philosophers—traditionally and notoriously Montesquieu and Locke but many others as well—than to the fact that the founders themselves (especially Franklin, Jefferson, and the authors of the *Federalist*) embodied a philosophical spirit and approached the construction of the new nation with resources of reflection and argument hardly equalled since in any comparable body of statesmen.

This interaction was celebrated in the Bicentennial Symposium of Philosophy held in New York in 1976. The working title for that symposium was "Philosophy in the Life of a Nation," by which was meant not merely philosophy in American life but philosophy as a component in any fully realized and responsible national life. Given the profile of the participants, however, the papers presented, as well as the resulting book, inevitably emphasized philosophy as such and, insofar as any national considerations were evoked, its relation to the American experience. Indeed, the book came to be called simply *Two Centuries of Philosophy in America.*[1]

In 1987 at the second Bicentennial, that of the Constitution, the question of philosophy in national life was certainly still pertinent. But in rethinking the issue, an international component imposed itself. If we ask what problems the Convention faced in 1787, the answer is, among other things, how to strike various national balances: balances between centralized and decentralized power, between popular government and a kind of representative meritocracy, between rights implicit and rights explicit, between peaceful commerce and military preparedness, and so on. But if we ask what comparable problems we face at the end of the twentieth century, the question has to be posed in a global context. The balances that now need to be struck are different: they concern the relation between world government, regional government, and the proliferation of small states; between the uncontrolled accumulation of riches and the forcible or voluntary distribution of goods with a view to the elimination of poverty; between old and new patterns of family life and population control; between individualism and collectivism; and finally and above all, between violence and negotiation as means of resolving conflicts, in view of potentialities for violence of new orders of magnitude.

Current conditions in the world, then, pose a challenge to philosophers to realize the connection between politics and philosophy in an international context. In particular, conceptual work on the nature of and conditions for peace continues to be needed. But that topic is strongly polarized in ideological terms: most of the putatively philosophical work devoted to it comes from ideologically committed or fringe groups, and the use of the term "peace" itself is automatically construed as a move in the cold war. This was brought home to me by one of the events that, along with the Bicentennial of the Constitution, provided the original stimulus for this book.

There were two such events, both personal, and they can be located precisely in time and place. One occurred in Montreal in August 1983, and the other in Palermo in September 1985. During the Seventeenth World Congress of Philosophy, in Montreal, there was a reception in the Soviet consulate. At an appropriate moment the consul raised his glass to "peace." We all drank, but I overheard some of my North American colleagues saying to one another that of course he hadn't really meant it, that one couldn't really trust him to have meant *peace*, not as we understand it at least. And I remembered a similar skepticism on the part of friends from the other side of the Iron Curtain about the use of that word by political figures in the West.

The semantic suspicion attaching to the use of the language of peace was still in my thoughts two years later when I was in Palermo for a meeting of the Steering Committee of the International Federation of Philosophical Societies. I had in the meantime proposed the concept of peace as a focus for the scholarly activity of the federation in the quinquennium 1983–88, but my suggestion had been received with a skepticism entirely consistent with that suspicion: the secretary-general of the federation dismissed the idea as politically dangerous, though whether he meant dangerous to the federation, to the profession, to philosophy itself, or indirectly to his own person, it was hard to tell.

Perhaps he did mean the latter, given the violence of Italian politics—though no danger seems to me to excuse the world's leading organization in philosophy from tackling the world's most serious problem. In Palermo there was a good deal of agitation focused on the forthcoming Mafia trials, and I came upon a poster advertising the position of a regional feminist group as "No alla Mafia" and expressing the hope that honest Sicilians might in the future live peaceably together free of this scourge. I began to reflect on what "mafia" meant. Like the French *défi* it means defiant bragging, but like *défi* and "defiance" it derives from *fides*, or "faith." The original mafiosi defied the law because they had no faith in it, no confidence in its justice.

Since part of the agenda in Palermo had to do with the planning of the World Congress of 1988, and since 1988 would be the quatercentenary of the birth of Hobbes, I was thinking about Hobbes too. The notion of "diffidence" as one of the causes of quarrel in his *Leviathan* suddenly joined itself to the lexical cluster on which I had been meditating. It seemed to me that here might be an approach to the problem of peace, not as an absence of hostility but as a condition of mutual confidence. The idea of trust, of covenant (*covenant*, a coming together in mutual trust), obviously belongs to the very word "peace," *pax* being connected to *pango pangere*, "to fasten or fix," in its perfect form *pepigi pactum*, "to settle or agree upon." To address issues of confidence, agreement, understanding, and their negatives seemed to be a way into the subject that might be free of ideological snares. Further, Hobbes's unease in the face of the risk of civil war bore, I thought, an uncanny resemblance to our unease at similar risks of world war. "Fear and I were twins," said he, speaking of his birth in the year of the Armada. In our case, fear of a nuclear holocaust has become everyone's familiar (and the contempt that such familiarity breeds is one aspect of the problem).

These, then, were some of the considerations that led me to convene, in Washington in the summer of 1987, a colloquium on the "causes of quarrel" in Hobbes's *Leviathan*, which gave rise to this book. Hobbes's three candidates for this category are *competition, diffidence,* and *glory.* All three are complex concepts as he uses them, but all are relevant, some in unexpected ways, to international disputes as well as to the civil conflicts in which he saw them operating. It is perhaps easiest to see the importance of the idea of competition, as embodied in armies, markets, and games. But the idea of diffidence clearly applies to defense, espionage, treaty obligations, and indeed to the cold war in general (including mistrust of others' use of the rhetoric of peace). The idea of glory as Hobbes understands it is also of striking interest in connection with religious, ethnic, and political pride, which actively impede peaceful moves in some notorious local conflicts (Ireland, the Middle East) but also play a role in nationalistic and ideological confrontations across major world boundaries.

Hobbes is sometimes considered to have been on the wrong side in the political debate that led to the American Revolution and the founding of the United States; his doctrine of absolute sovereignty seems too closely allied with the hereditary monarchy from which the colonies were struggling to liberate themselves. But the founders learned from him, more or less directly (Madison's preoccupation in the *Federalist* with "the design of political institutions to manage social conflict" is said by Frank Coleman, for example, to be "derived from Hobbes"),[2] and the problem he addressed, of the uncertainty of civilized life under the constant threat of war, is still with us.

The kind of war Hobbes had chiefly in mind was civil war, but by now, with the reduced effective size of the planet (to the dimensions of a "global village" in one popular if melodramatic formulation), many of us experience his uneasiness in a world context. And if we cannot accept his solution to the problem (there being apart from all the other relevant considerations no satisfactory analogue of the sovereign at the international level), we can still learn from his formulation of it.

Hobbes, then, is an essential part of the background to the eighteenth-century problem of the political foundations of civil order; the Constitution of the United States is to date, and at the national level, the most successful and most enduring solution to that problem. What the Constitution succeeded in doing was to create *a federation without a sovereign*—that is, a set of mutual covenants that would hold, regionally at least, without a higher power to enforce them, something Hobbes thought impossible. (The question as to what happened to this arrangement over the course of time— whether, for example, the defense of the Union in 1861–65 counted as an exercise of Hobbesian sovereignty—will not be pursued here.)

The Pursuit of Peace

What if we could bring to bear on the generalized or international form of Hobbes's problem the kind of attention the founders of the United States brought to bear on its national form? Of course the concept of international organization is ideologically loaded, especially in view of the various Internationals active in the late nineteenth and early twentieth centuries. American politics has often been (understandably if not always justifiably) uneasy in an international context, as among other things the histories of the League of Nations and UNESCO and the World Court demonstrate.

Pursuing peace is therefore easier said than done. In organizing the colloquium and preparing this book, I must admit to having sometimes been prey to a very complex set of feelings, which ranged from unreality and futility on the one hand to possibility and hope on the other. The sense of unreality was, I think, partly because of the location of the university in which the colloquium was held and in which I work. The State Department and the White House are within ten minutes' walk, and what is done there surely has momentous consequences for world peace. What, by contrast, could possibly be the consequences of what we might say? Yet we felt impelled to speak, and we feel impelled to keep thinking and talking about peace as long as war continues to be a risk.

This sense of unreality was compounded by the fact that part of our implicit agenda dealt with something that none of us knew directly. There may, to be sure, have been some combat veterans among us—as far as that goes, I myself have vivid memories of the German bombing of London—so it is not a question of being wholly inexperienced. Still, we all realize that war and peace would not be the issues they are if it were not for the nuclear threat, and none of us knows at first hand what nuclear war is like. I have argued elsewhere that we can't even imagine it—it's what I call an "off-scale" concept, and that means that people manage quite comfortably not to think about it at all most of the time. Our insistence on thinking about it serves perhaps some need to testify. Sartre, writing about writing in 1947, says in effect that his generation will not be forgiven if future generations have to say of it: They saw disaster coming and said nothing.

But by now nobody can complain that nothing is being said—the problem is that huge numbers of people are saying things and still the risk looms. I was struck, in preparing the colloquium, by the massive proliferation of concerned if sometimes eccentric groups of well-intentioned people devoted to peace. If, for example, we could only have had our meeting a few weeks later, we would have been able to spend seven minutes, along with a great many other people, visualizing "Earth being calm and serene and Earth, sun and humanity being in harmonious confluence." We would thus, according to one of the more exotic of these groups, have had a causal influence on the chances for peace—not only because warlike events are correlated to sunspot activity (a fact that, if shown, we would certainly have to consider for what it was worth), but because the Academy for Peace Research, from whose literature I quote, was conducting a "three-year study to see if people, by consciously visualizing, meditating, or praying together *in time synchronization,* could quiet Earth's magnetic field or the Sun's activity and thereby help to bring about more peaceful conditions." (The moving spirit behind this study wrote, in regretting his absence from our Washington meeting, that he had gone to California and was temporarily without funds or gainful employment; he also said that, being acquainted with the philosophy of science, I could probably sense the difficulties he encountered in getting the results of this experiment published.)

I really do not mean to make fun here, since any benign intention, no matter how bizarrely expressed, deserves respect. It also must be conceded that even more sober groups, and there are many of them, have not had much better luck in getting their point across. On the other hand, the claim might equally well be made that these groups are all immensely successful, since there hasn't yet been a full-scale nuclear war. An acquaintance of mine who also regretted his inability to attend the colloquium, an executive of a large foundation who runs its program "Avoiding Nuclear War"—that is what it says on his letterhead—tells me that every morning he congratulates himself, observing that the world is still in one piece, on the continuing success of his mission. However, there is too much extant hardware, and too much research and money devoted to improving and deploying it, to inspire this kind of confidence generally. Such an attitude can be (and in the case in question presumably is) adopted ironically, but it represents all the same, in most cases, a way of dealing with reality by refusing or making light of our danger.

Hobbes and Political Realism

One thing that Hobbes cannot be accused of is self-deception about the political realities of his time. He has a somber view of the human condition unconstrained by covenants; like Rousseau he believes in taking "men as they are" and is willing to think of "laws as they might be."[3] But unlike Rousseau, Hobbes refrains from romanticizing the men. The nature of the human he reads unapologetically from himself. It isn't a matter of observing the behavior of others, which can only lead to varied results according to "the constitution individuall, and particular education" of this person or nation and that, but of recognizing "the similitude of *Passions*" that each of us can find within; these passions arise from a material base, the motion of inward parts, which is common to humankind.[4]

It is from such inwardly observed facts about the human beings we are that Hobbes derives the state of nature, that is, the condition of species life before society, which would (and indeed sometimes does) obtain in the absence of agreed political order. State-of-nature arguments are a stock in trade of political philosophy; they represent a return to the elements of the problem, starting from which a reconstruction of the actual situation can produce new understanding and perhaps new strategies for action. The familiar features of Hobbes's state of nature, which have by now become clichés, are that it is a war of all against all, and that in it "the life of man [is] solitary, poore, nasty, brutish, and short" (p. 186). But for Hobbes there is a more fundamental human characteristic than these, one indeed that in the absence of social bonds precisely explains that war and that misery of life. It is that human beings have been created *equal.*

My use of "created" here is deliberate but not Hobbesian. Hobbes says, at the very beginning of the chapter in his *Leviathan* entitled "Of the NATURALL CONDITION of Mankind, as concerning their Felicity, and Misery":

> Nature hath made men so equall, in the faculties of body, and mind; as that though there bee found one man sometimes manifestly stronger in body, or of quicker mind then another; yet when all is reckoned together, the difference between man, and man, is not so considerable, as that one man can thereupon claim to himselfe any benefit, to which another may not pretend, as well as he. (p. 183)

"Created" is intended to link this passage with another, more simply expressed, which at a distance of 126 years is almost certainly its direct descendant. I mean, of course, "We hold these truths to be self-evident, that all men are created equal . . ."[5] Hobbes's argument for the principle of equality, at least in mental faculties, follows strictly from his principle of self-observation: everyone observes this equality in himself or herself, and this is shown by a general unwillingness to admit that anyone else is wiser than oneself: "For there is not ordinarily a greater signe of the equall distribution of any thing, than that every man is contented with his share" (p. 184).

It is just this equality that, unconstrained, makes people prey on one another's goods, anticipate such predations, and hence mistrust one another and vie with one another: thus competition, diffidence, and glory emerge as the causes of quarrel. The only way that Hobbes can see to constrain equality is to have individuals mutually renounce their claims to individual sovereignty, vesting collective sovereignty in the Leviathan. Hobbes seems to have chosen this name for its allusion to size and strength, and to underscore the futility of individual efforts at influence or control, believing as he clearly did that in the modern state the power and apparatus of government would have to be of monstrous proportions and overwhelmingly convincing authority. In Hebrew the word means "sea monster," and the whole of the forty-first chapter of the book of Job is devoted to God's recital of Leviathan's awesome characteristics, of which the last is "He is a king over all the children of pride" (Job 41:34). Its other biblical connotations, which would have been immediately recognized by Hobbes's readers—and which were certainly not overlooked by Hobbes—include both playfulness ("This great and wide sea, wherein are things creeping innumerable, both small and great beasts. There go the ships: there is that leviathan, whom thou hast made to play therein," Psalms 104:25–26) and crookedness ("In that day the LORD with his sore and great and strong sword shall punish leviathan the piercing serpent, even leviathan that crooked serpent," Isaiah 27:1). But these playful and crooked hermeneutic readings of the Leviathan are of less interest here than its embodiment of authority.

Leviathan is called by Hobbes an "Artificiall Man," that is, an agent formed by (political) art, who will exercise sovereignty on everyone's behalf so as to restrain violence and establish justice. It is worth noting here that in spite of an understandable prejudice that links sovereignty with the idea of kingship, (to the extent of inserting a spurious "g" into the very word, by analogy with "reign"), the term "sovereign" actually derives from Latin *superanus*, or "highest one" (from *super*, "above"). So negotiations about sovereignty and the creation of the Leviathan mean, in effect, that instead of everyone's scrambling to be higher than anyone else, a manifestly contradictory and chaotic state of affairs, all agree to make one (whether an individual or small group) higher than the rest, conferring on it the position and power that will enable it to "keep them all in awe."

Competition for superiority, mistrust of foreign powers, national pride: these remain causes of quarrel at the international level. Reflection on the world situation since 1945 suggests that a partial sovereign has in fact emerged, to the degree at least that it represents the required power to keep all in awe: I mean nuclear weapons themselves, which have kept us all in exactly that posture. Such a sovereign is obviously not an agent, but its sovereignty (in the strict sense just specified) applies even with respect to the powers that manufacture and deploy it: they will not be fully in control if its force is unleashed. The description of Leviathan in Job is uncannily apt:

> By his neesings [sneezings] a light doth shine, and his eyes are like the eyelids of the morning.
> Out of his mouth go burning lamps, and sparks of fire leap out.
> Out of his nostrils goeth smoke, as out of a seething pot or cauldron.
> His breath kindleth coals, and a flame goeth out of his mouth.
> . . . .
> The sword of him that layeth at him cannot hold: the spear, the dart, nor the habergeon.
> He esteemeth iron as straw, and brass as rotten wood.

Just as Hobbes had to acknowledge the reality of human passions, so we have in the postwar world to acknowledge the superadded reality of the destructive energy that can be released in nuclear reactions.

The combination of traditional political realism, of which Hobbes was one of the earliest expositors, with what might be called "nuclear realism," yields a product that may be either most terrifying or most hopeful, according to the manner of the combination. Political realists (like Reinhold Niebuhr, Hans Morgenthau, George Kennan, and others) insist, like Hobbes, on the constitutive self-interest of human beings, and also on the role of power in resolving disputes between states. They are not moralists but pragmatists. In Niebuhr's words:

> What is lacking among . . . moralists, whether religious or rational, is an understanding of the brutal character of the behavior of all human collectivities, and the power of self-interest and collective egoism in all inter-group relations. Failure to recognize the stubborn resistance of group egoism to all moral and inclusive social objectives inevitably involves them in unrealistic and confused political thought. . . . They do not see that the limitations of the human imagination, the easy subservience of reason to prejudice and passion, and the consequent persistence of irrational egoism, particularly in group behavior, make social conflict an inevitability in human history, probably to its end.[6]

Combine this brutal nature with nuclear weapons as the means of conflict and the result is doomsday. But allow the reality of nuclear weapons to contradict the inevitability of conflict and the result is something like deterrence theory.

Now it was, as we have seen, the *reality* of conflict and of the human disposition to it that inspired Hobbes to devise the Leviathan, whose function was nevertheless to override the *inevitability* of conflict. Hobbes's realism consisted not merely in acknowledging the passions but in appreciating the possibility of a balance of forces between them. Nature is not abolished by politics but harnessed; what causes quarrel in the state of nature produces, once that waste of effort has been eliminated, just the things whose absence in a time of war or primitive insecurity Hobbes laments in a famous passage, which I paraphrase positively: "Industry; Culture of the Earth; Navigation, and use of commodities that may be imported by Sea; commodious Building; Instruments of moving and removing such things as require much force; Knowledge of the face of the Earth; an account of Time; Arts; Letters; and Society" (p. 186)—a veritable catalog of peace.

Given that that sinister quasi-sovereign, the Bomb, has in some measure left us free domestically to cultivate the fruits of peace, is there no better way to organize matters at the end of the first nuclear century? Hobbes's sovereign, whether individual or joint, was at least envisaged as being human, not some raging monster who would annihilate us all if not restrained. Can we learn anything in this matter from bodies of political thought that sprang from the civil conditions of England in the seventeenth century, bearing in mind that the same thought underlies our own Constitution? These were the background questions at the colloquium whose proceedings occupy the following pages. Not surprisingly it happened in this case, just as with the Bicentennial symposium to which I referred earlier, that the contributors, for the most part professional philosophers with specialist preoccupations, paid more attention to philosophical than to constitutional questions, so that the promise of the full title of the colloquium—"The Causes of Quarrel: Constitutional Sovereignty and International [Mis]Understanding"—was only partly realized. For obvious reasons, I have retained the American connection in this introduction, but it is not uniformly present throughout the remainder of the work.

The essays, most of which have been extensively rewritten by their authors since the colloquium, occur in the order in which the original papers were presented. They begin with a rousing challenge by Paul Churchill to the very foundations of political realism in the Hobbesian account of human nature, and a call for rethinking the moralist approach to peace and war in Tolstoy, among others. In the next chapter, Charles Griswold deals explicitly with the framing of the Constitution, with special reference to the founders' attitude to religious conflict, finding that it follows a middle way between the utopianism of Plato and the realism of Hobbes (the latter has to be supplemented, he suggests, if not by outright moralism, at least by a conception of good as well as of evil). In the third chapter, Rex Martin concentrates on some fruitful difficulties in Hobbes's doctrine of sovereignty in the context of a more general conception of authority.

There follow two essays that take the discussion into international territory, as it were: Anthony de Reuck's analysis of conflict as illuminated by a general theory of culture, and Daniel Farrell's careful working-out of the domestic/international parallel in Hobbesian terms, modifying the structure of (national) equality and leaving open the question of Hobbesian construal of a disposition to war in the international case. Jean Hampton and William Sacksteder next take up the most neglected of the causes of quarrel, namely, glory: Hampton conducts a penetrating and subtle analysis of the concept, concluding with its application to nations, as Hobbes might have seen them if he had been less radically individualist, while Sacksteder works out a scheme of international relations in terms of "rating," closely following Hobbes. Andrew Altman's chapter was originally a response to Hampton and Sacksteder and has kept that relationship in its enlarged form, noting that although the mutual esteem that holds between liberal democracies maintains peace even without military equality, there are still features of human nature whose malice makes Hobbes look like an optimist.

Margaret Chatterjee's contribution again takes up the theme of putative Hobbesian relations in a multinational world, finding that the war of all against all has given way to a "war of some against others," in which new strategies, democratic or nonviolent or both, make the situation more complex and perhaps in some ways more hopeful than it was in Hobbes's time. Charles Landesman, reminding us that Hobbes really did live hundreds of years ago and could not have anticipated some of the outrages of powerful and unrestrained sovereignty, invites a new look at anarchy as an alternative to the nation-state. And Peter Henrici brackets Hobbes historically, contrasting the modern view of war, mainly in Hegel, with the medieval Christian view in which peace is rooted in human nature as something independent of and deeper than the mere absence of war.

The conception of peace as positive is, again and finally, taken up by Gray Cox, with principled objections to the merely privative definition of peace as well as to the assumption that conflict is constitutive of the human condition. My own chapter, from which parts of this introductory essay have been detached (so that the two

11

can in some measure be read as one, anecdote and summary apart),
examines some of the warlike features of what we commonly call
peace and questions their necessity, with special reference to the
structure of command and countermand. The book closes with
Steven Lee's argument for positive peace, originally, again, a comment on the previous two papers as presented at the colloquium but
serving now as a reflective anchor for the collection as a whole.

Two

Hobbes and the Assumption of Power

R. Paul Churchill

It has been observed that while professional philosophy has not yet had a leading role in the analysis of the causes of international tension, many other disciplines are already deployed in this domain, among which military science, political science, sociology, conflict resolution, psychology, anthropology, systems analysis, international law, and history are only those that most readily come to mind. Faced with the need to assimilate the overwhelming body of information generated in these fields, it hardly should be surprising that, despite the renown of philosophy for its synthetical activities, individual philosophers have found this Herculean undertaking daunting. It is therefore hardly surprising that philosophy, as one discipline among many, has had a small role in increasing enlightenment about the causes of quarrel and international misunderstanding.

Furthermore, the fragmentation of intellectual activity is a distressingly pervasive experience shared by everyone who has attempted a serious study of the causes of war and the opportunities for peace among nations. This fragmentation registers at one extreme as the failure of many professional warriors and "nuclear theologians" to comprehend the human realities of war as represented by the horror of the concentration camp museum at Dachau, for example, or the shadows of human beings scorched onto concrete in Hiroshima. This fragmentation is more commonly the cause of the frustration and despair we experience in going from one book or report to the next and finding that the truth continues to be elusive because each study allows us to see the subject only through a narrow disciplinary slit. Thus despite our awareness of the commonality of problems and the overlay of themes in all of these studies, we have difficulty discovering through them a more fundamental, unified, and comprehensive understanding of the problems of war and peace.

This book draws together elements of discussion and research—the experience of constitutional order in the United States, Hobbes's study of human psychology and politics, and the uneasy coexistence of the superpowers—that are all fragments of the larger problem of world order. The hope of the conference from which this book emerged was that the synthetical activity of philosophy, understood in a broad sense, will help us overcome this fragmentation. Our purpose now is not only to encourage the cross-fertilization of ideas from different domains, but also to search for an underlying conceptual structure. Philosophy does not inquire into facts in the way that other disciplines do; rather, it asks about the methods by which we search for such facts, the grounds or reasons on the basis of which we assert them, and the concepts we use in formulating them. Thus, as philosophers, we will not in any straightforward way be thinking about the world as the military historian or psychologist does, for example; rather, what we will be thinking about is thinking about the world.[1] The results we seek therefore do not take the form of new facts. We hope instead to establish a new clarity about what are and aren't the old facts, and about the ways certain models or theories gain legitimization as a point of view while alternative models do not. In this way philosophy is both the critical study of existing conceptual structures and the speculative source of new ones.[2]

But perhaps the major task before us is not so much to grasp what is inherently difficult to understand as it is to see some familiar things in a new way, and to take a new attitude toward them. The ancient philosopher Heraclitus noted, "Men are estranged from what is most familiar and they must seek out what is in itself evident," and Norman Angell has written, "It is quite in keeping with man's curious intellectual history that the simplest and most important questions are those he asks least often."[3] Thus perhaps what we need most is a kind of awakening, to see familiar experiences in a new light, to view them from a perspective that is possible only by bringing together different orientations to the common problems of war and international order.

In my view, there is a major challenge to the success of this enterprise, that is, a major challenge to a philosophical inquiry about the causes of quarrel, and especially the attempt to evaluate ethically the uneasy coexistence of the great powers. This challenge comes from those who style themselves "political realists." Having taught

a graduate seminar on normative issues in U.S. foreign po
come to appreciate just how recalcitrant the realist posit
I would like to discuss briefly the realists' challenge, n
cause it may help frame some of the major issues witl. ..
are concerned, but in order to clarify what I mean by "understanding
in a new light."

The realist position, which has been especially influential since
the end of World War II, is represented by the works of Reinhold
Niebuhr, Hans Morgenthau, Kenneth Waltz, and George Kennan. It
is associated in the popular culture with Bismarck's concept of *real-
politik* and the notion of *raison d'etat*. The view maintains that
international politics is a struggle for survival, and it rejects both
the claim that moral judgment is applicable to diplomacy and the
claim that the actions of statesmen ought to be guided by moral
principles. Instead, realists argue that it is the responsibility of a
nation's leaders to seek the national interest with nothing more
than prudential concern for the interests of other actors in the international arena. Morgenthau puts this point very strongly: There
is, he says, for the nation, "but one guiding star, one standard for
thought, one rule for action, the national interest".[4]

The philosophical foundations of realism go all the way back to
Thrasymachus and Callicles in the dialogues of Plato and to the
Athenian generals of the Melian dialogue recorded by Thucydides.
The influence of Machiavelli, who proclaimed, "It is necessary for
a prince who wishes to maintain his position to learn how not to
be good", also cannot be overlooked.[5] But the major philosophical
support, the philosopher whom the realists might claim as their
very own, is Thomas Hobbes. The necessity of "national egoism"—
the view that a state's pursuit of its own interests justifies disregard
for moral standards that would otherwise constrain its actions—is
said to derive logically from the alleged Hobbesian "state of nature,"
which rules among nation-states.

This state of nature is said to be a state of war characterized
both by the expectation that every state, as an actor in the international arena, will behave as an egoist, and by the expectation that,
if a state fails to act egoistically, it will be victimized by other states.
Moreover, it is claimed as a condition of rationality that one must
have adequate assurance of the compliance of others before acting
on moral rules. Thus it is argued that while there are moral principles
or laws of nature in the state of nature, they do not bind to action
in the absence of a common power to ensure general compliance.
Indeed, no arrangement other than a supreme world government can
defeat the expectation of egoism, although the realists usually go
on to argue pessimistically, as Morgenthau does, that world govern-

ment is impossible either because no state will agree to an arrangement that will diminish its national sovereignty or because the effort
to achieve partial collective security will inevitably end in a world
war.

By relying upon the analogy between international affairs and
the Hobbesian state of nature, the so-called domestic analogy, the
political realist makes an interesting case for national egoism and
the skepticism of international morality that it entails. This is an
important argument because it links rationality with morality in an
apparently persuasive manner. In effect, the realist argues that there
is insufficient reason to accept moral rules unless it can be shown
that it is rational to do so. But given the state of nature, as a Hobbesian war of all against all, it is not rational to abandon national egoism
and adhere to moral rules.

What response can be made to the realists' appropriation of
Hobbes's philosophy? Among the alternatives, three are well known
and deserve brief comment. One response is to accept the domestic
analogy as an accurate description of international affairs and accept
Hobbes's view that the state of war can be ended only with the
creation of a sovereign capable of overawing all other actors. One
might go on to argue, as some world federalists seem to do, that
contrary to the realists, a world government is possible. But however
desirable a world government might be for other reasons, it seems
to me that this position concedes far too much to the realists. It
assumes the correctness of the domestic analogy; it assumes that
the only viable world government is some form of absolutism; and
it fails to consider that there may be alternative roads to peace that
do not require world government.

Another response is to challenge the realists' claim that Hobbes's
model gives a correct account of the justification of moral principles
for international affairs. Why should we accept the Hobbesian view
that moral rules impose obligations only when they can be shown
to be in the interests of everyone to whom they apply? Why take
the view, in short, that ethics is based only on enlightened self-
interest? After all, there are examples of "natural moral requirements," that is, certain principles that seem intuitively to impose
requirements on our actions regardless of considerations of possible
benefit and regardless of the presence or absence of expectations of reciprocal compliance. For example, the principle that one ought not
to cause unnecessary suffering and the principle that one ought to
help save a life if it can be done at acceptable cost and risk seem to
be candidates for status as natural moral requirements in this sense.

This response may be attractive to those who would adopt as
their model the example of the peaceful evolution of federation

offered by the Constitution of the United States. But as a genuine alternative to a Hobbesian sovereign who would compel compliance, the constitutional pattern seems to presuppose that independent and sovereign nation-states will have formed a constitutional order only because they have decided that such a system will promote their particular interests better than an anarchical state of nature. Thus, in addition to leaving the relationship between rationality and morality problematical, advocates of this alternative fail to prove that moral rules obligate states even when observing them is not perceived to be in the national interest. Moreover, from the point of view of leaders of countries like the United States and the Soviet Union, who prefer to believe that the best mix of national self-interest and morality comes from continuing present policies, those who make this response to the realists fail to give motivating or persuasive reasons why these political entities should leave the present "state of nature" and comply with rules governing just participation in institutions designed to produce a more lasting peace.

A third response to the realists involves challenging the empirical premise that international affairs is analogous to a Hobbesian state of nature; that is, it challenges the domestic analogy itself. It might be argued that states are not equals, that they are not the only significant actors in international affairs, that they are not analogous to individuals, and finally, that relations between states closely approximate an international community of interests because there are reliable expectations of reciprocal compliance.

It is something of a historical irony that the international tumult and disorder that was known as the Thirty Years' War, which made such a strong impression on Hobbes while he was writing *Leviathan*, was succeeded by a system of international order in Europe that lasted for almost one hundred years, although without the presence of an overwhelming Hobbesian sovereign. The *Leviathan* was published in 1651, but three years earlier, in 1648, the Peace of Westphalia had laid the foundations for the modern state system.

The Westphalian system was based on the identification of the nation with the state, the concept of the state as a sovereign or supreme authority over a defensible, largely impermeable territory, and equality among sovereign states. The system was a response to the fragmentation of traditional authority resulting from the Thirty Years' War and the consequent decentralization of power in Europe. But to a large extent, it was also a system of ordered expectations that involved, at least partially, the normative principles of neutrality and nonintervention and the doctrine of just war, a system that attempted to avert catastrophic major wars through mechanisms such as the "balance of power."

17

Today there is much interest among international economists and political scientists in the way monetary policies, trade practices, and other cooperative activities have led to the emergence of new "regimes" that are understood to be "sets of recognized principles, norms, and decision-making procedures around which actors' expectations converge in a given area of international relations."[6] The existence of these "regimes" indicates an element of complexity in international affairs that is not captured by the realists' extension of the Hobbesian model and about which ordered expectations may continue to develop. But it remains to be seen whether these extra-governmental regimes can supply norms or principles rich enough to lead to permanent forms of association or federation that will offer some promise of averting a nuclear holocaust or of systematically reducing the tendency of states to resort to violence in the pursuit of their interests.

The history of the Westphalian system illustrates at least the rudiments of an international order in which the relations between European states were deftly manipulated by statesmen to minimize the chances that the equal pursuit of national interests would result in the open hostility of armed aggression. Yet it must be remembered that the Westphalian system twice broke down badly. It was initially undone by the imperialism of Napoleon, and later, after being reinstalled by the Congress of Vienna, it collapsed on the eve of World War I. Indeed, some historians believe that the reliance of key statesmen on an outdated Westphalian model was a major cause of World War I. They argue first that technological changes had made the model's prescriptions for averting a major war by threatening war wholly inappropriate, and second, that nationalistic forces, together with technological changes in weaponry, meant that if any war should break out, it would certainly become a total war. And yet the Westphalian model of international relations as the exclusive affair of sovereign states still influences statesmen (as it seems to have influenced Henry Kissinger), even though concepts like the "balance of power" are woefully inadequate to describe a bipolar world dominated by superpowers.

It is part of the legacy of the Westphalian system that we think of the legitimacy of governing order as arising from its identification with a nation and its de facto control of a geographical region rather than from a government's willingness to satisfy universal human needs or to facilitate the achievement of transnational values. It is a tragic remnant of that legacy that we have difficulty even conceiving of solutions to international problems except for those that involve states as the major actors and that allow major governments to have a controlling influence. Thus the Westphalian paradigm, which may have been a major cause of the absence of war in Europe through long stretches of the eighteenth and nineteenth centuries, may be a major obstacle today to the discovery of a more lasting peace.

Questions about the extent to which solutions to the problems of international tension require continued reliance upon state governments is directly related to a further, but more innovative, response to realism that I believe we should consider. This innovative approach also illustrates the point I made earlier about philosophy's role in helping us see familiar things in a new light. The familiar, indeed pervasive, phenomenon that we need to understand in a new light is power. Underlying all of Hobbes's political philosophy is a certain logic of power and a set of assumptions about the effectiveness of force and coercion and, by implication, about the ineffectiveness of nonviolence and peaceful resistance. The hard core of the Hobbesian perspective is a belief in the significance of violence in human life—both in the individual's personal life and in his communal life. For Hobbes, the individual even in the state of nature is absolutely subjected to violence, for he or she is completely determined in thought and behavior by the impact of the changing universe on his or her consciousness and the subsequent generation of the appetites and aversions. As for man's communal and political relations, Hobbes's own analysis shows that competition, diffidence, and glory are only indirect or secondary causes of dangerous quarrels, for the truly proximate cause of aggression and war is what first disposes men to compete, to be diffident, and to seek glory, and what renders ineffective all attempts to avert the inevitable effects of competition, diffidence, and glory. And this cause is nothing other than the unending will to power in humankind. Hobbes makes this clear in a telling passage in which he proclaims, "In the first place, I put for a general inclination of all mankind a perpetual and restless desire of power after power that ceaseth only in death." He goes on to point out that this perpetual desire exists not because the individual hopes for more intensive pleasure, "but because he cannot assure the power and means to live well which he has present without the acquisition of more. And from hence it is that kings, whose power is greatest, turn their endeavors to the ensuring it at home by laws or abroad by wars."[7]

All realists and almost all anti-realists who have responded to the realist challenge accept without question Hobbes's analysis of power and his assumptions about its effectiveness. Anti-realists may reject Hobbes's determinism, his psychological egoism, or (as we have seen) the application of his contractarian logic to international affairs. But they do not question his assumptions about the logic of

19

power relationships. After all, what could be more obvious, more certain, than this simple, most evident, and familiar aspect of experience? It is hardly surprising, after all, that we are intellectually unprepared and almost emotionally incapable of conceiving of any interpersonal problem in other than power terms. Children of our culture are sedulously taught throughout their educative years that the purpose of life is, so far as possible, to excel others. We are so conditioned to find security in success in competition that for the rest of our lives we are prone to react with symptoms of severe anxiety to anything or anyone who appears to threaten the hierarchical system of values by which we define our places in life. But this is precisely why we need to be reminded of Heraclitus's simple point about our reawakening. Isn't it just possible that the logic of the Hobbesian position—the logic of power that we so easily assume—involves a great central illusion, namely, the illusion that problems which have all been caused by the will to aggrandizement and power in man can be solved by further applications of power?[8]

If one reads Tolstoy philosophically, especially the great novel *War and Peace* and the nonfiction works on nonresistance, one feels awakened to the possibility that this great, central "truth" of Western political philosophy may indeed be illusory. One is impressed by the extent to which the cataclysmic episodes of the Napoleonic Wars, such as the Battle of Borodino and the evacuation of Moscow, were not brought about or directed by the allegedly "great" generals Napoleon and Kutuzov. One feels persuaded by Tolstoy's view that the association of power with an individual is a function of the ability of that individual (or the imputation of ability to him) to express opinions, predictions, and justifications about a collective action over which he has no real control.[9] Tolstoy argues in *War and Peace* that war is a peculiar combination of human activities: a minority who take responsibility, elaborate justifications, and define purposes combine with a majority who actually perform the necessary actions, although they seek to relieve themselves of all responsibility for performing them. But war is actually the work of common soldiers, who determine the outcome by their killing activities, while the responsibility for the war belongs only ostensibly to the statesmen and generals. Tolstoy attacks the great commanders for their arrogance in naively believing that they can order and thus cause momentous historical events, made up of the contributions of thousands of men. Their hubris rests on the illusion of power, which in reality they do not possess. Tolstoy concludes that there is no metaphysical reality to power, that it is a myth, a cheat, a fraud.

In *The Politics of Non-Violent Action,* a work very different from a Tolstoy novel, Gene Sharp presents an analysis of power that nevertheless reinforces aspects of Tolstoy's view.[10] Sharp finds that power, as a social phenomenon, always involves two-sided relationships. A "superior's" power always depends upon the voluntary compliance of a majority of those who accept their positions as "subordinates." By contrast, Sharp identifies the traditional Western view of power, the view shared by Hobbes, as the "monolith theory." Power is thought to be monolithic, possessed by or coming from a few men, and existing as a fixed quantum of independent and durable force. If this monolith theory is assumed, then one accepts, almost as an axiom, that in a severe crisis a government's power can be significantly reduced or demolished only by greater physical force. War is based on this view of the nature of political power, since the objective is to possess greater destructive capacity than the enemy, and nuclear weapons are the extreme development of this approach to power.

In one of Tolstoy's nonfictional works, the reader comes across Tolstoy's own observation about Hobbes's philosophy. He says that the Hobbesian perspective is one that would be adopted retrospectively by statesmen who attribute to men generally those qualities that have most formed them as leaders and that offer the strongest defense of their own assumptions about human nature and the justification of their own actions.[11] From Tolstoy's vantage point, one comes to suspect that the very people who are allegedly trying to solve the problems of the world conflict by the wisdom of their policies imposed and executed by coercion and threats of violence— the presidents, premiers, ministers, generals, and national security advisors—are themselves, by the perpetuation of false assumptions, a major cause of the problems their offices exist to "solve".[12] One comes to see the reasonableness of Tolstoy's pacifist position that violence is not only morally illegitimate but also morally self-defeating; that humans cannot be changed for the better by external coercive means; and that the only way genuine improvement can be brought about is by each person's making the one change that is legitimate—change from within.[13]

Someone will surely say that what seems like a reawakening or a new vision to me is merely a philosophical dream. I confess that I don't really know which it is, for if one accepts Tolstoy's vision, then what sense can be made of those experiences in which force or coercive threats seem so clearly to produce social benefits, such as the criminal law or the practice of nuclear deterrence? And what about instances in which the use of force seems unquestionably morally legitimate, such as self-defense? When we reflect on such examples, we may indeed find that the pacifist vision is a dream in the end. But even so, I would maintain that such visions are beneficial and salutary dreams, for they make us reexamine our most basic assumptions. When we do this, we find that much intellectual work that seemed only remotely connected to the problems of international peace and order is very centrally related. I have in mind, in addition to Tolstoy, not only the works of Gandhi and Martin Luther King, Jr., but also studies of violence such as those of Simone Weil and Hannah Arendt, Albert Camus's study of rebellion, Elias Canetti's study of crowds and power, and the study of power and nonviolent resistance made by Gene Sharp.[14]

The study of these works may not convince us that central concepts, such as power, that we have been assuming in our analyses are wholly wrong, but they may help us accept the possibly unwelcome truth that the responsibility for ending the evils in the universal body politic rests inescapably on each of us and that we may contribute most successfully to moral progress in the community by first correcting confused and distorted ways of understanding human experience. Second, these works may help us discover new, alternative solutions to the problems of war and international order that will remain unavailable to us as long as we are blinkered by old ways of looking at those problems. New solutions may not depend, as the failed "solutions" have, on states as the major actors in the international arena or on the traditional trappings of national status and prestige.

Three

War, Competition, and Religion: Hobbes and the American Founding

Charles L. Griswold, Jr.

In Plato's *Laws*, the Athenian Stranger ominously predicts that "there can be no rest from evils and toils for those cities in which some mortal rules rather than a god" (713e4–6).[1] War is chief among these evils. Two thousand years later, when the weapons for destruction have reached nearly unimaginable power, we wonder whether war will not soon see to the end of the human race altogether.

War does not manifest itself on the international level alone, of course. While its consequences may not be global, civil strife is *the* plague of efforts to sustain civilized communities. In this essay, I would like to focus primarily but not exclusively on one particular type of civil conflict, namely, religious war. At this writing, Ireland, India, and Lebanon offer examples of the miserable consequences of this type of civil war. I suppose that the United States offers a good example of the near disappearance of religious warfare. Other nations maintain peace between religions as well as between religion and the government. But the United States is remarkable for the sheer multiplicity of the religions it fosters, for the passion with which its citizens pursue their faiths, and for the relative lack of out-and-out religious persecution. I shall want to say something about the causes of this laudable achievement. I begin with some observations about that great theorist of civil war and, if I may put it thus, the patron saint of this volume of essays, namely, Thomas Hobbes. In part 1, I contrast his solution to the problem of civil war with differing solutions proposed in Plato's dialogues and in the American founding. Then in part 2, I shall focus on the issue of religious civil war, a cure for which was worked out by John Locke and Adam Smith among others, and instituted in the American founding.

I

In the *Leviathan* Hobbes distinguishes between three "causes of quarrel." The first is competition, which results from the pursuit of gain. The second is diffidence, which results from desire for safety. And the third is glory, which results from desire for recognition.[2] All three are, as Hobbes also tells us, reflections of human nature. "Quarrel" does not quite convey man's natural propensity; "war of every man against every man" is more accurate. The most basic of the three causes of war is diffidence, and Hobbes derives competition and glory-seeking from it (chap. 13, pp. 183–85). Diffidence, in turn, is rooted in the desire for power. The desire for power is without limit (chap. 11, p. 161), for the fear of death is without limit. That is, power is valuable not because there exists a *summum bonum*— Hobbes explicitly denies such a thing (chap. 11, p. 160)—but because the fundamental desire of humankind is for self-preservation, and power is the means to that end. The striving for self-preservation leads to war, Hobbes says, because human beings are roughly equal by nature in terms of their desires and abilities, because no one can entirely make himself safe from all others, and finally because power is a relative and changeable thing. We are thus compelled perpetually to seek more power over our fellows than we perceive them to have (either actually or potentially) over us. For Hobbes the battle is ubiquitous, since he claims that reputation, prudence, nobility, science, honor, dignity, and magnanimity are all to be understood as kinds of power (chap. 10, pp. 150–60). The natural and comprehensive condition of humankind is that of war. Nature is not beneficent.

It comes as no surprise that Hobbes views religion as an effort to increase one's power. Each individual contemplates the present situation and future prospects, and "hath his heart all the day long, gnawed on by feare of death, poverty, or other calamity" (chap. 12, p. 169). A belief in God helps quiet the anxious premonitions of power, that is, of death. As Hobbes says, "The End of Worship amongst men, is Power" (chap. 31, p. 401). Those who provide religion are moved, Hobbes says, by the desire to control others. Hobbes plainly views tenets of religious credo, such as the immortality of the soul and indeed the existence of a "soul" (chap. 12, pp. 170–71), as politically useful superstition (chap. 12, p. 177), the origin of which lies in our imaginations (chap. 11, p. 168). Hobbes even proposes that God is to be understood as possessing "Irresistible

Aristotle and others produced a host of further reasons showing that the sort of solution to war proposed in the *Republic* is not feasible.

These observations seem to lend force to Hobbes's "realistic" approach to the problem. Instead of attempting to reform human nature, Hobbes counts on its most fundamental passion—the fear of death—to ensure peace. Hobbes argues that the simplest calculations of utility show that the chances for survival are better under a social contract in which the rules are vigorously and impartially enforced than under the conditions of a state of nature in which there are no laws in effect (chap. 14, p. 190). Vigorous enforcement requires a centralized and irrevocable authority powerful enough to suppress conflicts within the realm. This authority is the "Leviathan."

However, Hobbes's argument makes several doubtful assumptions. One is that fear of death really is our fundamental passion. Given that premise, Hobbes is unable to explain why anyone would want to go to war to defend the nation. It would make little sense to give one's life in the name of a social contract whose justification is its ability to protect one's life. It would be more rational to switch loyalties.[4] Further, the phenomenon of religious warfare suggests that humans do not always regard death as the *summum malum*, for that sort of war can be distinguished by fanaticism fueled by visions of an afterlife. Threatening disobedient religious believers with death may be equivalent to promising them salvation, which would provoke rather than quiet them. Our era provides ample evidence that religious passion can overcome the fear of death. One might also point to the striving for fame or for the other sorts of "immortality" discussed in Plato's *Symposium* (208e–212b) as evidence of the same. Furthermore, a perpetually instituted sovereign would, as John Locke pointed out, soon abuse its power rather than administer the law fairly.[5] The old Platonic problem of reforming the revolutionary rulers remains.

Finally, it could be objected to Hobbes that his attempt to reconcile on doctrinal grounds the demands of religious authority with those of political obedience fails. This objection goes to the root of Hobbes's conventionalism and calls into question his view that justice or injustice can only be defined relative to the performance or nonperformance of contracts (chap. 13, p. 188; chap. 15, p. 202). This would certainly be a Platonic objection to Hobbes. Carried out fully, this objection would necessarily focus on Hobbes's definition of the liberty of the individual. In the *Leviathan* we are told that "liberty" is to be understood as "the absence of externall Impediments" to using one's power as one judges most advantageous. "Natural right" simply means "the liberty to do, or to forbeare" (chap. 14, p. 189).

Power" and, he argues, that fact explains why all of God's actions are morally right (chap. 31, p. 397). The phenomenon of power is thus basic in Hobbes's analysis of religion and religious strife.

Hobbes argues that the proximate cause of religious warfare—specifically warfare between the sovereign of a state and the religious authorities—lies in the claim of individual religious bodies to represent the kingdom of God (chap. 44, pp. 628–29; chap. 47, p. 708). Since that claim is articulated in what Hobbes thinks of as unreal and absurd abstractions—an entire section of the *Leviathan*, entitled "Of Darknesse," is devoted to heaping scorn on Aristotelian Christianity in particular—religious wars will be waged in the name of meaningless doctrines and in the cause of raw power.

Hobbes's solution to religious warfare, is, as I understand it, twofold. First, he seeks to persuade us that commonly received dogma—both Christian and non-Christian—is by and large meaningless. Second, he argues on both biblical and independent grounds that no sect can claim to represent the kingdom of God. There is no "spiritual" authority above the temporal (chap. 42, pp. 600–603), and ecclesiastics have authority to teach and nothing more (chap. 42, pp. 524–25). Heresy is whatever the political sovereign says it is (chap. 42, p. 605). True piety consists in obeying the laws and keeping faith in Christ, for there are no other divine precepts that should be obeyed (chap. 43, pp. 610, 624). Hobbes goes on to argue the extraordinary view that it is never inconsistent with piety to obey the sovereign, whether the sovereign is a believer or not, and indeed that to oppose even the sovereign who is a nonbeliever is to sin against the laws of God, that is, of nature (chap. 43, pp. 624–25). This solution to the problem of religious warfare is an extension of Hobbes's general analysis of civil strife, and so of human nature.

At a very general level, Hobbes's solution to the problem of civil war is one of at least three possible types of solution. A first type of solution, proposed by Hobbes, seeks to put those aspects of human nature that cause war into the service of peace. A second type, proposed in Plato's dialogues, and later by Marx, is premised on the possibility of changing, or at least significantly reforming, human nature. A third is that exhibited by the American founding. In order to bring out more clearly some of the general assumptions of Hobbes's account, I should like to say a few words about these contrasting views.

In the second book of the *Republic*, Socrates and his interlocutors set themselves the task of showing that justice is something good in and of itself—a task that from Hobbes's standpoint (represented, in the *Republic*, by Thrasymachus) is utterly impossible. On the assumption that it is easier to see the nature of justice against the backdrop of the vast canvas of political life, Socrates and friends create a "city in speech." The earliest form of community they represent is a rustic, peaceable village, whose inhabitants worship the gods, live according to need, sleep in the open on beds of "rushes strewn with yew and myrtle" (372b), bear children, and so forth.[3] Glaucon objects that this is a "city of sows," and so these rustics are allowed to acquire desires for the unnecessaries. They now desire spices, houses, money, artisans; and they now are in need of artists, doctors, lawyers, and the rest. This "feverish" rather than "healthy" (372e) city has the advantage of illustrating the difference between justice and injustice, a difference previously invisible. For expanding desires require more land and riches to be satisfied, and therein lies, we are told, the origin of war (373e).

The cure for war is to change the self-interested part of human nature, that is, to change the "self" (or the "part of the soul") in which we are interested. This requires the restriction of desire, which is to be achieved in part through education, through selective breeding, and (at least for the guardian class) by removing the objects of temptation. The abolition of every form of private property (including the family), as well as the institution of a civic religion that requires all the citizens to regard each other as brothers born of the same earth and serving the same divinities, is supposed to generate the cohesiveness needed to silence the dog of civil war. The *Republic*'s civic religion (quite different from the prevalent conventional religion, as book 2 of the *Republic* shows) is intended to convey basic moral truths in a rhetorically effective manner. Plato's Socrates tries to overcome everything that lets selves oppose themselves to others. Particularly in the case of the guardians, citizens are not allowed to create any life plans for themselves that are out of tune with the whole polis. As in Hobbes, religion is permitted only to the extent that it is purified and that it is under the sovereign's control. Like Marxist communism and unlike Hobbesian individualism, Platonic communism proposes that war can be suppressed only if human nature is improved.

Objections to that solution to the problem of war and justice are evident in the *Republic* itself, most obviously in the proviso that the "just" city will come about only if everyone over the age of ten is expelled from it (541a). The proviso is necessary if the traditional obstacle to successful revolutions is to be removed, namely, the obstacle created by the fact that the reformers are not themselves reformed and that persons past a given age tend to be unreformable. Having instituted their reforms, they carry on in an unimproved, prerevolutionary way. But since Socrates' proviso is impossible to carry out, the reforming revolution he proposes is impossible.

A "natural right" entails no obligation whatever; "liberty" is "license." The "individual," correspondingly, has no intrinsic moral status for Hobbes. "The *Value*, or WORTH of a man, is as of all other things, his Price; that is to say, so much as would be given for the use of his Power" (chap. 10, p. 151). To call into question Hobbes's thesis that death is the *summum malum* is ultimately to call into question his estimate of the liberty and worth of the individual.

Is there a middle way between Plato's "utopian" and Hobbes's "realistic" solution to the problem of war, between the demands of philosophic virtue and of self-interest, of objectivist metaphysics and conventionalism? Plato's solution seems to extinguish, in the name of hierarchical nature and peace, all claims to the liberty of the individual. Hobbes's solution reduces justice to a means to the accumulation of power and to self-preservation. For the one, the greatest evil is corruption of soul. For the other, death is the greatest evil, and neither "corruption" nor "soul" have meaning.

It seems to me that the American founding does offer us a middle way. It constitutes a third type of solution to the problem of war. Specifying it precisely is among the most vexed problems facing students of the founding. Such a task is far beyond the modest scope of this essay. My comments on this matter are correspondingly preparatory.

Let me begin by observing that Jefferson and Adams (to name only two) read the *Republic* and detested its communitarian recommendations as well as the process by which the recommendations were reached.[6] Furthermore, Jefferson and Madison were acquainted with Frances Wright's arguments in favor of, and efforts to establish, utopian socialist communities.[7] On 1 September 1825, Madison wrote Wright a letter in response to her proposals in which he questioned her suggestions for the emancipation of the slaves, as well as her thesis that the abolition of private property—at least in the absence of a common religious impulse—would be compatible with productive labor.[8] Madison took an equally glum view of Robert Dale Owen's "New Harmony" community in Indiana, a key premise of which was the possibility of changing human nature as we have observed that nature through time. Madison commented: "Mr. Owen's remedy for these vicissitudes [scarcity and changeable economic conditions combined with fast population growth] implies that labour will be relished without the ordinary impulses to it; that the love of equality will supersede the desire of distinction; and that the increasing leisure, from the improvements of machinery, will promote intellectual cultivation, moral enjoyment, and innocent amusements, without any of the vicious resorts, for the ennui of idleness. Custom is properly called a second nature; Mr. Owen makes it nature herself."[9]

At the same time, Madison and colleagues cannot be cast as outright Hobbesians, though *Federalist* no. 10 has long encouraged that reading.[10] One reason the founding is not simply Hobbesian is that the doctrine of natural rights enshrined in the Declaration of Independence contains a deontological dimension. That is, natural rights thus understood impose moral "claims." Possessors of these rights can claim that others ought to respect the freedoms defined by the rights, independent of reasons of utility. In Ronald Dworkin's language, these are "rights" in the "strong" sense of the term.[11] Correspondingly, freedom or liberty cannot mean, for the founders, just "license." The Declaration's propositions are presented as and were understood to be claims to objective truth, not just "rational" expressions of desire à la Hobbes. Implicit in the Declaration is a view of the worth of the individual as not reducible to any given "price." On that rests the criticism of slavery that Jefferson included in his draft of the Declaration.

Let me bring this discussion back to the question of war, to civil war in particular. If the Constitution had been built on Hobbesian premises (and so death supposedly the *summum malum*), then it would have failed to avert the perpetual civil war (let alone religious civil war) that Hobbes tells us is the natural condition of mankind (this is at least the inference a Jefferson or Madison would probably have drawn). But the Constitution did not establish anything like a "Leviathan," and it does not just balance Hobbesian self-interests against each other. I suggest that the Constitution's war-averting power rests on a blend of Hobbesian self-interest and Platonic education of soul, a mix of a deontological theory of natural rights and appeals to social utility. As Madison writes in *Federalist* no. 51, for a free republic to survive, "Ambition must be made to counteract ambition. The interest of the man must be connected with the constitutional rights of the place."[12] The connection requires that the people learn to take an interest in the (natural, deontological) rights underlying the Constitution.

Further prima facie evidence for the rather general suggestion concerning the mediating role of the founding may be found in Madison's essay entitled "Universal Peace" (1792), in which Madison offers some critical reflections on Rousseau's "Paix Perpétuelle" (1761). Madison distinguishes between war that flows from the will of the government, and that which flows from the will of society. The former is to be cured by rightly structuring government (e.g., by making sure that only the people can declare war, and that those who declare it must pay for it). The latter is harder to cure, and Madison indicates that in addition to balancing self-interest against self-interest, the citizens must become habituated to conducting themselves reasonably.[13]

I would like to flesh out this "middle way" between Hobbes and Plato in terms of the disease of religious civil war and the American antidote to it. I am aware of the complexity of the topic and offer the following as a propaedeutic to a full-fledged treatment of the matter.

II

Three of the fundamental texts concerning the solution to the problem of religious conflict are Locke's *A Letter Concerning Toleration* (1689), Jefferson's "Statute for Establishing Religious Freedom" (1777; enacted 1786), and Madison's essay "Memorial and Remonstrance against Religious Assessments" (1785). All three documents argue for the separation of church and state, that is, for freedom of religious belief from political controls. Civil peace, as well as purity of religion and morals, are proposed as major consequences of this separation. The argument has two sides to it: one side is pragmatic, based on experience, utilitarian. The other amounts to a sort of theological argument. While the first seems Hobbesian in spirit, the second is essentially Platonic. Let us look first at the pragmatic argument.

Experience teaches that when churches are permitted to gain political power, that is, to claim that they unite spiritual and temporal authority, both religion and politics are corrupted. Priests and ministers alike begin to think more about their possessions than about the rigors of worship. Assured of a steady stream of consumers, they concentrate more on accumulating power than on pleasing God. Religion becomes a veil for self-interest, mere rhetoric, and that corrupts the language of piety as well as of politics. Further, the purpose of the political association is lost; no longer intent on "securing" basic rights for the citizens, the church that is in power does its best to crush those rights. For that reason, and also because more than one religion is bound to exist, the inevitable result is political instability, the prelude to civil war. As Madison puts it in the "Memorial and Remonstrance" essay, "Torrents of blood have been spilt in the old world, by vain attempts of the secular arm to extinguish Religious discord, by proscribing all difference in Religious opinions."[14]

Let us grant that this argument is sound. Why should the separation of church and state constitute an improvement? Here the American founders assume an argument (I still limit myself, for the moment, to "pragmatic" considerations) that finds its fullest formulation in book 5 of Adam Smith's *Wealth of Nations*. Smith there argues that competition between churches results in both peace and purer religion, so long as it is clear that no church is permitted to avail itself of the power of the state—that is, so long as it is clear that state-sanctioned monopolies are forbidden. Religions compete for disciples; the product is a conception of life and afterlife; the salesmen are the priests. In an unregulated marketplace, churches will succeed only so long as they persuade by example and words that their claims lead to morality and happiness. Just as a baker who sold adulterated bread would find his customers flocking to his competitors, so too would a church. Competition between a multiplicity of churches will force them to moderate their claims, live up to generally acceptable standards, and generate honest piety. Not required to buy into a particular church, consumers will espouse those they truly believe in. Adam Smith, for one, thought that the result of such a process would be the elimination of fanatic and bizarre religious doctrines, and the production of what he calls "pure and rational religion."[15] Further, churches will compete with and so control each other, thus preventing any of them from obtaining an exclusive monopoly. A tolerable war of words will replace intolerable inquisitions. In a way strongly reminiscent of Hobbes, the Smithean marketplace of religions turns self-interest on itself so as to moderate the negative effects of the striving for power. Pragmatic reasons such as these are intended to convince us that a Platonic use of religion by the state is to be rejected.

These pragmatic reasons do not suffice, however. One can easily imagine a religion that holds that the risk of corruption within the church can be minimized by Draconian measures for dealing with the corrupted, and that it is the duty of every God-fearing person to take every step humanly possible to ensure that God's word is implemented throughout the community. A powerful tool for eliminating evil as well as dissent—and so for ensuring both goodness and peace—is the sword, and control of the state provides just that. *Not* to unite church and state would be a sin on this account; all those who sacrifice their lives in the name of uniting church and state will be blessed eternally. As for "liberty of the individual," that would be condemned as a relativistic, perhaps Satanic, creation of nonbelievers.

In order to counter the view I have just sketched, and so to argue for the separation of church and state, something more than pragmatic reasons must be offered. Here we come to what I referred to

31

as the "theological" argument, whose main points are laid out in
Jefferson's "Statute for Establishing Religious Freedom": "Almighty
God hath created the mind free," and intends the mind to be influenced by reason alone; it is a sin "to compel a man to furnish
contributions of money for the propagation of opinions which he
disbelieves"; God is not interested in forced professions of belief;
human beings are "fallible"; "our civil rights have no dependence
on our religious opinions"; and "truth is great and will prevail if left
to herself."[16] Or as Madison puts it in the "Memorial and Remonstrance" essay, the right of everyone to exercise religious conviction as conscience dictates is unalienable because "it is the duty
of every man to render to the Creator such homage, and such only,
as he believes to be acceptable to him."

> Whilst we assert for ourselves a freedom to embrace, to profess and
> to observe the Religion which we believe to be of divine origin, we
> cannot deny an equal freedom to those whose minds have not
> yielded to the evidence which has convinced us. If this freedom be
> abused, it is an offence against God, not against man.[17]

The Jeffersonian and Madisonian line of reasoning assumes both
the existence of God and a particular notion of God, a notion that
is not reconcilable with that of a number of religions. Very generally
put, Jefferson and Madison are assuming a Christian notion of God.
But to say that is not to say enough, for it is a notion that seems
more Protestant than Catholic, thanks to the implicit emphasis on
the directness of the relationship between God and an individual's
conscience. Of course, it does not suffice to just label it "Protestant."
Quite possibly the emphasis on fallibility and the freedom of the
mind is compatible only with Protestantism understood in a specific
way. One historian of religion argues that Jefferson's appeal to the
liberty of individual conscience is strongly connected to doctrines
advanced by Roger Williams, Puritan founder of the Rhode Island
colony in the 1630s.[18] However one might wish to specify the particular notion of God assumed by Jefferson's and Madison's famous
argument for the separation of church and state, my point is that
some such particular notion is assumed by their public arguments
for toleration. So far as I know, this assumption was widely shared
at the time.

References to the divine in the course of arguments for the liberty of the individual exist in other documents central to the American founding. The Declaration of Independence informs us that
peoples are entitled to "assume among the powers of the earth the
separate and equal station to which the laws of nature and of nature's
God entitle them." It is striking that this political equality is jus-

tified by reference to "nature and nature's God." The divine is not explicitly named in the sentences establishing the moral equality of individuals that underlies political equality, but it seems probable that the phrasing of the first two of the "self-evident" truths was intended to allude to "nature's God" ("all men are created equal; that they are endowed by their creator with certain inalienable rights"). Again, the founders' argument for liberty—including religious liberty—is publicly stated by them so as to require a fairly specific theological doctrine that is not compatible with every alternative doctrine. It seems to me that the core of this doctrine is the notion of the individual as an irreducibly moral entity responsible for its own self, answerable to its own conscience, and capable of—to state the point in religious vocabulary—facing nature and nature's God.

All this suggests that, for the founders, propagation—albeit through mostly private means—of a civic religion that articulates basic and objective moral principles is necessary to institute the sorts of liberties proclaimed by the Declaration and Constitution, liberties (natural rights) that are crucial to peace. That is, in addition to various "inventions of prudence" (Madison's phrase in *Federalist* no. 51), the founders propose a religion of tolerance in order to solve the problem of religious war. In its essentials, the argument for this civic religion sounds Platonic, since it requires educating people to harness self-interest to other-regarding morality.

On this account, market processes and self-interest are a necessary but not sufficient condition for the extirpation of religious strife. We require not so much a Hobbesian notion of the *summum malum* (death) as an idea of the *summum bonum*—say, the "happiness of the individual." In the American Enlightenment, that notion of the highest good is often couched in religious language, the implication being that some reformation of self-interest through education and habituation is indispensable. The reason for this is in the first instance a motivational one; given that death is not the *summum malum*, Hobbesian "prudence" does not suffice to control the tendency to war.[19] But theoretical reasons for introducing talk about "objective norms"—whether or not such talk is cast in religious terms—have also been offered. Locke, Jefferson, and Madison evidently thought they had to say something about "nature" to ground their theories of justice. Similarly, in Plato's dialogues we are told that an "ascent" to first principles is philosophically unavoidable and that civil war will never cease until those principles are implemented in the *polis*.

Let me state the "theoretical" aspect of the issue in different, though again much abbreviated, terms. Jefferson and his colleagues argue that the citizens must believe that it is right, and not just to their individual advantage narrowly understood, to tolerate competing beliefs. On this view, the citizenry ought to ascribe to a nonrelativistic doctrine of natural rights, and hence of moral duties, in order to generate a regime in which citizens are free to follow their own lights, and in which limits to liberty can be argued for. If the value of toleration were conceived as a subjective matter, a value one might be free to hold or to reject, we would be left with what Karl Popper called the "paradox of tolerance," namely, that tolerance would require tolerating intolerance, or differently put, that freedom would be compatible with the liberty to enslave others.[20] This point was fundamental in the debates of 1858 between Abraham Lincoln and Stephen A. Douglas.[21] It therefore seems implausible to claim that the separation between church and state is based on the thesis that all moral values are matters of convention, that they are finally relative to the individual. At some point, commitment to a distinction between the tolerable and intolerable is necessary, and the Hobbesian "fear of death" will not do.

On the other hand, it cannot be correct to claim that the supposed truth of a civic religion warrants the state's establishment of any particular church or organized religion. That Platonic line of reasoning also leads to the war of all against all, as Locke, Jefferson, Madison, and other Enlightenment figures urged. The discussion of civic religion and objective values provides a basis for the separation of church and state, just as affirming that separation requires (on the Platonic view shared by Locke and others) affirming some overarching notion of natural rights, moral equality, and so forth. This suggests that, properly understood, contemporary American "liberal" and "conservative" positions on the church/state issue actually require each other to form a coherent doctrine. The "liberal" claim to strict separation of church and state requires the "conservative" affirmation of objective value, while the "conservative" claim leads to the strict separation of church and state.

My unavoidably telegraphic reflections on civil war, religious civil war in particular, obviously leave many critical questions unanswered, indeed, unasked. By way of conclusion, let me raise one of these questions. If it is true that the solution to religious strife hinges in part on a civic religion that entails a determinate notion of the divine, can liberty of religious belief extend to those who reject even the general propositions of a civic religion? Recall that no less a libertarian than John Locke concludes his argument for religious freedom and separation of church and state by holding that while all varieties of beliefs (except the intolerant) are to be tolerated, publicly professed atheism is to be censored by the state.[22]

However, one can rephrase the point without reference to religion, since one can argue that whatever may be the case historically in the United States, from a philosophical point of view the affirmation of objective moral values as a basis for liberty of the individual need not be based on any religious notions. Perhaps there are indeed better incentives to morality than those of religion, and considerably better arguments for the liberty of the individual than the religious ones. Many philosophers have argued for both propositions, and nothing I have said above was intended to call either into question. What then of persons (say, representatives of the Ku Klux Klan) who publicly attack founding moral propositions (such as those of human equality enunciated in the Declaration of Independence) and so, on the argument sketched above, threaten the basis for peace?[23] Questions of this sort represent unavoidable quandaries for all communities that try to answer civil war with liberty.

Four

Authority and Sovereignty

Rex Martin

I

The notion of the state has three main elements: the issuing of rules, the expectation of general compliance, and the possession by government of a monopoly in the use of coercive force. Moreover, if the claim is sound that the notion of political authority should be mapped onto that of the state, it would follow that the notion of political authority has these same three parts. Where that notion is made normative, as it would be in the idea of a justified political authority, these three elements will still be present.

The notion of a justified political authority is a systematic one, and the logic of its justification must involve establishing systematic connections between its elements. What we have to show, then, is that a rightful license to issue rules does connect with a rightful presumption of compliance and that this connection does confer a possible title to back up these rules coercively.

Now it might be contended that I am here alleging a problem in relating two notions—the rightful license to issue rules and the obligation to obey them—although no such problem exists. The two notions are already connected, by virtue of their meaning, and the problem vanishes simply in seeing this. It is a persuasive reply and has considerable vogue among contemporary political philosophers; hence it might be worth examining at some length. Even so, it will not allow us to dispense with the problem I have raised, for there remains the question of a connection between the rule-issuing license and the citizen's obligation to obey, on the one hand, and the coercive enforcement of these rules, on the other. But here I want to deal only with the linkage between rule-issuing and obligation.

Many contemporary political philosophers see a close connection between the rule-issuing authority of government and the obligation of the citizen. It is, for them, a two-way analytic connection. To say that a government has such authority means, or entails, that every citizen has an obligation to obey its particular laws, and vice versa. The stick can be picked up from either end. Accordingly, in this essay I will investigate just the second of these mutual entail-ments—that obligation to obey rules implies rule-issuing authority.

One of the traditional positions in political philosophy on the question we want to address, the question of whether a citizen is bound to obey all laws merely because they are laws, is that of the obligationist. The essence of the obligationist position is the notion that citizens have a special obligation toward the laws as such, as distinct from an obligation to do a certain thing whether it is pre-scribed by law or not. The nature of this obligation is that we must do what we are told to do simply because it is mandated by law. The obligation is a strict one; it attaches to all laws and can be overridden, if at all, only in exceptional cases. How might one come to hold such a position, or to support it? There are surely many answers to this question, but I am mainly interested in one answer—or, better, type of answer—that has actually been advanced historically.

In the obligationist perspective, the issue of justifying political authority is focused on the question of whether citizens have a strict obligation to obey laws just insofar as they are valid laws. Since obligation is made the eligible issue here, the justification of strict political obligation has become central and the question of the jus-tification of political authority is thought to turn on it. But since obligation is now logically prior to any other political concept, the task of justifying it requires that we go outside the whole system of political concepts and institutions. Hence the justification, whether it can be accomplished or not, must be attempted by ref-erence to some external, nonpolitical standard.

Here one goes outside the political system, outside the idea of the state, to find the ground of political obligation. One looks for an obligation-conferring trait external to the body politic and brings that to bear on the issue of the citizen's standing before the law. Thus one could allege that a person has a standing of obligation toward the law if it is divinely commanded that people obey laws, that is, obey laws simply insofar as they are laws. Or, again, the person who was bound to obedience by an oath or some sort of formal promise would have an external ground of obligation to obey all particular laws.

Perhaps the best example, though, is the well-known theory—usually associated with Hobbes and Locke—in which a contract or other act of consent is said both to authorize a government to make laws and to bind subjects to strict obedience. However, the theories of Hobbes and Locke may not be quite so simple as this.

37

Locke, for example, could be taken to argue that at a certain point (i.e., upon reaching the age of adulthood and then by staying on more or less voluntarily), people become members or parts of a particular body politic. The main function of any such body is to create a constitution or form of government. Presumably, there is a consensus (what Locke calls a majority) among the citizens as to where—that is, in what institutions—the main powers of government (legislative, executive, etc.) have been lodged. Indeed, Locke says, if there were not this consensus the body politic would come apart, would simply disintegrate, and could only be held together by obvious and clearly improper force. Now, from these two facts—that one is a member of a body politic and that there is a constitutional government for it—it follows for Locke that each citizen is strictly bound to obey the laws duly issued by the constitutional government. Or it follows logically from these two facts plus one other—if laws were not obeyed people would in effect have returned to the unwanted state of nature—that each citizen has the strict obligation in question. One has, in short, not consented in so many words to obey the laws; rather, one has consented to be a member of a body politic and from that fact, plus one or two others, it follows as a matter of logical entailment that the citizen has a strict duty to obey laws duly issued. One is thus obliged *as if* one had in fact expressly consented to obey.[1]

The doctrine of consent in Hobbes is, on the face of it, simpler. He dispenses with such ideas as the body politic (as something conceptually prior to government) and legitimate or constitutional rulership and argues that all subjects consent in one and the same fundamental respect. Each "stands aside" from the exercise of natural rights and thus consents (or, in effect, promises) permanently but conditionally to defer to the exercise of those selfsame rights by the governmental person(s), the sovereign. Thus the subject consents to be under the sovereign's will and is obliged to comply with it in all or almost all cases.[2]

One could contend, consistent with Hobbes's basic account, that the duties of subjects are not implied by the sovereign's natural right but are merely superadded to it (for reasons of prudence) in civil society. Even so, it could still be said that there is at least one implied duty here. The subjects' willingness to defer to the sovereign does create an obligation on their part: that they not exercise their rights as rights. That is, the waiving of a right, or its exercise, by A implies such a duty of A. But whether A must conform in conduct to the sovereign's will may not be a logical implication.

Even so, when we consider that for Hobbes the sovereign's natural right is what it is in civil society only because the subjects' duty to conform is attached to that right, then it becomes imperative to say that the sovereign's right is always paired with such a duty. That the duty to conform is mediated by arguments of prudence and is not, unlike the duty of not exercising one's rights, a matter of logical entailment is a point of no great consequence.

It can be said, then, that both Hobbes and Locke ground political obligation in consent, but not straightforwardly, as the traditional interpretation would have it. Thus Hume, who is of course no partisan of the original contract theory, interprets the theory as asserting that citizens have an obligation to obey because they have, in effect, promised to do so.[3] This is perhaps closer to the mark as an account (and ultimately a criticism) of Rousseau than it is of Hobbes or Locke, but clearly, in all these cases, the theories do ground obligation in some specific undertaking by the citizen-member of the body politic.

The crucial point in this theory is that the citizens' obligation to law is derived from their being a party to a promise or a contract—or from their being treated as such. The social contract governs the relevant obligation just as any contract, whatever its nature or whoever the contracting parties, would in establishing the duties that attend it. Political obligation is here a species of contractual or consensual obligation. Where it is indeed the presumed fact of a contractual relationship that establishes the citizens' obligation to law, then clearly such obligation is conceived as externally grounded. It is evident that in many theories the relationship of citizens to the government is construed as a case of some nonpolitical undertaking, like promising or signing a contract, which is obligation-creating in character.

However, I would argue that an external ground of political obligation never creates an obligation to obey laws as such. To take a religious analogy, when God commands us to obey all laws, we obey them because God says so. Our obligation is to what God commands and not principally to the laws at all. Nothing about law itself or about the system of political concepts, without the superaddition of the will of God, makes obeying laws obligatory. Similarly, when utility commands us to obey all laws, we obey them because it is useful to the end of the greatest happiness of the greatest number. Our obligation is, logically, to the principle of utility; our obligation to subordinate rules holds only insofar as they accord with it. Again, nothing about law, except under the superordinate principle of utility, makes obedience obligatory. And the same could be said for the categorical imperative as a ground of political obligation.[4]

This analysis of the external grounds of political obedience rules out the notion of a special obligation to laws as laws. The very procedure of justification creates a deep conceptual problem. As we have seen, the ground for a strict obligation to obey law on this view lies in some politically external standard (like a promise, contract, agreement, or understanding). But to repair to this standard, as the logic of the externalist justificatory argument requires, is to treat these obligations as nonpolitically derived. Hence all external grounds exclude political obligation, that is, special obligations to obey laws qua laws, in principle. It follows, then, that although we may have obligations to the law, they can never be special ones; thus none of the strict obligations we have can be obligations to the laws per se. We are left with only one conclusion: that we can have no strict *political* obligations at all.

The perception of this fact has been seized upon by the philosophical anarchist. Although the claim that where we have external justifying grounds we have no political obligations is merely a re-description of the contention that our standing before the law is governed by external grounds of obligation, philosophical anarchists need nothing more to introduce their arguments. Nonetheless, this capacity of anarchism represents not so much the peculiar vulnerability of political obligation to critique as it does the exploitation by the anarchist of inherent defects in the externalist program for justifying political obligation, and hence authority.

Locating these inherent defects is another matter. I don't think the defect lies in making political obligation the prior concept over rule-issuing authority rather than the other way around. The same problem clearly exists under either option. In both cases we first establish (on *external* grounds) the justification of a single focal element, either (a) rule-issuing authority or (b) a strict obligation for citizens to obey the laws issued. We reason from there, using the idea of a mutual entailment between rule-issuing authority and obligation. In case a, we say that citizens thus must have a strict obligation of obedience; in case b, we say that since they do have a strict obligation to obey laws, government must have a title to issue such rules in the first place.

These two "prior element" approaches have constituted, I would say, the traditional and standard answers to the ancient question of whether citizens are strictly bound in conscience to obey the laws of the land. But as I have shown, these standard answers are deeply problematic, for each is committed to the externalist program.

That program requires that we take one element in the idea of political authority—say, the license to issue rules or the reasonable expectation of compliance—and lift it clean out of the realm of the political to bring it under some external normative standard, such as the divine will or an ultimate ethical principle (like that of utility).

Hence the externalist program commits us to a piecemeal treatment of the constituent features of the notion of political authority. More important, by removing elements of that notion from the particular theoretic system in which they are located, we sunder the connections that any such element has within that system to the other conceptual elements ingredient there.

External justification, in short, makes it impossible to exhibit the systematic connections that yield a distinctive notion of political authority. Instead, it singles out some element within the notion and moralizes it, or baptizes it; but what it takes out of the system, no longer having its systematic connections and its place there, is no longer characteristically political. Thus the obligation to obey the law is not treated in the accounts we have examined as a political obligation. On the contrary, it is treated exclusively as a moral one, or as a divinely commanded one, and it takes its place, if it has one, in a list of moral rules, on a par with the obligation to keep promises.

The defect of the externalist program as regards obligation, then, is that it makes it systematically impossible to determine whether the peculiar political standing of a citizen before the law can be morally approved. It is never determined, and never could be, that, for example, some specific obligation is inherent in the citizen's standing before the law in a system determined by a given set of political concepts and institutions. Similarly, the question whether some authoritative rule-issuing agency is actually required by such a set, and hence is a necessary feature of any state so organized, cannot be answered in the externalist program.

Nevertheless, a solution to the problem is perhaps suggested by these very considerations. Rather than take one of the elements in the idea of political authority—whether it is the title to issue rules or the reasonable presumption of compliance or, for that matter, the government's rightful monopoly in the use of coercive force—and ground it in some external normative source, we might consider working up the elements together. To be precise, we must contemplate working up a theoretic system of political concepts in which these three elements would be seen to be in place once the system is fully described and hence could be said to be required for that system to be instantiated. Here, in contrast to the externalist program for justifying political authority, is the germ of an alternative scheme: a program for an *internal* justification of political authority—and hence of obligation.

On this view, the justification of political authority involves establishing systematic connections between the three elements (in normative form) in the notion of authority. The intuitive point of internal justification is that the connection is mediated through a

41

background theory. Thus it is the coherence of a particular theoretic system, in which subsequently each of the authority elements can be shown to have a necessary place, that justifies political authority, not in general but within that particular system. For it is within such a system that the authority elements have been successfully linked together.

As I see it, then, the question of strict or of absolute political obligation, whether or not it is an intrinsic feature in a theoretic system of political concepts and institutions, really depends on what the system is. Hence, to see if a particular theoretic system really can support the category of strict political obligation, we would need to give body to the notions that actually make up that system.

II

Hobbes's doctrine of consent is complex, as I have indicated. Accordingly, it might be possible to construct a small-scale model system from it. The question is, would that system support the elements of authority? It would only if it is a well-ordered, coherent system in which each of the authority elements can be shown to be ingredient.

Now Hobbes used a somewhat stronger idea than authority; he used the notion of sovereignty. He would, of course, make no significant distinction between the two. But my point remains the same. It would still be necessary to show that the background theory for the model system is coherent and hence able to support the three elements of sovereignty—(a) that lawmaking is rightfully concentrated in a single governmental body, which is all-powerful (and therefore has a title to issue rules on any subject); (b) that there is a reasonable presumption that citizens are absolutely or, at least, strictly bound to obey these rules; and (c) that government has a rightful monopoly in the use of coercive force and is thereby able to back up its laws with punitive sanctions. My claim here, and my criticism of Hobbes, is that his background theory is not coherent.

For Hobbes, government is the rational means to enforce the rational end of civil association, namely, peace. Peace, in effect, is no more than the keeping of the terms of the contract, terms that mandate a complete, mutual, and permanent renunciation of a policy of boundless and unending violence. No such contract is valid unless it makes sense to keep it—which requires that its terms can be maintained and enforced. Here government enters as a means to that end. A valid contract then would entail for me and everyone else as well that each one of us gives up the policy of first-strike violence on which we operated in the state of nature. My license, and that of others, to do just anything has been renounced.

The doctrine of consent in Hobbes amounts fundamentally to consent to be under government, where government is conceived as a rational means to a rational end and where government is always said to be constituted by someone in particular. I would suggest that how this consent is given—whether by open residence or by submission to a conqueror—is not the essence of Hobbes's theory of consent and that, if it were, the theory would be at best paradoxical and at worst merely Pickwickian. Rather, the essential point is what one is said to consent to.

Each person, as subject, voluntarily consents to stand aside, that is, to renounce a policy of first-strike violence, the natural license to do anything, vis-à-vis that person who is the sovereign. Hence the sovereign is and remains someone whose liberty to act, with respect to his (or her) subjects, is still in the state of nature, though they, of course, are not similarly free to act toward their sovereign or toward each other. The upshot of this curious convention is that the conditions of the state of nature carry over unilaterally in the relation between the government and its subjects.

Thus, from Hobbes's argument, the power of government is not something to be settled at a constitutional convention; it is decided at the very outset. Government can do anything by virtue of the retention by the governmental person(s) of the right of the state of nature. This power is not conferred, for it is already there in what is called natural right. This right merely carries over into the civil condition. All governments have the same power whether they are elective or not, or whether they are government by one or by many or even by all persons. Governments all have the same power, whether they use it ill or well, to serve this end or that.

By standing aside, we as subjects author each act of government, for we voluntarily allow the exercise of what we know to be a wholly unlimited power. Consent here does not confer the power but only allows it. We authorize each act of the sovereign as *de jure*, as coming under a rule of reason that we acknowledge and that defines (in the state of nature) appropriate conduct.

In Hobbes's view, governments can do anything, and nothing they do can ever be wrong in the sense of unjust. This is so, not because of the consent of the government's subjects, but by reference to a prior theory of natural right—with the added claim that governments are to be conceived as remaining, with respect to their liberty of action vis-à-vis their subjects, in a state of nature. That Hobbes regarded such liberty as both necessary and rational for the sovereign in a civil association is, I think, evident from the text of *Leviathan.*

But we need to examine this view one step further, for it is not the case that the subjects, in standing aside, permit or acquiesce in everything government might do. They may authorize it inasmuch as they recognize it as rational; they may be unable to call it unjust. They may even be unable to stop it. But they do not have to like or even comply with it. This is so because Hobbes did allow for a narrow range of cases in which, even though the law by definition could not be "unjust," it was "right" to disobey the law, the "right" in question being neither political nor moral but a "right of nature," the right of self-preservation (chap. 21, pp. 141–43). I have in mind such cases of resistance as immediately involve, in Hobbes's words, "death, wounds, and imprisonment" (chap. 14, p. 91). Thus anyone might resist being executed, might flee the scene of battle though commanded to stay, or might refuse to give testimony that could be self-incriminatory and hence punishable (chap. 14, pp. 86–87, 91–92; chap. 21, p. 142).

What we have in these cases is a conflict of natural rights between the sovereign, whose act is authorized by all as reasonable and in any case never unjust, and the subject whose act clearly serves to preserve life and limb. The action of neither one here is unjust, for in each case, the agent is regarded as being in a state of nature respecting the other person. That the subject no longer is willing to stand aside, no longer defers to the sovereign, is immaterial from the perspective of rights. The sovereign does not possess the rights by conferral; consent is no part of actually having or understanding the sovereign's power. Nor is it by action of the sovereign that the subject has the rights here exercised. The natural rights of each antedate the social contract and depend in no way on the consent or recognition of any other person.

The sovereign or government cannot be said to gain or lose anything respecting its natural rights by reference to the so-called consent of the subject. Nor can the subject be thought to gain or lose by the withdrawal of consent. All that changes is what the subject is willing to allow. What the sovereign wants to do is as authorized without the subject's consent as it was with it, for it is authorized by a rule of reason, insofar as such rules can be said to operate in a state of nature. The only change is in the subject's willingness to exercise an individual right (of nature) against the sovereign.

But is Hobbes consistent at this point? Most theoreticians, seizing on Hobbes's own language, have contended that he regarded the subject's natural rights as somehow renounced or transferred in every case where it is proper to speak of sovereign and subjects. The standard view is that all natural rights have been transferred to the sovereign, at least in the sense that only the sovereign has the disposal of such rights; the subject, simply in virtue of being subject, does not.[5] In this view, in a conflict between subject and sovereign, it is difficult to see how so-called natural rights could be called upon by subjects at all, let alone *against* the sovereign. It would seem that once renounced, those rights would no longer be available to the subject; when transferred, they would be the sovereign's alone.

Even on the most generous of readings, then, a question remains for Hobbes whether one can transfer one's natural rights to the sovereign without alienating them entirely. The best Hobbesian answer to this question is that we are really concerned here, not with a right proper, but with its exercise.[6] I would suggest that a more refined statement of the transfer of the subject's natural rights to the sovereign is required than Hobbes gave.

The subjects may be said to transfer the right of striking first to the sovereign and do so with the intention that the sovereign will protect each individual's vital interests. But what each subject actually does is simply stand aside: "The transfer of a right can only mean that the transferor will stand aside from the exploitation of [the sovereign's] preexisting right."[7] It follows that the subjects voluntarily allow for the sovereign to do anything, for this is his or her preexisting right, that is, natural right; and this could clearly jeopardize the vital interests of any one of the subjects.

Indeed, the position of Hobbes here, though it is not his language, is to say that the natural right of each to protect his or her vital interests has been waived. But this contention requires care, for when such a right is said to be waived, it has not been surrendered or renounced; rather, the right is retained but its exercise is forgone.[8] This waiving, for Hobbes, is permanent but conditional. That is, the right is held throughout, while the *exercise* of the right is extinguished permanently but conditionally—the condition here being the sovereign's respect of the subject's unmistakably vital interests.

It is plausible, then, and not inconsistent with Hobbes's basic theory to regard the invasion of the subject's vital interests, when "death, wounds, and imprisonment" are faced at the hands of the sovereign, as the trigger for the subject's exercise of his or her natural rights. It is plausible and consistent, that is, so long as the subject's renunciation and transfer of natural rights is construed as being merely a conditional, albeit perpetual, waiving.

The potential for conflict between sovereign and subject here is properly described as a conflict of natural rights. But how is this any different from the anarchic state of nature from which Hobbes starts?

45

It differs in two important respects. (1) Only the sovereign retains a policy of first-strike violence—a policy that the citizens as subjects have renounced for themselves in permitting it solely to the sovereign. (2) The citizen can resume a policy of violence against the sovereign only in the face of an active threat to life and limb. The sovereign is, respecting all the subjects, always in a state of nature toward each of them; but they are individually not in a state of nature toward it or toward each other. Each subject can, however, resume a policy of violence against an active threat of violence to life and limb, and when resumed, the policy of violence could be as extensive as it was in the state of nature.

Hence there is in Hobbes's theory of civil association an unresolved residue of the state of war. Hobbes allows for an impasse between rights in the civil condition that can only be resolved by a partial reversion to the strategies of the state of nature. To the extent that Leviathan was intended to be "Lord of the Proud" (chap. 28, p. 209), disallowing all active resistance or dissent by the subjects to the sovereign will, Hobbes's theory is defective.

Indeed, there is a further incoherence in Hobbes's theory. It has been correctly observed that if "there are natural rights of men, . . . there must equally be a possibility of collision between the sovereign power and these natural rights, which would justify a resistance to it."[9] One can thus argue that Hobbes's theory does not show, despite Hobbes's intent that it do so, that rebellion is always wrong. It could be noted, by way of reply, that the reversion to war that Hobbes contemplated was not a return to the state of nature per se; it was, rather, a one-to-one resistance of the sovereign by an aggrieved subject. It is not clear that Hobbes ever considered permissible a collective resistance to the sovereign by an army of subjects; indeed, one would expect that he was never willing to allow for this. But if my reading here is correct, then Hobbes's theory does not rule out even collective rebellion.

If a ruler were sufficiently inept or sufficiently evil or sufficiently hard-nosed to threaten the vital interests (regarding death, wounds, imprisonment) of many subjects, and to do so at roughly the same time, then each of them could justifiably resist. Given the reasonableness here of their resisting *together* (as offering the only hope of successfully repelling the sovereign's threatened invasion of the vital interests of each), they could and should make common cause by raising an army against the ruler. Here the sovereign's mighty power to overawe each subject, taken individually, would be countered in the only way it could be, by collective resistance. The appeal would then be to arms, and the king, if he would be king, must necessarily meet this army of subjects (now enemies) in battle. Right has been replaced by might. Thus we would have civil war—the paradigm of the anarchic state of nature for Hobbes and the very thing his theory was meant to rule out (chap. 13, p. 83).

The crucial disability in Hobbes's theory is the inability to satisfy its own terms of analysis, the projects it sets itself. It is the inability to rule out reversion either to a one-on-one state of war or to collective resistance to the sovereign—and hence a return to the state of nature—that marks the crucial failure. Hobbes's theory cannot meet its own standards for success as a theory. The theory is internally flawed and ultimately incoherent.

III

The linchpin idea in Hobbes's account is that subjects consent to government by "standing aside" from their own exercise of their natural rights; thus they waive, as I argued, any such exercise permanently but conditionally. On the basis of this account of consent, Hobbes's theory of sovereignty records two successes and a resounding failure. First, he does provide an interesting ground for the claim that the government must be all-powerful. The retention by governmental persons of their full natural rights implies, given Hobbes's account of natural rights, that they can do anything. Second, he does provide an interesting reason for saying that there can be only one topmost or fundamental governmental body (made up of one natural person, or a few, or all); for, if there were more than one such body, there would necessarily be conflict between them (since each would be normatively capable of doing anything). The problem of the state of nature, moved to the level of governmental bodies, would now be duplicated by them.

But the reason he gives for there being only one ruling body proves fatal to his theory of the potential conflict of natural rights between the citizen (in extremis) and the sovereign. The state of nature has not been fully overcome, for such conflicts must inevitably occur even in civil society.

Suppose, then, we fall back from Hobbes's claims and content ourselves with saying simply that his theory, while failing as a theory of sovereignty, shows some viability as a theory of political authority. (This, of course, is a distinction Hobbes himself would not make.) I do not think we can advance even such a modest claim, however.

First, Hobbes's theory is conceptually defective as one example of an externalist program for justifying political authority. Too much is allowed to ride on the idea of consent (where consent is assimilated to a promise, agreement, or contract). Hobbes often seems to take the in-effect promise of obedience to be normatively conclusive as regards the obligation of subjects and hence the rule-issuing authority of government. Second, where we flesh out the details of Hobbes's background theory in what I earlier called his model system, we find that it does not constitute a coherent set of ideas. Lacking systematic coherence, it cannot support (as systematically grounded) the main notions of political authority. Hobbes's theory consequently fails to justify political authority in the way mandated by the internalist program.

Specifically, Hobbes tries to combine natural rights of individuals both with the normative capacity of a government to issue rules—any rules—and with the strict obligation of subjects to obey those rules. My point is simply that such natural rights, presuming them to be retained throughout (as Hobbes did), would constrain both the government's capacity to issue rules and the citizen's strict obligation to obey the rules actually issued. (Hobbes could, of course, have recognized these constraints. If he had, his theory would be more like Locke's theory or like Rawls's today. But it would not be a Hobbesian theory of authority, not a theory of sovereignty.)[10]

Nor is my basic criticism changed if we put human rights in place of natural rights. For human rights (that is, ways of acting or of being treated that can be claimed for each individual, on general moral grounds, and that should be maintained by governmental action) would put the same constraints on laws issued and on the citizens' strict obligation to obey them.[11] Thus it cannot be argued, starting from individual natural or human rights, that we must end up with a single all-powerful governmental body, the laws of which the citizen has a strict obligation to obey.

The failure of Hobbes's account has an important implication for the establishment of governments. It is now possible that, starting from individual natural or human rights, we could end up with a plurality of more or less equal bodies, each one of which has restricted powers (constrained by the rights themselves), and some laws of which citizens would not have a strict obligation to obey. We can arrive at such a conclusion, I would add, only if we can show that basic rights, when thought through consistently, are part of a coherent system of concepts the instantiation of which involves the normative elements of a justified political authority. That is, it involves the presence of an authorized agency for making rules (or a coordinated set of such agencies), a reasonable presumption of citizen compliance with these rules, and the government's rightful use of coercion to prevent or punish noncompliance.

I will not, of course, attempt to construct such a system in this essay. But the failure of Hobbes's program, as demonstrated by

Locke, and the sense (however dim) that individual rights and representative, multibody government can form part of a program for justified political authority radically different from Hobbes's sovereignty theory was surely part of the background of what happened in Philadelphia in 1787–89, with the emergence of the doctrines of separation of powers and federalism and the Bill of Rights in that period.[12]

Five

Culture in Conflict

Anthony de Reuck

Thomas Hobbes, whose work we celebrate, has been appropriated by the political philosophers. He is accounted one of the founding fathers of English political thought. But he wrote at precisely that time when medieval scholasticism was giving way to "natural philosophy"—to what is now called "science." Galileo died and Newton was born in the year 1642, in which Hobbes first published *De Cive*, in Latin. It was also the year of the outbreak of the English Civil War, which so influenced Hobbes's thinking and which ended in the execution of the king and the creation of a republican Commonwealth. It might be taken to mark a watershed between the medieval and the modern traditions of politics, of philosophy, and of science.

The problems to which Hobbes addressed himself—the paradoxical functions of conflict in creating human groups, and the role of leadership in controlling conflict, for example—are now centrally located within the province of the social sciences. Though Hobbes's intentions were manifestly scientific, his intellectual system fell short of his scientific aspirations because it involved a confusion—universal before Leibniz—of logical or mathematical analysis with empirical or scientific inference. Hobbes's method was fundamentally deductive; nevertheless he can justly be claimed in kinship by the social scientists, as an intellectual forebear, together with Comte and Marx, Durkheim and Weber, at the foot of the tree of sociology.

It is as a political sociologist rather than as a philosopher that I appear in these pages: a trifle self-conscious as one uncertain of his role. What I want to do is to present to you, in deductive guise, an outrageously compressed argument derived from the sociology of conflict, which has grown out of the soil originally dug over by Hobbes.

Conflict as a Complement of Social Change

Briefly then, I wish to assert that, properly understood, all conflict is always about social change.[1] Specifically, conflict is both a cause and a consequence of changes in social structure, later to be strictly defined. Patterns of relations constitute social structures, and social structures form systems for the allocation of the means of production, persuasion, and coercion throughout society—indeed between societies. Thus conflict is about changing social roles or relations and the redistribution of human resources, material and symbolic.

Moreover, our social relations define both our personal and our group identities: our relations are constitutive of our selves. Our very identities are constituted by our families, our friends, our professions, our congregations, our communities, our nations. To change our social connections, to reconstitute our social milieux, is to change our roles, reshape our values, remake our identities. This is by no means impossible—indeed, it must be the aim of some parties to any conflict—but when it is too deeply disturbing to others whose identities are also at stake, it may be resisted even unto death.

Thus every conflict is liable to have a cultural dimension, not merely at the level of mutual misperceptions between opponents—though misperceptions there will surely be—but a culture clash at the subliminal level, at least partly unconscious, embedded in the *Weltanschauungen* of the protagonists, involving their concepts of order, of justice, and of morality.

Neither the connections nor the identities of any two people or any two groups can be the same; nor can they possess the same world view. The world in which we live is not our own mental creation: we inherit it as part and parcel of our language and culture. As Mary Douglas has said, "Individual thought is but social thought writ small." We do not decide or create or even choose for ourselves either our identities or our values—except in a limited contingent sense or in rare cases of genius. We are taught who "we" are, who "they" are, and how we should relate to others, for good or for ill. But we are nonetheless each uniquely situated both physically and mentally. We may share a culture, a world picture, but our point of view, our perspective, is uniquely our own. The greater our social and cultural separation, the wider the difference between us in outlook.

The Structure of Social Relations

This brings us to the question of social structure.[2] How are people bonded together and banded into groups? The explanation in terms

51

of calculated self-interest favored by Hobbes, or by Mancur Olson in his rational choice theory, are inadequate, on their own at least. Naturally there is some meeting of minds out of pure self-interest, as in deals among entrepreneurs or military alliances. But public spiritedness and even self-sacrifice are better diagnostic criteria of social bonding than free-riding on the system; and however unfashionable it may be to say so, altruism is a most striking feature of our dealings with each other, particularly in intimate human relations.

We are bonded together both by what we share and by what we exchange. We are linked by our interdependence in the social division of labor and by our shared codes and categories, ways of thinking and acting, which enable us to communicate together whether in order to collaborate or to compete.[3] The essence of all human relations is reciprocity, either of sharing or exchange, in more or less extended networks of social, cultural, political and, of course, economic indebtedness. Every persistent group can be envisaged as a marketplace comprising at least four analytically distinct subsystems, each distinguished by the form of symbolic credit it employs—social connection, cultural prestige, political legitimacy, or financial credit—to mediate the distribution of the corresponding productive outputs.[4] It is a virtue of this approach that all human relationships, whether in the fields of kinship, society, culture, religion, law, politics, or economics, are seen as versions of the same basic process. Each mode of relationship is metaphoric of all the others, and their inner dynamics and rationales are essentially homologous.

Social structures are thus envisaged as more or less persistent networks of exchanges. They therefore assume the configurations characteristic of markets, hierarchical, segmented, with all manner of market imperfections. This significantly new definition of social structure is the key to all that follows.[5] The ground rule of all relationships is reciprocity in quantity and in quality (of amity or of enmity). This is not a moral injunction; it is mere self-interest. We pay our debts so that we may borrow again; we retaliate under attack to deter further aggression. The object is to maintain our credit or our credibility: positive reciprocity sustains valued relations; negative reciprocity seeks to repudiate unsatisfactory ones. Balanced reciprocity is difficult to attain, however, and power inheres in relations of continual indebtedness. The incapacity of some to give as good as they get, their inability either to requite or to repudiate their debts—social, cultural, political, or economic—renders them dependent on their creditors. Power is the capacity to secure compliance from those to whom one is indispensable.[6] Whoever is the less dependent upon a relationship is the more powerful; it is clearly a matter of degree. Asymmetrical exchanges in value or in kind usually signal inequalities of status or power in the relationship. A patron, said Dr. Samuel Johnson, is one who supports with insolence and is repaid with flattery—and one is reminded of much international aid.

So it comes about that, as with all markets subject to a Pareto distribution, social stratification develops. To every human value there corresponds a social hierarchy; to every hierarchy must correspond a value. In a sense, these are tautologies. Wherever reputations are to be made or lost, there will be social ranking. How reputations are made—whether as prophets or warriors, as entrepreneurs or statesmen, as scholars or sportsmen—depends upon the local culture. But all values, all evaluations for better or worse, spell hierarchy. Those who pursue society's values most successfully rank highest in the eyes of their fellows; the hierarchy represents the current "state of the field" in the pursuit of that value.

For what do men strive but for fame, for fortune, for power, or for the love of women (and of course, *mutatis mutandis*, between the sexes)? Our four subsystems correspond to these representative values—cultural prestige (fame), economic fortune, political legitimacy (power) and social connection (affection)—which stand as surrogates for any number of possible values.[7] In addition, those of sanctity and honor in religious and military cultures come to mind. Each value represents a motivation system; each hierarchy represents an axial gradient, a drive to ascend, which constitutes achievement or "progress." The climb may be steep or shallow; the cone may be tall or short: these are social parameters to be determined empirically in any particular instance. But every ascent in social space must be paid for in work, in expenditure of energy over time; and since structural movement is implied, it also involves potential conflict and, at the least, competitive effort to outstrip other climbers. It may be observed that the urge to ascend or to compete must itself be partly a matter for cultural prescription (or proscription); where everyone else is climbing, it may be necessary to do so too merely in order to stand still relative to the rest, in the fashion of the Red Queen.

All social systems, at every level, tend to be stratified; most are also segmented. Universities are likely to be stratified by rank and attainment, and to be segmented into faculties of (say) sciences, technologies, medicine, and humanities. The British people are stratified by class and segmented into English, Irish, Scots, and Welsh. The global society of nations may be viewed as stratified into developing and developed countries and the superpowers, and also segmented into Western, Eastern, and Nonaligned blocs.

In each society, those who interact frequently and intensely form close relationships; those who interact less are socially, culturally, politically, or economically more distant. Thus the relations and distances between members of a social group may be mapped upon a center-periphery model (or, alternatively, within a stratified cone of which the center-periphery is a contour map), a radial plot with close and intense relations in the middle and those more sparse or attenuated around the margins. An egalitarian group would be represented by a flat disk, the limiting case of a cone with no height. The height of the cone, the width of the contours, will vary with each instance.

At the center are mapped people involved in dense and extensive networks. They are most active because they are best endowed and most productive. In the lower strata on the periphery will be those less well connected socially, less creative culturally, unproductive politically or economically because they are ill endowed and so have least to offer in exchanges.

Social structure is, by definition, this more or less persistent pattern of transactions, which like a waterfall retains its general form over time while continuously changing in content and in detail. The social system is thus a process rather than an entity, a process that shows many of the structural and dynamic properties of a market. The market structure creates the circumstances within which its members must choose strategically how they shall act or react to the moves of others.

Culture and Social Structure

Social structure is thus a map of relations in behavioral or social space, which implies that it is also a plan of culture, because patterned behavior must reflect shared patterns of thought.[8] Structured relations represent a pattern of ideas in action. A culture is a program for living. What it means to the community and how it works in practice are made manifest in their actions, in their structured relations. Because cultural norms and values are the rules for regulating the behavior, the relations that shape the social structure and determine its boundaries, so values and structure must be mutually consistent, or one or both would have to change. But since neither relations nor resources are uniformly distributed through society, neither are values. The different strata or segments in any complex social grouping represent different variants of the range of value sets. The social mosaic is also a cultural mosaic.[9]

For example, in Belfast, where most Catholics and Protestants prefer to patronize schools, shops and clubs, and to form friendships within their respective communities, transaction patterns faithfully mirror cultural polarization. The social structure makes manifest the perceptions, motivations, evaluations, and distinctions between people that make up their worlds of meanings. To a first approximation, in equilibrium, structure and culture must be congruent because culture is the text of the play "acted out" in the structure. Any mismatch between them heralds a mutual readjustment—and a potential occasion for conflict during the process of change.

Boundaries between communities are marked in social space by watersheds, where relations are so few or attenuated as to leave gaps in the network, or where the bonds are so weak that the preponderant valencies belong to another society.

Social, cultural, political, and economic boundaries do not necessarily coincide because their respective relationships operate over increasing ranges, so that each of the corresponding subsystems can encompass a larger domain. Social connections create a circle of intimates. Culture links us to a wider community, political bonds can extend to a whole nation, and economic transactions know almost no bounds. But nationalism has operated over two centuries to bring these domains together, so that now ethnic and national frontiers tend to coincide, at least in Europe.

Now we have defined and depicted social structure. And we can see at once that the relations between people or between groups vary according to their relative positions in that structure which includes them both—depending, for example, on whether they are above/below/beside or near/far from each other or approaching/receding, rising/falling, moving rapidly/slowly.

Social theory asserts that the social system can be both described and explained as a market structure involving at least four categories of transactions.[10] These transaction systems account both for the patterns of behavior and resources (the "objective" circumstances), on the one hand, and for the distribution of cultural values and identities (the "subjective" perceptions and motivations), on the other. Social relations are functions of the relative locations of the actors concerned. Consequently, changes in relations are correlated with their relative movements—and it is with such changes and movements that conflict is concerned.

Community and Association

Now let us turn to consider the cultural concomitants of structural location. We have seen that the warp and weft of the social fabric comprises two sets of interwoven connections. People are connected by their similarities, by their shared values and culture, on the one hand; and by their differences, by their complementary roles and skills through the division of labor, on the other hand.

Community, or *Gemeinschaft*, consists of people joined together by their common culture and the symbols they share, which enable them to operate a communication network with a common code. This is a largely expressive process, and one that affords people their sense of identity, often ascribed and indelible. So congregations in churches, ethnic groups within communities, and politicians in parties come together in the satisfaction of sharing and for mutual support.

Association, or *Gesellschaft*, concerns people made interdependent by their specialization in the division of labor, who are thus drawn into a trading network for the production and mutual exchange of goods and services. This network is largely instrumental in function: personal evaluations are based upon achievement criteria rather than ascriptive (inherited) values. Nevertheless, the goods and services need not be solely economic in essence. They may also be social or cultural or political in nature. Complementary exchange of nurturance in families or of instrumental performances in orchestras, as well as alliances in politics, are of this type.

The underlying factor distinguishing *gemeinschaftlich* from *gesellschaftlich* culture is primarily the degree of specialization of roles. The differentiation of roles and the extent of specialization in the division of labor is of course much higher in modern urban industrial societies than in traditional agraria. In *Gesellschaften* many social relations are single-stranded, in some cases purely social or familial, in others purely occupational or economic, and in still others largely religious or cultural, for example. Imperial China, though an agrarian economy, was strongly *gesellschaftlich*, with a highly developed Mandarin bureaucracy that ultimately became the model for the British civil service. In *Gemeinschaften*, on the other hand, where people are relatively unspecialized, relationships tend to be more complex. In one pair of persons, for example, elements of kinship and occupation may be combined. One may have both a cultural role as a teacher and political authority as an elder, for example.

Gemeinschaft and *Gesellschaft* together in varying proportions make up the fabric of every social group, however great or small. Between them, these two networks determine the allocation of the means of production, persuasion, and coercion (in Runciman's felicitous phrase) among the incumbents of the various roles that their economic, cultural, and political subsystems comprise.

In general, the core of virtually any social group is liable to be relatively more specialized and so more *gesellschaftlich* than the periphery, which is relatively unspecialized and *gemeinschaftlich*. By contrast, at the very center or apex of the group, the leadership may form an island of undifferentiated *Gemeinschaft*. That aside, we may say that stratification represents a cultural succession. The passage from periphery to center implies in general—there must be exceptions—a developmental sequence of increasing role differentiation and a steady decline in the proportion of *Gemeinschaft* to *Gesellschaft*.

The international system displays these features on a global scale, involving the world society of all humankind. The progression from Third World periphery to advanced industrial core forms a developmental sequence. It runs socially from the intimacy of rural communities to the anonymity of urban crowds, economically from subsistence farming to industrial manufacture for the market, politically from subjecthood in a traditional autocracy to citizenship in a bureaucratic republic. Culturally it marks a shift from emphasis at the agrarian periphery on the communal and the customary, on ascriptive roles, and on the sacred in both law and morality to a reliance in the industrialized core on bureaucracy, on achievement and meritocracy, and on the political and secular in the conduct of public affairs.

Those at the center of domestic societies, or indeed of world society, have one subset of values, and those at the periphery another. Those near the center are likely to be meliorist in aim and pragmatic in strategy, while those toward the periphery may have radical aspirations and espouse revolutionary means. When it comes to initiating social change, it will often be that the periphery proposes and the center disposes. Their respective views on justice are also likely to differ, sufficiently so as to ensure that a conflict of value will confuse every conflict of interest that arises between them.

Culture and the Conduct of Conflict

The degree of violence culturally sanctioned between social groups depends partly on the sociocultural distance between them.[11] Violence, broadly speaking, is outlawed *within* the community (e.g., murder) but in certain circumstances approved *between* communities (e.g., in war). This has important implications for social relations between industrial and agrarian societies, which are separated by a wide cultural divide.

Within all social groups, as Radcliffe-Brown observed, there is a distinction to be made between public and private delicts. Public transgressions of customary rules are likely to be punished as threats to society at large. They are crimes. This is in contrast with private trespasses for which society at large takes only limited responsibility, usually only to mediate. These are torts.[12] The distinction is fundamental to conflict analysis, particularly where what to one side is a crime is to the other a tort.

Prototypical public, that is, criminal offenses in all the urban *Gesellschaften* of Europe and America are homicide and theft, whereas private delicts leading only to civil actions at law are typically breaches of contract, including contracts of marital fidelity. At the opposite pole of the cultural spectrum, in many *gemeinschaftlich* rural societies, the culture provides for a reverse value discrimination. Incest rather than murder is the prototypical crime together with other breaches of the ascribed social order (e.g., adultery), whereas offences against persons or property are rated only as civil trespasses to be settled privately, torts in which society at large has no more than a mediatory interest.

If the cultural ideal of agrarian society is one in which everyone is connected, say by kinship or by feudal ties, in an ascriptive relationship to everyone else, then incest and adultery are the supreme threats to public order because they confuse kinship relations and disturb the proper stations from which life is conducted. In a technocratic culture constructed upon the premises of individuality and reciprocity, murder and theft become the supreme offences against the prevailing cultural ideals of the person and of achievement through honest dealing.

Observe now what happens when such cultures conflict. One may discern a binary opposition between two types of warfare. First, there is war between close neighbors sharing common cultural presuppositions—as in Europe, for example—competing within a partly tacit framework of received rules. This conflict is readily encompassed by the culture as a reciprocal exchange of violence between formally equal partners. Second, there is war between imperial and colonial societies, where the "superior" party makes its own rules, conceding no rights and precious little humanity to its "inferior" opponents. The cultural contrast exacerbates the conflict.

The first type of warfare corresponds in world society to private delicts and domestic quarrels, which are settled by civil suit on the assumption of symmetrically situated opponents willing to abide by the agreed rules of the game. The second can be likened to public delicts, matters for criminal jurisdiction, on the basis that "we," the authorities, make the law. In this light, breaches of the "law" by the "lawless" (or Kipling's "lesser breeds without the law") are an attack upon the foundations of the "natural" social ordering of affairs.

Palace rebellions and neighborly wars represent conflicts of interest in which the dispute is not about the rules of the game but about the distribution of the prizes. In contrast, revolutionary insurrections and wars of distant conquest are also conflicts of value in which the rules of the game are themselves at stake, particularly the ground-rule about who makes the rules for whom.

At the *gemeinschaftlich* peripheral pole, culture reverses the values of the *gesellschaftlich* central pole. In *Custom, Law, and Terrorist Violence* (1975), Edmund Leach suggests that this has a bearing on terrorism. Western society lives in vast, loosely knit, impersonal associations of relative strangers, who attach prime importance to individual achievement and to property relations. But there exist in their midst alienated people, damaged in dignity and identity by cultural rejection and effective exclusion from the rewards and therefore from the motivations of the established system. Thus, for example, many people of color are excluded from wealth, from power or prestige, in Britain and America. To this state of affairs there are several possible responses, including retreatism and counterrejection. Many such people retreat into a microculture shielding a relatively small, intimate, and closely knit community with an almost religious attachment to expressive relationships (loyalty, obedience, or doctrinal purity, for example) rather than to the received instrumentalities.

This cultural value–reversal reinforces the boundary and increases the sociocultural distance separating alienated groups from the larger society. For both sides it appears that "we" operate one set of rules, and "they" operate another—what is conformist in one may well be deviant in the other. And since members of the established system and of the minority society ambivalently both claim and reject membership of the other, each group claims the right to "legislate" for and to punish the other's deviance. The counterculture thus engenders a frenzied counterrejection.

In order for this reaction to occur, it is essential that members of the peripheral culture should at some stage have internalized the values of the macroculture by which they feel rejected. Exclusion from or even denigration by cultures to which we are not affiliated are rarely experienced as a deprivation. It is the circumstance of repudiation by their own reference group that forces people either to self-rejection or to the creation for themselves of a counteridentity repudiating the repudiators. These processes are reflected at different levels and in different ways in, for example, terrorism in Ulster, polarization in Cyprus, the revolution in Iran, and in much of the ambivalent culture-clash between the Third World and the industrialized world. Anomic violence is thus often rooted in the inversion of values across the *Gemeinschaft/Gesellschaft* interface—the discordant clash between the individualistic and instrumental Enlightenment politics of the center and the collectivist and expressive Romanticist or "religious" values of the margin—emerging at a level beneath the threshold of consciousness as a semi-impotent repudiation of an otherwise inescapable relationship.

Microcultural Contrasts

In the macrocultural contrast between center and periphery, we encounter the most obvious polarization of thought-and-feeling and structural situation. More subtle and interesting conflicts of value are to be discerned within any considerable social grouping, since every such structure comprises a mosaic of microsocial structures, like the clusters of crystals that go to make up a chandelier. Mary Douglas has been teasing out the corresponding microcultural climates of these small-scale structures in a notable series of publications.[13] In her analyses we are shown how the microstructure of social relations at any point within a larger society must correspond to a local cultural "dialect" or "sociolect." This correspondence carries with it profound implications for potential clashes of perception and of evaluation in disputes with other people, differently situated.

Consider Mary Douglas's four principal localized structural configurations. People, by choice or by chance, may find themselves members of an egalitarian group, or of an ascribed hierarchy, or operating in an individualistic and competitive arena. Or they may find themselves isolated, encapsulated in roles among the loftiest or lowliest in a social pyramid. Let us briefly consider each in turn in order to illustrate by example what should in future be the subject of study in depth.

Small-scale egalitarian groups are met with, for example, in political activist cells, in religious sects, in academic schools, or in hippy communes. Such collectivities tend to be characterized by constant, often implicit, threats by members to withdraw from the group, and by insistent norms of complete equality and total participation by everyone in group affairs and responsibilities. As a consequence, the group has a weak leadership—authority is itself likely to be an anathema—but a very hard and sharp boundary between members and outsiders. Deviance from the collectivist ethos is likely to be perceived not as innovation or ambition but as heresy or treachery. Individual initiative may be felt very intensely by other members as a disloyal challenge to both their collective and their individual identities. A "witch-hunt" may ensue—suspicion may indeed be endemic—ending in the only sanction open to the group, namely, expulsion of the guilty. For such groups, the world is divided between "them" and "us," the moral order between black and white, pollution and purity. The group and its categories alike are clearly bounded.

The strife notoriously encountered within and between charitable committees that, say, raise funds for hospitals or animal welfare, or that campaign on environmental or feminist issues, are often reflections of this type of structure; and their militant relations with the outside world may sometimes seem at odds with their expressed ideals.

Hierarchies, by contrast, say in firms or schools or regiments, are sustained by displaying an ethos that includes a compulsion both to conform and to ascend, ambition both engendered and moderated by respect for rank and authority. Each level (except the highest and lowest) implies alternative relations of superiority and subordination, preferably under the aegis of a strong central leadership. Arrested promotion is the principal sanction against deviance, viewed either as incompetence or as insubordination. Typically, strong elitist sentiments are allied to a disciplined group loyalty, often expressed through collective ritual observances. The world is ideally viewed as a march of progress, involving harmonious collaboration in a specialized division of labor, with meritocratic evaluation of achievement and worth. The universe exists chiefly to be exploited.

Those at the very top and very bottom of any hierarchy are often uniquely situated in profound insulation from those below or above them, possibly involving a social isolation in which virtually every relationship open to them is formalized, ritualized, and closely prescribed. The queen of England and the most junior maidservant in a great aristocratic household have this in common, that their range of acquaintances is strictly delimited by their roles and neither is really free to negotiate the smallest deviations from those roles, even down to the form and content of their most trivial conversations.

For *Homo aequalis* in his collectivist group, the universe, like society at large, is "outside," potentially hostile, perhaps to be wooed, but certainly not a passive entity to be exploited. "Outside" is potential pollution and danger, especially if nature falls prey to the exploiters, themselves dangerous "outsiders" and polluters. Anxiety lurks close beneath the surface of the mind about industrial pollution, nuclear accidents, resource depletion, ecological catastrophe. For *Homo hierarchicus*, on the other hand, the universe, like society at large, is potentially harmonious, benign if it is correctly controlled, profitable if it is properly exploited. Confidence persists in professional management, in the "technological fix," in resource substitution, and in environmental conservation.

Structural predispositions to a conflict of values on environmental issues may readily be discerned in the deep-seated and persistent tensions between the Friends of the Earth and their allies on the one hand and the nuclear-industrial lobby on the other, at perceptual and cultural levels that are manifestly distinct from (though probably congruent with) material or professional interests, and notoriously impervious on each side to rational persuasion. Equally notorious are our skewed perceptions of risk so that (relatively probable) road accidents lie beneath the threshold of consciousness while (relatively remote) dangers from nuclear contamination are very real in many minds. These paradoxes have also been the subject of structural analysis by Mary Douglas.[14]

The individualistic and competitive arena, in which people compete under the norms of laissez-faire enterprise, occur, for example, in many branches of scholarship and the arts, among politicians, publicists, and sportsmen, and of course in actual market trading. That situation affords members the utmost freedom to negotiate with each other to form or to swap alliances, with no effective group boundaries and no generalized constraints on private dealings. The group exercises few collective sanctions, but individuals who fail to compete successfully or to secure recognition are liable to be driven to the periphery, there to be subjected to ruthless exploitation. This is a Hobbesian environment of piratical self-help, and the moral order is primarily viewed as a race for prizes that properly fall to the swift and the strong.

Is it not fair to see former president Reagan's advisors on the National Security Council as wheeler-dealers operating in such a free-enterprise arena, and to observe that they were judged by hierarchically minded organization-men on the Congressional committees investigating the "Irangate affair," employing a different set of values and inhabiting a different perceptual world?

Douglas's four configurations are "ideal types" intended to exhaust the structural possibilities but perhaps rarely to be encountered in their pure forms. Any actual society may be expected to show some complex mixtures of them in varying proportions. Together they certainly subsume an extraordinarily wide variety of recognizable milieux within which people live out their daily lives and quarrels. They may gravitate deliberately to one rather than another of these situations, even converting one into another. Most people, of course, spend part of their lives, part of their days, in one type of structure and the remainder in another. Few people exist in "total institutions"—such as convents or prisons—that command every aspect of their activity and time. *Mentalités* are formed by a variety of experiences and situations, and to each social configuration there corresponds a "cosmology," as Douglas calls them. The point is not that people are trapped in these sociocultural structures, but that for those who are content to continue within them, each structural situation induces a cognitive consonance between thought and action in its members, so as to endow their mental worlds with different styles of intellectual coherence—and also with different and possibly troublesome styles of perceptual incoherence with their neighbors. We are, incidentally, here on the threshold of a cultural anthropology of philosophical controversy. But that, as they say, is another story!

Six

Hobbes and International Relations: The War of All against All

Daniel M. Farrell

Hobbes is well known for arguing that rational, self-interested individuals situated in a "state of nature" amid conditions of moderate scarcity would choose to leave the state of nature in order to form a commonwealth in which the power and rights of each individual are subordinated to the power and sovereign authority of an absolute ruler (or ruling body). And while some writers have claimed to see little importance in Hobbes's reflections in this regard, I think it is clear that if Hobbes's argument were sound, it would be very important indeed. For it would show that inasmuch as we, like Hobbes's imaginary egoists, want to preserve ourselves and, if possible, to prosper, we will, if rational, support either the continuation or the establishment of something pretty much like the sovereign that Hobbes set out to defend.

Of the many interesting things that Hobbes says in his discussion of these matters, one that particularly interests me is a point he makes almost in passing. Imagining himself pressed to give an example of parties who would actually face the sorts of difficulties he imagines people facing in a state of nature, Hobbes declares that all *sovereign states* are in the state of nature relative to each other, inasmuch as such states exist in a situation where there is no single sovereign power to which each of them can appeal in settlement of its quarrels with the others.[1]

What are we to make of this claim? It is certainly true, given Hobbes's way of thinking, that the nations of the world were in the "state of nature" relative to each other in the seventeenth century.

It is true as well that, relative to each other, the nations of the world are in the state of nature today.[2] Is it also true, though, that because they are in the state of nature, the nations of the world are inevitably involved in a "state of war"? Supposing they are, does it follow that if they are rational, the nations of the world will agree to leave the state of nature and submit themselves to the authority and power of an international version of the absolute Hobbesian sovereign? Or must we say that Hobbes's argument for the rationality of leaving the state of nature does not apply to nation-states, perhaps because of some important difference between individuals and nations? Finally, supposing we take this latter tack, what exactly shall we say are those differences that make it rational for individuals to support the relevant form of national sovereignty but not rational for nations to support an analogous form of international sovereignty?

In what follows I want to explore these questions, with an eye to determining whether Hobbes's arguments for the rationality of submitting to absolute authority can be applied on the international level and whether, supposing they can, we must conclude from this that it is just as irrational for nations to refuse to submit to an all-powerful international sovereign as it is for individuals to refuse to submit to an all-powerful national sovereign. Of course, not everyone agrees that Hobbes is right in what he says about the rationality of submitting, as individuals, to a form of absolute sovereignty. However, most writers do agree that when the proper qualifications have been made, Hobbes has formulated a compelling argument for submitting to something very much like his favored form of sovereignty. Hence it would be interesting to know whether something like an international "supersovereign" can be rationally justified, even if the exact form of sovereignty that our argument establishes is not quite the form that Hobbes himself might have favored.

I

Let us begin by rehearsing Hobbes's argument for the claim that individuals would make the choice he favors, supposing they found themselves in the sorts of circumstances his famous thought-experiment requires. Very briefly, the argument is that if we begin with individuals who are basically rational, predominantly self-interested, and roughly equal in their mental and physical abilities, and if we suppose that these individuals are situated, without a government, amid conditions of moderate scarcity, we will see that what Hobbes calls a "state of war" must inevitably ensue. This being so, the argument continues, we must ask what these individuals could do to avoid this state of war and, given whatever options would be open to them, whether any one of these options would be clearly preferable to the others and preferable, as well, to remaining in the state of war. As is well-known, Hobbes's view is that there is really only one alternative to remaining in the state of war, that being the alternative wherein we choose to leave the state of nature by agreeing to submit ourselves to the power of an absolute sovereign.

A few comments are in order before we go on to ask whether this argument can plausibly be extended to the situation that arises when, with Hobbes, we imagine the state of nature populated, not by individual human beings, but by a group of nation-states. First, we should note that when Hobbes argues for the inevitability of what he calls a "state of war," he is arguing, not for the inevitability of constant interpersonal violence, but for the inevitability of a certain attitude or dispositional state. "For war consisteth," Hobbes says,

> not in battle only, or the act of fighting, but in a tract of time wherein the will to contend by battle is sufficiently known; and therefore the notion of *time* is to be considered in the nature of war, as it is in the nature of weather. For as the nature of foul weather lieth not in a shower or two of rain, but in an inclination thereto of many days together, so the nature of war consisteth not in actual fighting but in the known disposition thereto, during all the time there is no assurance to the contrary. (chap. 13, p. 100)

This point, of course, will be quite important when we come to ask whether the international order really is inevitably a state of war and, if it is, whether it is such a war as to make it irrational for nations to prefer remaining at war over avoiding war by submitting to some form of international sovereignty.

Second, we should note that while, given Hobbes's assumptions, many writers are willing to concede that war in this sense is inevitable for imperfectly rational individuals, or even for perfectly rational individuals with imperfect awareness of each other's rationality, there is considerable controversy over the question of whether perfectly rational individuals with full awareness of one another's rationality would in fact be driven inevitably (in a Hobbesian state of nature) into a Hobbesian state of war.[3] This point, unlike the previous point, will not have much effect on our reflections on the rationality of nations' submitting to international sovereignty, since the assumption of perfect rationality, with perfect reciprocal knowledge of perfect rationality, is not an assumption that will have much interest in application to the international realm. Still, it is important to bear in mind that Hobbes's conclusions about what individuals would do, were they situated in a state of nature, are accepted by many writers only with the provisos just described.

Third, we should also note that Hobbes is not required to deny, by anything he argues in *Leviathan*, that cooperation is possible in the state of nature, even for imperfectly rational individuals with imperfect knowledge of each others' rationality. On the contrary, Hobbes himself describes cases where rational cooperation will occur, even among individuals who are apparently assumed to be only imperfectly rational (i.e., who are not necessarily assumed to act rationally all the time) and who are also apparently assumed to be less than fully confident of the rationality of their peers.[4] The point is simply that, despite whatever cooperation will occur, the state of war is nonetheless inevitable, in Hobbes's view, given the conditions we have assumed will hold in the state of nature.

Finally, we should note that what most commentators are willing to concede, in response to the argument sketched above, is not that submission to an *absolute* sovereign is shown to be rational by Hobbes's argument, but that submission to some form of limited (but still quite powerful) sovereignty is what that argument forces us to accept.[5] This point will of course be quite important in our deliberations below, where we will eventually want to ask, supposing the international state of nature is inevitably a Hobbesian state of war, whether leaving that state of war, by submitting to an international analogue of Hobbes's civil sovereign, really would be preferable, to strictly self-interested nation-states, to remaining in the state of war.

II

Let us assume that, understood as an argument for the desirability of submitting to some sort of limited sovereignty, the argument sketched above is sound. The question we want to ask, in light of this assumption, is whether an analogous argument can be constructed to prove the desirability of submitting to a similar sort of (limited) sovereignty when the parties in question are taken to be nations, or nation-states, rather than the individuals that Hobbes appears to have had in mind in most parts of *Leviathan*.

Now I shall assume without argument that the situation of the nations of the world satisfies at least three of the four conditions that Hobbes imagines holding for individuals in the state of nature and leading inevitably to war: the relevant nations are predominantly self-interested, they are basically rational, at least in the sense that they are capable of reasoning from ends to means in the standard decision-theoretic sense, and they are faced with a moderate scarcity of the resources that they need to satisfy their national aspirations.

More problematic is the question of whether we can plausibly suppose that nations meet the fourth condition Hobbes imagines and that his account in fact requires if the state of nature is plausibly to be said inevitably to lead to a state of war: namely, the condition of rough equality.[6]

At first blush, of course, it would appear that rough equality is something that we clearly cannot attribute to nations. For some nations are quite clearly more powerful than others militarily, and more powerful in ways that give them clear advantages over other nations. Hence it is tempting to conclude that Hobbes's argument simply cannot get off the ground.

This conclusion, however, would be premature. For one thing, it would overlook the fact that at least some of the nations of our own world are roughly equal militarily, and hence could plausibly be said to constitute, relative to each other, a world in which all four of Hobbes's conditions for war hold. Of course, this would be uninteresting if these happened to be relatively weak nations, since we could then imagine that some stronger nation would inevitably end their state of war by reducing them all to submission to its own power. However, as it happens, at least two (and possibly more) of the strongest nations in our own world are themselves in fact roughly equal in military power. Hence it seems reasonable to think of these nations as constituting a genuinely interesting example of nations that exist together in a state of nature and that meet the conditions that Hobbes thinks must inevitably generate a state of war.

I shall pursue this line of thought in a moment. First, though, we need to say something about where it leaves the weaker nations. Do they just fall out of our conceptual picture, so far as our interest in a Hobbesian theory of international relations is concerned, or is there some way in which they too can be seen as involved, and involved in interesting ways, in the world in which we imagine the superpowers contending for power?

I think it can be shown that these other states do not necessarily fall out of the picture and, moreover, that they remain in the picture in ways that make their presence interesting and important as regards the issues that will concern us below. To see this, we need to note, first, that to parallel conditions in the interpersonal state of nature, we need to suppose that every nation is driven by a desire to survive—that is, to preserve itself and its own national identity. Thus we must suppose that as long as they survive, the less powerful nations will do what they can to continue to survive, despite their inferior position relative to the larger states; and of course we must suppose as well that the more powerful nations will do the same.

But now consider the following possibility: suppose that in the world we are imagining, the smaller nations, or some of them at any rate, take advantage of the fact that none of the larger nations wants the other larger nations to become too strong (i.e., strong enough to be in a position to make a credible attempt to dominate the other stronger nations). Suppose, in particular, that at least some smaller nations get themselves, individually, into a position where one or another of the larger nations is willing to grant them a certain amount of independence provided they do not get too close, politically, to the other larger nations. In such an eventuality, we would end up with a world where more than just large nations survive and where some smaller nations have a kind of threat capacity relative to the larger nations: they can affect the behavior of one nation by seeming to get closer to another.

Let us suppose, then, that something like this picture is true of our contemporary world. The larger nations—the so-called super-powers—enjoy the rough equality that Hobbes's account requires. The smaller nations, on the other hand, while not enjoying anything like equality relative to the larger nations, nonetheless manage to survive with their own national identities intact, rather than being swallowed up by one or the other of the larger nations, because they are able to take advantage of the fact that none of the larger powers is willing to allow the other larger powers to enhance its own power, through international aggression, beyond a certain point.

Our interest here, of course, is in whether a Hobbesian state of war is indeed inevitable in the world just described. First, though, one final preliminary point must be made. We have thus far avoided mention of what some writers see as the salient feature of contemporary international relations, at least when viewed from the standpoint we have been taking: I refer to the existence and possession, by any number of nation-states, of nuclear weapons, weapons with an extraordinary destructive capacity and yet that are, by conventional standards, relatively cheap.[7] How, it might be asked, does the fact that such weapons are part of the arsenals of both of the superpowers, and of some of the smaller powers as well, affect the picture we have sketched so far?

My remarks on this score must necessarily be rather cursory. But this much seems clear. The existence and possession of nuclear weapons does not significantly alter the picture we have painted, so far as relations between the superpowers is concerned. Whether a nation has a military capacity roughly similar to another, both being among the most powerful nations in a given world, is independent, logically, of just what sorts of weapons account for the fact that this is so. Of course, the number of nations that could plausibly be said to be included in the number of roughly equal, and equally superior, national powers might be importantly affected by the availability of nuclear arms. But this is consistent with the point just made: from the Hobbesian perspective that currently interests us, the sources of military might are not nearly as important as the fact of rough equality between two or more independent nations. I return to this point below.

Equally clearly, though, the existence of nuclear arms does seem to be relevant to the second part of the picture we have painted. For we supposed that it was a significant feature of the contemporary world that certain smaller nations manage to survive, and thus avoid being entirely dominated by aggressive larger nations, by playing the larger nations off against each other in a way that effectively makes certain larger nations the "patrons" of certain smaller nations. This process, it seems to me, might well be significantly affected if smaller nations come to possess even moderate arsenals of nuclear arms. For in possessing such arms, along with a suitable means of using them, smaller nations will come to possess a second way to threaten larger nations with harm: just as they could previously threaten to align themselves with competing larger nations, thereby getting a given nation to respect their national integrity, so now they can threaten at least limited (but very extensive) military damage as a way of protecting themselves against their larger neighbors.[8] To be sure, their threat capacity will not be anything like that of the larger nations, and in any case they will use their threat capacity knowing that if they ever do what they have threatened, they will be annihilated in turn. Still, the possession of nuclear weapons does seem to have given certain smaller nations in our own world an extra measure of security, so it seems reasonable to suppose that this is something we can plausibly build into our picture.

III

What we have seen thus far is that it is possible to think of the major powers in today's world as occupying a Hobbesian state of nature and as satisfying, at the same time, the conditions that Hobbes claimed were sufficient to make inevitable an interpersonal state of war. What's more, we have seen that it is consistent with viewing the modern international order in this way to imagine that, although they are the strongest, the major powers are not the only players in the international game. I now want to turn to the question of whether a Hobbesian state of war really is inevitable in such a situation, given the assumptions we have made, and then to the question of whether the only reasonable choice for the relevant states, supposing the state of war is inevitable, is to leave the state of nature by forming and submitting to some analogue of the Hobbesian sovereign.

It might at first seem obvious, given Hobbes's way of conceiving of the state of war, that the state of nature will inevitably be a state of war. It might also seem obvious that this is bound to be so whether we populate the state of nature with individual human beings or with sovereign states, for the state of nature is by definition a situation where the relevant parties are imagined to coexist without a common power to which to appeal for enforceable adjudication of interpersonal or international disputes. In a situation where there is no such common power, how else are we to imagine the relevant disputes being settled except by force of arms?

This argument for the transition from the state of nature to the state of war moves much too quickly, though. Among other things, it overlooks the distinction between being in the state of nature, on the one hand, and satisfying there, on the other hand, the conditions that Hobbes postulates in his account of the inevitability of war. It would be easy to show, though space prohibits our actually doing so here, that parties who fail to satisfy some or all of the conditions that Hobbes postulates might readily exist in a state of nature without thereby succumbing to a state of war. If we suppose that the relevant parties are benevolent, for example, or live amid extraordinary abundance, it is fairly easy to see how they might avoid the state of war. The question therefore is why we should suppose that nations that satisfy our four conditions must inevitably find themselves in a Hobbesian state of war.

Now despite the existence of the very rich and complicated literature that has developed on this question, I think the answer is actually quite simple: war (in Hobbes's sense) is inevitable in the state of nature, given our assumptions, because in the final analysis the parties there will simply not be able to trust each other not to resort to violence when conditions suggest to one or more of them that resorting to violence will help them advance their aims (particularly that most fundamental of aims, both individual and national, which is to secure one's own existence and to secure oneself at the same time against possible attacks by others). Of course, to say that lack of trust is a salient feature in the state of nature as we have imagined it, and that it is in fact responsible for the inevitability of the Hobbesian state of war, is not to say that trust—or at least rational expectation of a certain sort—is impossible there. We know from the theory of games that under certain circumstances—for example, the circumstances that are characterized by an iterated Prisoner's Dilemma of unknown length—egoists situated as we have imagined our egoists situated can in fact cooperate effectively to advance their own ends. Still, it is consistent with recognizing this fact to recognize as well that under certain other circumstances— for example, circumstances characterized by noniterated Prisoner's Dilemmas or by an iterated Prisoner's Dilemma of known length— cooperation will not be possible, at least for rational egoists of the sort we are imagining here. Hence, as long as we accept Hobbes's definition of war—namely, a willingness to do battle should one's welfare appear to require it—we must say that nations in a Hobbesian state of nature *will* inevitably be at war, given our assumptions, and will inevitably be at war for exactly the reasons Hobbes's original argument suggests.[9]

IV

Suppose everything we have said thus far is right: some of the largest and most powerful nations in the contemporary world are roughly equal militarily; many of the smaller nations, while not even remotely equal to these larger nations in military might, nonetheless manage to survive, both by virtue of playing the larger nations off against each other and, in some cases, by accumulating a nuclear arsenal that gives them at least a moderately enhanced threat-capacity relative to the larger nations; and finally, "war" in Hobbes's sense is indeed present and inevitable in our world, inasmuch as we exist in a situation where at least a good number of the nations of our world are ready to do battle with each other if a point arrives where it appears their national interests require it. Obviously, it does not follow from this that it would be irrational for the nations of the world to refuse to create an international sovereign of some sort—a sovereign world-government, for example, analogous to the national governments that make it possible for individuals to avoid the state of war. It remains an open question at this point whether subjection to such an international form of sovereignty would appear, to rational nation-states, preferable to their condition in the international state of nature. Even if the (international) state of nature is (inevitably) a state of war, and even if the only way to avoid this state of war is to agree to submit to a world state of some sort, it follows that we rationally ought to form (and submit to) a world state only if it can be shown that our prospects as members of a world state would be better than our prospects as separate nations in the condition of war that we are supposing is consequent upon remaining in the international state of nature.

Can this be shown? Clearly, any account that purports to show it would have to provide us, among other things, with compelling answers to the following questions: (1) What would establishment of the requisite form of international sovereignty involve, and what would international life be like under it? (2) What exactly are the disadvantages of our present international arrangements that this new arrangement would arguably remedy? (3) Why should we suppose that those disadvantages—particularly the evident presence of the Hobbesian state of war—cannot be eliminated without establishment of the international sovereign that direct application of Hobbes's argument entails? Needless to say, in this essay we will not be able to address these questions in anything like the detail they deserve. Indeed, the third question will have to be avoided altogether: I shall simply assume without argument, given our remarks above, that regardless of whatever cooperative efforts and international restraint our present condition may allow, it will indeed be impossible to eliminate the state of war, as Hobbes conceives it, without the establishment of some quite powerful form of international sovereignty.[10] What about the first two questions, though? What can we say, even briefly, about what would be involved in establishing an international analogue of Hobbes's sovereign and how plausible is the claim that a world in which a sovereign existed would be preferable to the world imagined above (very roughly, the world we now in fact inhabit)?

As for the question of just what we would be agreeing to, as nations, if we were to agree to an international analogue of Hobbes's sovereign state, the following two points will have to suffice for now. First, I shall suppose that this international state would not be an "absolute" state of the sort Hobbes himself favored, at least in the domestic version of his argument, since we are supposing that Hobbes's modern critics are right in saying that an absolute state is not supported by Hobbes's otherwise quite compelling argument. Thus, while we can suppose that the member states would have to give this "superstate" the power to do the job they are creating it to do—to keep them out of the state of war—I shall suppose they would not have to yield to it all the rights and powers Hobbes imagines us yielding to the sovereign described in chapter 18 of Leviathan. Second, though, we must suppose that even though an absolute state is not supported by Hobbes's arguments, a state of a very formidable sort would have to be created if it is to be able to achieve the task we would be creating it to achieve. In particular, we must suppose that any state that is going to be able to end the state of war is going to have to have a more or less effective monopoly on the use of force. In the present context, therefore, we must suppose that while the superstate we are imagining will not be the absolute superstate that an exact analogue of Hobbes's argument would require, it will nonetheless be a sovereign body that has at its disposal force sufficient to see to it that any of its member-states will do its bidding when told what to do. And what this means, I shall suppose, is that at least the following two conditions will have to hold: (1) no member nation will be allowed to retain nuclear weapons, so far as it is possible to see to it that this is the case; and (2) no member nation will be allowed to retain a balance of conventional forces sufficient to enable it to resist the orders of the sovereign. In the absence of either of these conditions, it seems to me, it would be impossible to say that we had created anything like an analogue of Hobbes's sovereign, even a limited one, and anything like what will be required to bring us out of the state of nature and put an end to the state of war.

Our question, then, is whether, given a choice between the sort of international arrangement just described and the sort of arrangement that in fact currently prevails, it would arguably be irrational for the nations of the world not to choose the former over the latter. As indicated above, the answer to this question will presumably depend on what the relevant nation-states can reasonably expect their lives to be like under each arrangement.

Now I shall suppose that the primary advantage of the first sort of arrangement is that it effectively ends the international state of war. What this means, among other things, is that the fear of actual war, both nuclear and non-nuclear, which we have supposed to be inevitable in the current state of affairs, will be eliminated. (Or, at any rate, the rational grounds for such a fear will have been removed.)[11] Against this advantage, however, which certainly must count as extremely important, we must balance whatever disadvantages might accrue to the arrangement. And then, of course, we must weigh the totality of expected advantages and disadvantages thus conceived against the totality of advantages and disadvantages, so far as we can determine them, of remaining in the international state of nature and thus in the international state of war.

How are we to determine what the disadvantages of the relevant sort of international regime would be, given that such a regime has never existed and hence is not something about which we have a great deal of first-hand experience? The answer, obviously, is that we have to ask what it is reasonable for potential members of this regime to *expect* its disadvantages to be—what fears it would be reasonable for them to entertain as they contemplate the prospect of creating such a regime and compare that prospect to what they have (i.e., international anarchy and the Hobbesian state of war). Of course, when we imagine the nations of the world doing this, the worry that immediately comes to mind is exactly the worry Hobbes himself imagined when, in chapter 18 of *Leviathan*, he tried to anticipate objections to the creation of the domestic version of the kind of sovereign we are now considering: surely we have at least as much to lose, through abuse of the power that will be conferred on the rulers of the imagined state, as we have to gain through the existence of that state, supposing its powers are not abused.

It seems, then, that nations contemplating the sort of move we are considering are in the following situation: they know what the disadvantages of their present condition are, and they assume that these can be remedied only via submission to a form of international sovereignty. However, at least two outcomes are possible should they make this move: a more or less benevolent international state, on the order of a more or less benevolent domestic government, or a tyrannical international state, analogous to the tyrannical domestic government that Hobbes imagines in chapter 18.[12] What's more, we may suppose they know that while their present condition is bearable—after all, this is how they are presently living—they also know, especially given the existence of nuclear weapons, that that condition could easily get much worse. Unfortunately, we must suppose as well that while they know all these things are possible, they have no idea just how probable the various outcomes are. No doubt, they may think they have reason to believe—and they may indeed be right in this assumption—that certain outcomes (e.g., the development of a tyrannical superstate, should they choose to create such a superstate) are much likelier than others (e.g., a more or less benevolent superstate). However, to grant this is consistent with saying that they have very little idea, if any, exactly what the relevant probabilities are.

What is it reasonable for them to do under these circumstances? It is clear, I think, that the large (i.e., militarily strongest) nations will choose to stay with the status quo. Despite the disadvantages of remaining in the state of war, the prospect of becoming victims of the sort of tyranny to which they themselves may well have subjected the smaller states will presumably prevent them from taking a chance on ending the state of war at the risk of becoming tyrannized themselves.

What about the smaller states? They, it seems to me, will take much more seriously the option of submitting to the sort of state we have in mind, since they have less to lose should that move not work out for the best. Of course, should the superstate turn out to be tyrannical, the condition of at least many smaller states will turn out to be worse than it was in the international state of nature. (After all, we are supposing that many smaller nations are managing, through a variety of means, to keep themselves intact and relatively independent in the state of nature.) Still, it might be argued that if transition to a superstate is possible, it would be rational for the smaller states to support its creation, taking a chance on the more acceptable outcomes being realized.[13]

But even if the smaller states do see taking this sort of chance as rational, the transition cannot be made, since we must assume that as long as the larger states choose not to take the same chance, all the nations must remain as they were. Thus, as long as we assume that the larger nations will not take this chance, and will not take it because of the rationality of keeping what they have rather than taking a chance on an alternative, we must assume that the transition in question will not occur. What's more, if we assume that the larger states are right to suppose that taking this chance would not be rational, we must conclude that Hobbes's argument cannot be extended to the international state of nature, even if we suppose that argument to be sound when applied to the interpersonal state of nature that Hobbes actually had in mind.

V

What have we learned? Two points, it seems to me, stand out. First, though it is possible to construe the situation of nations in our present world as analogous, in important respects, to the situation of individuals in Hobbes's state of nature, the inequalities in military power that characterize our present world appear to be great enough to keep a Hobbesian argument for some serious form of international sovereignty from going through. To be sure, the relevant inequalities are in many cases not great enough to keep us from saying that a rough international equality of power is present in our own world (at least as regards a fairly large number of nations). As we have seen, none of the more powerful nations seems to be in a position to impose its will on all other nations, not even on all of the smaller (or weaker) nations; and given the presence and possession of nuclear weapons, a number of smaller nations seem to have exactly the capacity that Hobbes himself regarded as decisive in determining when two or more parties could be said to be roughly equal in power: that is, the capacity to threaten the very existence of other parties (chap. 13, p. 98). Still, the fact that we must distinguish, at least in our own world, between militarily "weak" nations and "strong" ones, seems to have the result that the "strength" of the strong nations will inevitably appear to them to be a reason for resisting the move from an international state of nature to some form of international sovereignty.

The second point to be made in light of our argument above is importantly related to this first point. In alleging that the so-called stronger nations might reasonably believe their prospects to be better if they remain in the international state of nature, rather than accepting some international (but nonabsolute) equivalent of Hobbes's civil sovereign, we ignored the question of just how likely actual warfare is in the present (or any other possible) international realm. Of course, we ignored this, at least in part, because Hobbes's definition of the state of war invites us to ignore it: we are "at war," on his view, at least as long as we are in the state of nature, just in case each of us is indeed willing, when our interests appear to require it, to do battle with the others. Clearly, though, it makes a great deal of difference, so far as concerns the relative desirability of remaining or not remaining outside a coercive international order, just how likely actual warfare is so long as we remain in the state of nature and hence in the Hobbesian state of war. If the probability of actual warfare is high enough, and the consequences of such warfare (for any given nation) are bad enough, it will presumably be reasonable even for the stronger nations to agree to leave the state of nature, despite the risks that this will entail.

We can see, then, how Hobbes, or a modern-day follower of Hobbes, might attempt to show that it is irrational for the stronger nations to refuse to support the creation of the relevant form of international sovereignty, despite the fact that in supporting it they run the risk, along with the weaker nations, of creating a monster that may well attempt to devour them. For if it can be shown that the risks of actual warfare are great enough, in the absence of the creation of such a sovereign, and that the consequences of such warfare would be bad enough—even for the stronger states—it can be shown that for any given state the expectable utility of moving out of the state of nature is greater than the expectable utility of remaining in it. Unfortunately, the question of whether the relevant probabilities currently obtain—I shall suppose that the consequences, should certain forms of warfare actually occur, are indeed sufficiently grotesque—is a question we cannot pursue here. We may simply note, for now, that until this question is resolved, the question of whether it would in fact be rational for the nations of the world to accept an international "superstate" is one that must remain unresolved.[14]

Seven

Hobbesian Reflections on Glory as a Cause of Conflict

Jean Hampton

In a particularly cynical passage of Hobbes's book *De Cive,* the philosopher declares that there is a "natural proclivity of men, to hurt each other, which they derive from their passions, but chiefly from a vain esteem of themselves."[1] It is this cause of conflict that I want to discuss in this essay. The desire for glory is problematic in the context of Hobbes's political writings. Insofar as it is different from, and a competitor with, the desire for self-preservation, glory-pursuit can (and does) disrupt the rational pursuit of self-preservation by precipitating conflict. And because Hobbes finally appeals to the rational pursuit of self-preservation to justify the institution of a sovereign, then to the extent that people are prone to the desire for glory, they may find their attempts to institute a sovereign disrupted. Hence, after heavy emphasis on glory as a cause of conflict in Hobbes's early writings, it is downplayed in *Leviathan.* That book emphasizes instead the way in which the rational pursuit of self-preservation precipitates warfare by prompting competitive aggression and defensive responses to such aggression, both of which can only be stopped (and self-preservation finally secured) through the institution of a ruler with absolute power. In my previous writings on Hobbes's political thought, I have been primarily concerned with the structure of Hobbes's argument for absolute sovereignty—not only the structure it has in *Leviathan* but also the structure it *ought* to have if his argument is going to succeed, and thus I too have had to downplay the impact of glory-pursuit on warfare on Hobbes's behalf in order to ensure that it is not so powerful as to make the institution of a sovereign-remedy for conflict impossible. But in this essay, I want to put aside Hobbes's argument and discuss his various remarks on the desire for glory in and of themselves. Generations of readers of *Leviathan* have found these remarks fascinating, insightful, and yet somewhat mysterious. We seem to know the desire he is trying to describe, and yet it is hard to understand the nature of the object of the desire. Just what is the glory that all of us want? Precisely how does our pursuit of glory place us in conflict with one another? And can we understand the conflict between nations by reflecting on the glory-pursuit of individuals?

I. Hobbes's Characterization of Glory

In *Leviathan*, Hobbes defines two kinds of "glorying"—a healthy sort, and an unhealthy sort:

> *Joy*, arising from imagination of a man's own power and ability, is that exultation of the mind which is called GLORYING: which if grounded upon the experience of his own former action, is the same with CONFIDENCE: but if grounded on the flattery of others; or onely supposed by himself, for delight in the consequences of it, is called VAINE-GLORY.[2]

It appears from the tone of the discussion of glory in chapter 6 that Hobbes means us to understand it as a desire for personal advancement that is somehow biologically intrinsic and that is so strong in us that when we cannot see it satisfied by the reality of our own powers and abilities in the world, we lie to ourselves or seek out the lies of others in order to inflate our sense of who and what we are. Yet the intrinsic nature of this passion is certainly questionable, because glorying in our abilities—particularly the unhealthy kind of glorying based on the flattery of others—seems to presuppose a comparison with other human beings, which could only develop in a social context. Hobbes himself says in the *Elements of Law* that glory-pursuit can prompt "signs of contempt and hatred, which are incident to all comparison."[3] Such remarks provoked Rousseau to argue that Hobbesian people prone to this passion could not be isolated individuals in a presocial state of nature precisely because this passion can only arise after social interaction.[4] What is the desire for glory after all, but the desire for high esteem from one's fellow human beings? When we crave glory, do we not crave recognition, social esteem, a valuable reputation?

Yet if this is so, the desire for glory in human beings would seem to presuppose the existence of a human community, a state of affairs in which people peacefully interact with and talk with one another, in such a way that reputations can be formed and people held in high or low esteem. Certainly the state of nature is not such a community, but if the desire for glory assumes such a community, then Hobbes cannot argue that his "natural" people need a sovereign for *all* social interaction and development because they already display a passion that reflects quite considerable sociality before any sovereign is instituted. We thus find another reason for Hobbes to shy away from discussing this passion at any great length in his later writings: it may well be a passion whose presence in human beings is in and of itself an argument against Hobbes's anti-Aristotelian claim that our sociality is not fundamental to our nature and only possible after the invention of a certain kind of political institution by self-interested human beings.

Is Rousseau correct that the desire for glory is one that could only take root in people who were interacting with one another fairly extensively? In the rest of this essay, I shall pursue this question by exploring what we want when we say we want glory. However, I do so not only to resolve the question of how far this passion is socially derived, but also to understand how it precipitates conflict. In his definition of the passion for glory, Hobbes does not condemn the pursuit of this object in and of itself, but only a certain kind of pursuit of it. Glory-prone people who are right about their eminence are legitimately confident and reasonable people; but those whose good opinion of themselves is based on self-deception or the insincere flattery of others are vainglorious, and it is this latter group that Hobbes regards as dangerous. Because of their dependence on the opinion of others for their good opinion of themselves, they cannot take it when someone communicates a low opinion to them. A vainglorious person, writes Hobbes in *Leviathan*,

> looketh that his companion should value him, at the same rate he set upon himself: And upon all signes of contempt, or undervaluing, naturally endeavours, as far as he dares, . . . to extort a greater value from his contemners, by dommage; and from others, by the example. (chap. 13, par. 5, p. 61)

And in *De Cive*, he argues that a vainglorious person, "supposing himself above others, will have a license to do what he lists, and challenges respect and honour, as due him before others. . . . This man's will to hurt ariseth from vain glory, and the false esteem he hath of his own strength" (chap. 1, sec. 4, p. 7). In a passage from *Elements of Law*, Hobbes also suggests that vainglorious people fight with others after they become enraged by insults to their power, having "provoke(d) one another by words" (part 1, chap. 14, sec. 4, p. 54). But why should insults prompt fiery spirits to violence? Why is it that people who degrade us make us angry enough to hit back at them? And why should hurting others help someone to gain their esteem and self-respect?

Perhaps these questions strike the reader as strange. Of course we know all too well the anger that wells up inside us when we have been insulted, and we know all too well the competitive violence that many of us engage in to prove ourselves "the king of the hill." What I am trying to suggest, however, is that we do not understand very well what prompts the anger or the violent competition because we do not understand very well what these responses are *for*. So let us bring, as best we can, the desire for glory before us in our minds and examine what it is that we want so badly that it would cause us to hurt those who say we do not have it. In what follows, I will attempt to develop a Hobbes-inspired theory of glory and its role in precipitating conflict.

II. The Nature of Glory

In his definition of glorying, Hobbes maintains that when we achieve glory we experience great "joy" and "exultation of mind" arising from a contemplation of our power and ability. But we do not exult over the fact that we have any particular power or ability. Instead, the aptitudes we have give us glory because we take them to signify something deeper and more important about ourselves.

There is a television talk show host in Orange County, California, named Wally George. George is politically very far to the right, and behind his desk on the television set is a picture of the Apollo 11 rocket that landed the first human beings on the moon, on which is printed, "The USA is #1." I have often reflected on what those words are supposed to mean. It seems wrong to ask what the USA is number one *in*. The sign is not merely saying that the USA is best at space travel, or scientific achievement, or economic growth. Rather, it is by virtue of these achievements that *it* is number one. The country itself is what is supposed to be better than all the others—to rank highest on some status ladder. So that picture on Wally George's set makes a statement about this country's worth or value relative to the worth or value of other nations. I want to propose that when we pursue glory, either as individuals or as a nation, we are pursuing a high worth, or as Hobbes would put it, a "high valuation" relative to other individuals or nations. But how is it that worth is assessed? Must it be assessed relative to the worth of others?

We can better understand the nature of the worth we seek by exploring "insults," those actions or words that challenge our sense

81

of our own worth. Imagine someone who has received treatment that is perceived by her as "disrespectful" or even "abusive." The person who wronged her is essentially sending her a message through the insulting treatment that she is not worth better treatment. Now there are two ways that a victim can respond to this message: she can reject it as wrong and hence regard the action as inappropriate given her true (high) worth, or she can worry (or even believe) that the insulter is right, that she really isn't worth better treatment, so that his action is understandable and permissible.

If she responds in the first way, she perceives herself to have suffered no literal degradation as a result of the wrongdoing. Her high status is, she believes, unchanged despite the action. But she is nonetheless demeaned in the sense that she has been forced to endure treatment that is too low for her. So there is a difference between feeling *demeaned* and feeling literally *degraded*, lowered in status or value. A prince who is mistaken for a pauper and who therefore fails to receive royal treatment will feel demeaned by this treatment, not because he will believe the treatment makes him into a pauper and causes him to lose his princely status, but because he will believe that the treatment is too low for him given that princely status. That is, he does not regard himself as literally degraded; he only receives treatment that makes it appear as if he is lower in status. It is because he believes that he is *not* lower in status that he regards the treatment as insulting and, if others are aware of it, humiliating. Similarly, a victim who is demeaned by an immoral action believes she has experienced treatment that is insufficiently respectful of her true high moral standing. Hence she finds the treatment insulting (and, if others are aware of it, perhaps also humiliating).

Exactly when one will be demeaned depends upon the rank that one's "theory of human worth" accords one. A theory of human worth tells one what sort of treatment is appropriate, or required or prohibited, for certain types of individuals on the basis of an assessment of how valuable these individuals are. Some philosophers follow Hobbes in thinking that any assessments of our value as individuals can only be instrumental. According to Hobbes in *Leviathan*, "The value, or worth, of a man is, as of all other things, his price; that is to say, so much as would be given for the use of his power" (chap. 10, par. 16, p. 42). Other philosophers insist that regardless of our price, the value that determines the kind of respect we should be accorded as persons is noninstrumental and objective. For example, according to Kant, by virtue of having the property of rationality, we are ends-in-ourselves, and this fact makes every one of us equal in worth and standing.[5]

But Kant has other opponents: there are objective theories of our intrinsic worth that do not accord us equality, for example, views of human beings that propose that certain people, by being members of a certain race or caste or sex are higher in value and deserving of better treatment than human beings who are of a different race or caste or sex. The fact that women are more frequent targets than men for certain kinds of violence shows how many assailants see males, but not females, as having a value that rules out the infliction of this sort of violence. And those human beings (e.g., black people in America) who have suffered unequal treatment, even slavery, know what it is like to be accorded a worth, and hence a moral status, that is less than the status bestowed on other human beings (and that, in extreme cases, can be more like the status accorded to animals).

One's theory of human worth may also be nonobjective, denying that there are any properties that bestow upon us a certain value and status. A theorist of this sort may see existing notions of relative standing purportedly based on assessments of "intrinsic worth" as, in reality, a societal creation, connected with or perhaps even the same as social standing in that culture. Alternatively, he might perceive it as a ranking that reflects subjective assessments of individual value, or as a ranking that varies from individual to individual depending upon what properties each uses to construct it and his judgment of the extent to which different individuals manifest these properties.

Theories of human worth can also differ in the way moral ranking is assigned. Consider that when assigning grades to students a professor can either determine the "level" of their work according to certain criteria in such a way that it is possible in theory for every student to get an A; or she can grade her students using a curve system, a method that assumes that there can only be so many A's, so many B's, and so forth. The first method, which I shall call "critical grading" can be used to evaluate people either noncompetitively or competitively (depending upon whether the criteria for a high rank include "winning" in competition against the others); the second, which I will call "curve grading," is inherently competitive and comparative. Moral theories can grade human beings in either of these two ways. That is, people may be evaluated to see whether or not they meet the criteria required for a certain standing (e.g., do they qualify as ends-in-themselves, as natural slaves?); or they may be assessed to see how far they are better or worse than one another, such that their particular positions can be determined on a "value curve" (where different theories may have differently structured curves).

We are used to the idea of philosophy students and even philosophy departments being graded competitively; but many readers will likely disapprove of the idea that our standing as human beings might be so determined. The hierarchical mentality fundamental to this form of grading is not popular among moral theorists in this day and age, and indeed, this kind of grading is much more commonly used in assessments of value in nonmoral contexts. However, we shall also see that the form of evaluation we find intellectually plausible and the form of evaluation our emotions in moral contexts actually presuppose are not necessarily the same. Finally, a terminological point: in what follows, when I speak of people losing "rank and value" or losing "standing," I intend these phrases to be neutral between the two grading systems.

A person's view of her standing determines whether an action will be interpreted by her as demeaning. For example, she can feel demeaned by another's action if she believes that she is the superior of the other but has received treatment that accorded her mere equality. In this country twenty years ago, a white person who was forced to sit next to a black person on a bus might have felt demeaned insofar as this made it appear that they were of equal rank and value and hence to be treated equally. Alternatively, one's outlook can prevent one from feeling demeaned by treatment that is obviously insulting. A rape counselor once told me of a woman who failed to tell anyone that she had been raped by a man she knew because she thought this was the sort of thing women had to "take" from men.

The rape victim was actually an example of someone who has suffered a more severe kind of injury than simply being demeaned. Prior to the rape, she had not been treated in a way that would convince her of her own worth. Her reaction to the rape was thus not surprising. She was like a princess who believed, after receiving treatment appropriate only for a pauper, that she really was a pauper. Such a person cannot feel demeaned because she has already suffered injury to her sense of self-worth.

There are two ways in which a victim can come to have her sense of self-worth injured. First, she may take an insult as evidence that her standing is lower than she thought: this will lead her to worry that the insulter's message may be right and that she has incorrectly accorded herself a standing (associated with a certain level of treatment) she does not warrant. She does not believe the treatment has *effected* a lowering of status; instead she worries that it has *revealed* a status that is lower than she thought. The injury here is injury to her self-esteem, and if it is severe, she may fall considerably in her own estimation. However, this injury can come in degrees. As long as her faith in her own worth is not completely undermined, she will still have some degree of belief that the wrong-doer's treatment of her was inappropriate given that worth. But to the extent that her sense of self-worth is shaken, any emotional protest of the insult will be mixed in her with the fear that the action wasn't an insult after all, a fear frequently associated with the emotions of depression and despair. Subservience, servility, and slavish temperaments are produced in victims of substantial or repeated wrongdoing whenever they come to believe their assailants' message: "You're not worth enough for me not to do this to you."

Second, an insult can effect injury to one's sense of self-worth if it is perceived to have done something to change one's value. For example, a victim can come to fear that a wrongdoing has actually effected a lowering of moral status if he interprets the assault as a "loss" to the wrongdoer that makes him "not as good as" she is in the way that a boxer's loss to another in the ring will result in his being ranked lower than the victor. Or the victim may fear that the action effects his degradation through the physical or psychological harms it has caused. There are certain ideals current in our society toward which we strive: for example, being the ideal athlete, the perfect mother, a "real" man. Certain kinds of deeply insulting (and immoral) actions can rob us of properties necessary to realize these ideals. A man paralyzed from the waist down by a gunshot wound may feel that the paralysis robs him of his manhood, or destroys his athletic dreams. A woman whose injuries mean that she can no longer bear children may feel that she has become a biological failure as a female. Feeling lowered in quality (becoming less than one's ideal) as a result of these injuries does not, in and of itself, mean feeling that one has suffered a loss of value as a human being. But such injuries can be linked by these victims (falsely, most of us think) to their worth; they may worry or even believe that the injury from the immoral action that makes them less than their ideal thereby makes them less valuable as persons, so that they no longer merit the same kind of respectful treatment they did before the injury. It is popular these days for philosophers to propound theories of individual worth that make it something possessed by all human beings no matter how little excellence they manifest as members of the human species (assuming, of course, that the damage they sustain is not so severe as to make it questionable whether or not they *are* human beings). This happy message is not always one that victims are able to believe.[6]

Let me now apply these remarks to Hobbes's perspective on glory. I have argued that the pursuit of glory should be understood as the pursuit of a high valuation, or the pursuit of high worth as a person. However, what one takes that pursuit to be depends upon the theory of human worth that one has. The valuation one believes one has or that one seeks may or may not be comparatively defined, and it may be either intrinsic or instrumental in nature. However, Hobbes's instrumental approach to valuation and his emphasis on honor or worth as derived from preeminence show that for him glory is attained when one is highly valuable in the marketplace of people. When Hobbes says in *Leviathan* that the value of a man is his price, he notes that value is "therefore not absolute; but a thing dependent on the need and judgement of another. . . . As in other things, so in men, not the seller, but the buyer determines the Price" (chap. 10, par. 16, p. 42). So there seems no doubt that Rousseau is right: the desire for this kind of valuation can only arise in a social context, although Hobbes is understandably reluctant to admit it.

III. Glory as a Cause of Conflict

The emotions of resentment and hatred are often associated with challenges to our sense of worth. In our analysis of them, we shall see that someone who holds a Hobbesian theory of human worth has the kind of perspective on a person's value that is likely to result in violence. We shall also see that Hobbes is on the right track when he says that it is not glory-pursuit per se, but the *self-deceptive* pursuit of glory, that is most dangerous to the community.

Resentment is a kind of anger over an insult, a protest of the demeaning treatment, and this protest is frequently linked with a verbal rebuke, reprimand, or complaint directed at the insulter. Of course, we judge some forms of resentment as unreasonable (e.g., the resentment of a white woman at having to sit next to a black person on a bus), and we also criticize people on certain occasions for *not* feeling resentment (e.g., the rape victim in our previous example). In both instances, however, the ability to perceive a wrong-doing and to feel resentment depends upon one's having enough sense of one's own worth to believe that the treatment is inappropriate and deserves protest.

But resentment is more than just a protest. It is also an emotion that attempts a certain kind of personal defense. To see this, consider an insulting situation in a context in which there is *only* protest: Imagine the response of a mother to her small child who has just misbehaved by, let's say, lying to her. Of course it would be appropriate, even required, of the mother to protest the small child's action, which she would naturally do by rebuking the child. Such a protest is, in itself, a kind of defense of the moral rules according to which such behavior is wrong. But we would think it strange of the mother to resent the lie of a small child; surely, we would think, the mother is "above" resentment in such a situation. Indeed, if she did experience that emotion, we might speak of her as being "insecure."

People like this mother, who are "beyond resentment," experience the demeaning nature of the insulting action, and they protest it because they want to defend the moral rules condemning the immoral behavior. Of course, these rules accord them value, so that defending the rules is an indirect way of defending themselves, but self-defense is not the point of the protest. Their anger focuses on the fact that the wrongdoer made a moral mistake; it does not focus on their own hurt. Thus, unlike resentment, this anger is not felt as a personal anger and the protest it involves is not intended as a personal defense. I will use the word "indignation" to denote this kind of anger, although that word is generally reserved for a very severe form of such anger, which a nonresentful victim may not experience. Some readers may even think that "resentment" has a wide enough meaning to cover this impersonal form of protest, but because I want to distinguish the two forms, I will call the impersonal form "indignation" and reserve "resentment" for the personally defensive protest. Note that this analysis explains why indignation may be—and frequently is—experienced by someone who witnesses a wrongdoing committed against someone other than herself, whereas resentment is normally an emotion experienced only by the one who has been harmed.[7]

What does it mean to say that resentment is a personally defensive protest? I propose that resentment is not only a protest of the insulting action but also a defense against the action's attack on one's self-esteem. As we have already discussed, someone can come to believe one of three things about an insulter's action: (1) that the insulter has made a mistake about one's status and is treating one inappropriately given that status; (2) that the insulter is right to think that one's status is low; or (3) that the insulter is right to think that one's worth can be changed and that the mistreatment has successfully effected a lower standing. Those who cannot resent harmful treatment accept that either point 2 or point 3 is true. Those who are "beyond resentment" are certain that only 1 is true and that responses 2 and 3 are false. But those who do resent the harmful treatment have some degree of belief in point 1—indeed, they want to believe it wholeheartedly—but they nonetheless fear that 2 or 3 may be true. Their mistreatment has raised doubts about their status.

The emotion of resentment is thus complex. It not only consists of a characteristic "feeling" frequently associated with certain physiological changes (a flushed face, an increased heartbeat), but also includes the following components:

1. A fear that the insulter has shown you to be, or else made you, lower in rank and value on some moral or nonmoral scale. Your fear can be analyzed as involving (a) some degree of belief that the insulter has made or shown you to be lower in rank and value (i.e., you neither fully believe it, nor fully disbelieve it); and (b) a *wish* that the belief in (1a) is not true, such that you are not lower in rank and value (i.e., you wish to have little or no degree of belief that you are lower in rank and value).

2. An "act of defiance": You "would have it" that the belief in (1a) is false (i.e., you would have it that you are still high in rank and value).

This act of defiance is the heart of the emotion. The resenter denies that he is lower in rank and value, and thereby defies the appearance that he is. This defiance is engendered by his wish that the fall did not occur. It is what he is using both to defend himself and to protest the harmful action as wrong. It is the person's battle against accepting the lower standing.[8]

Hatred is also a response to insults, and it is frequently confused with resentment. But whereas the object of hatred can be and frequently is a person, the object of resentment is an action. When resentment is directed at a person, it is about what he did, not about who or what he is. Hence we say, "I hate you" and "I resent what you *did*," but generally not "I resent *you*."

The semantic difference directs us to the substantive difference between resentment and hatred. But to pursue this difference we first need to see how the word "hatred" covers a family of negative emotional responses. For example, I can hate a person in the way that I hate cloudy weather, or ski-mobiling, or mosquitoes. "I can't stand that man," I may tell my friend at a party, "he talks my ear off every time I meet him." This is what I will call "simple hatred": it is an intense dislike for or a strong aversion to an object perceived as profoundly unpleasant, accompanied by the wish to see the odious thing removed or eliminated. This sort of hatred is the opposite of "simple love," the attraction one feels toward objects one finds greatly pleasurable, from sunny weather and chocolate, to charming people at parties.

Much less simple is the kind of hatred toward human beings that is experienced in many moral contexts; for example, I may speak of hating the Nazis for what they did to the Jews, or of hating the South African whites for their violence against blacks. I will call this "moral" hatred: it is an aversion to someone who has identified himself with an immoral cause or practice, and it is prompted by moral indignation and accompanied by the wish to triumph over him and his cause or practice in the name of some fundamental moral principle or objective, most notably justice. Initially this kind of hatred seems surprisingly impersonal; one is not really attacking the person so much as the immoral principles with which he has identified himself. But these principles can get tangled up with his character and beliefs in the way that a cancer can get tangled up with the healthy cells of one's body, so that hating them can come to mean hating him. Moral hatred is the opposite of what one might call "moral love," the attraction one feels toward someone whom one believes has identified himself with a moral cause or objective, combined with the desire to see him and his moral cause prevail, the kind of emotion felt toward people like Martin Luther King, Jr., or Gandhi.

I do not have the space to discuss moral hatred in this essay, and in any case, it is an emotion that Hobbes shows little sign of recognizing. But I do want to distinguish both of these forms of aversion from the sort of hatred that Hobbes was very concerned to condemn, the hatred one tends to feel toward those who have personally brought harm to one (where that harm may or may not be a moral wrong)—the hatred I feel when I experience spite or malice toward someone or "nurse a grudge" against him. Note that one can only feel this form of hatred toward a *person*; it makes no sense to feel spite toward a crime. So this kind of hatred can only be a personal animosity, and as I shall now argue, this is because the person's action generates a *competitive response* to him.[9]

Resentment is an emotion that contains within it both the fear that one has been made or revealed to be lower in rank and value than one had believed previously, combined with a defiant denial of the fall. Clearly, a resenter is in an unstable situation—she is trying to defy what she half-believes. How does she keep from succumbing to what may be the unpleasant reality? The rational way of defending oneself would be to go out and secure evidence showing that the feared belief is false. The problem with this strategy, however, is that the evidence may point to the belief's being true. Hence our vulnerable resenter would prefer a strategy that will *ensure* that she finds support only for the belief's falsity.

Hatred is not only an emotion with a characteristic feeling and certain accompanying physiological changes, it is also a strategy for getting that support, and this introduction to it should already suggest my conclusion that it is an irrational strategy for restoring self-esteem. But I am getting ahead. In order to understand hatred, we need answers to three questions: How does this emotion "work"? How is it a "strategy"? And exactly how does it fail to achieve the hater's objective? Answering these questions is, I believe, the key to understanding how the pursuit of glory, interpreted as the pursuit of a high valuation, precipitates violent conflict.

Imagine someone who has hurt you badly—suppose he has physically assaulted you. If you hate him, you see him as "low" and "base." Your hatred may prompt you to try to "get him," or "hurt him back," or "get even." You vilify him either in private or to his face. You may seek his public censure and take pleasure in the thought of his humiliation. Whereas you seek to see a beloved one increase, you desire to see this hated person decrease. But what good does his diminishment bring you?

Perhaps you value that diminishment for its own sake, so that your hate is a display of what one might call "negative other-interestedness."[10] But this does not seem right; there is far too much human enthusiasm for this emotion (especially among the most selfish of us) to make it plausible that the only self-regarding benefit to be gained from it is an unintended side-effect of the pursuit of a disinterested objective. But to find the self-regarding good that haters pursue, we must figure out how diminishment of another can be a good for us. Only then will we discover the *point* of hatred.[11] Consider that one situation in which you are benefited by harm to another is when you are in competition with him. In a race you benefit from your opponents' exhaustion when it allows you to win. An orange grower in Florida benefits from the harm by frost to growers' crops in California if it allows him to sell his product at a higher price in a competitive market. So we have an explanation for a hater's pleasure at the thought of her opponent's demise if we see her as competing and wanting to win against this person.

For what is she competing? Consider again the two ways in which a wrongdoer's immoral action can damage the victim's self-esteem. She may worry that his action has effected a lowering of her status and value, or she may worry that his victory reveals that she has less value and status than she thought she had. A resentful victim who wishes to restore her self-esteem may not think the insulter has elevated himself by his insulting action—she may only fear or believe that she has been diminished by it, falling not only relative to him but to others. As long as she believes this, diminishing her opponent does not make sense; she wants to raise herself up, and she does nothing to achieve this objective if she works to bring him low. But if she interprets the injury in a competitive way, she will pursue the restoration of her standing by attacking the standing of her opponent. In other words, she begins to hate her opponent. A hater sees the assailant's action against her as representing a loss in a competition for rank with him. Her own fall was the means by which another elevated himself relative to her and to others. For example, if she believes she and others are evaluated for rank on a curve, her opponent's action represents a competitive victory over her that allows him to move up the ladder and forces her to move down. Alternatively, those who believe they are evaluated on a criterial-basis can read their loss in a competitive fashion if they see the wrongdoer's action against them as a victory that reveals qualities that place him higher and them lower on the ranking ladder than they were (or thought they were) previously. Compare the way in which tennis rankings work: a lower-ranked player who beats a higher-ranked player moves up in rank and causes the higher-ranked player to drop in standing; similarly, a hater may fear that the hated one has beaten her in a way that shows that he meets the criteria for a higher standing, and she the criteria for a lower standing.

Haters respond to this competitive threat in a competitive way. Like the resenter, haters "would have it" that the standings created by the hated one's triumph over them are not correct. Their hatred is a strategy for buttressing this defiance. The hater supports what he wishes to believe by reinterpreting the world so that his opponent is diminished, and this reinterpretation is frequently accompanied by action designed to reveal or effect that diminishment. The diminishment of the opponent is valued as a means to the hater's ultimate objective, namely, showing himself to have high rank (at the very least, a higher rank than it appears that he has, given what he has suffered).

What do I mean when I say that hatred involves a defiant reinterpretation of the world? Consider someone who inwardly seethes at an enemy whom she fears has "won" over her in some way. Using words that vilify her enemy and elevate herself, this person projects onto the world the rankings she would have them occupy. She "sees" him as low, and herself as high. Like an unscrupulous scientist casting around for evidence to support her theory, the hater uses anything that might count as evidence for what she wishes to be their relative value and rank to support her defiant view of their real standings. For example, she might make use of things she has heard people say about him, or psychological theories that call his achievements into question, or prominent character defects—anything that could be grist for her mill that he is really lower than he appears on the ranking ladder. She may also imagine herself winning various hypothetical contests with him, thereby lowering him and raising herself in her own mind. Her dim view of him may even arouse emotions of disgust and outrage at his action and character. And through it all, she takes pleasure in the thought of his diminishment because she believes it represents a relative gain for her on the ranking ladder.

But such private reinterpretations are rarely enough for the hater. The relative valuations she projects onto the world have their source in a wish. She cannot simply claim that she believes these valuations; the fear driving the defiance tends to undermine her belief in them, and her unscrupulous use of evidence does little to confirm them in her own mind. Hence, to make this buttress stronger, haters will frequently try to find new evidence for their reinterpretation of the world, so that the valuations they wish to be true are further supported.

To this purpose, a hater may attempt to persuade other people that despite, or even because of, what her opponent has done to her, he is a "low-down" character whereas she is fine. If they agree to her valuation, this provides evidence that it is true, helping her to believe what she wants to believe. Or she may vilify the opponent to his face, trying to extract from him a confession of his inferiority, which would be another kind of evidence that the relative valuations for which she hopes are indeed true.

More commonly, she engages in what are called "vengeful" actions that attempt to downgrade the opponent by controlling or harming or mastering him. For example, if she fears her opponent is right to say, in virtue of his action against her, that he is "up here" and she is "down there," she may welcome the chance to return the harm to him in order to send the reverse message. By "getting him the way he got her," she wins against him in the same way that he previously won against her, and this, she hopes, will provide evidence that she is now superior.

The action threatening the hater's sense of self-worth and relative standing need not be what we would normally consider to be immoral. For example, In 1 Samuel 17–18, King Saul is described as hating David (and seeking to have him killed) because of David's excellence as a warrior. In Saul's eyes such excellence was evidence that David was a superior leader. David thus became a hated rival for the highest rank in the community and the object of Saul's murderous intentions. Note, however, that although David's action was not immoral and was not even directed at Saul, it still threatened Saul's understanding of his social and political rank and value in his community, and hence was an action whose message he felt called upon to defy.

Nor is it necessary that the hater, in order to be threatened, fear that her assailant's action has shown her to be inferior to him; she need only fear that it has either changed or forced a reevaluation of their relative rankings, lowering her and raising him. To give an example, I once knew a teenage boy who was in the track club at school, and who decided that he wanted to race a female friend of his. They staged the race and, to his alarm, she won. He was mortified because he had lost to a girl, and very angry at her for what he thought she had done to him, but her victory did not suggest to him that she was of higher standing than he. Instead it suggested that relative to other males he was of rather low standing precisely because a female could beat him in a race. He responded to her hatefully, verbally abusing her in person and maligning her behind her back. The boy perceived her action as raising her status as a female while lowering his (still higher) status as a male; he believed that regaining the status that her victory had taken from him required that he master her on other playing fields.

One may even hate a person who one believes has a higher ranking than oneself if one takes exception to action which suggests that one is even more inferior than one thought. A peasant's hatred of the lord whose onerous taxes are hurting him may never dream of trying to prove himself the lord's superior, but he may still long to attack the lord and achieve victory over him in order to degrade the lord and upgrade himself.

Hatred thus involves the belief that the action of the hated person may have downgraded you, at the very least, relative to him, and probably also relative to others. This holds even where that behavior may not even have been directed toward you, as we saw in the case of Saul and David. You "would have it" that he is lower and you are higher; hence you seek the diminishment in status and value of the hated one because you believe yourself to be in competition with him. You attempt to "win" over him either through a reinterpretation of the world in your own mind, or through actions or events that confirm the reality of your faith in your higher standing relative to him (and thus to others). This is why we call haters "vindictive"—they are trying to vindicate a controversial faith in their own relative standing and value.

Because they are after this kind of vindication, haters always welcome any actions of others that might manifest the opponent's lowliness, and that therefore might be taken indirectly to suggest their own elevated status. But I suspect we tend to think that vindication is surest when we win a direct competition with the ones we hate. Their defeat at our hands provides the best evidence for our claims not only that they are lower, but that we are higher.

I have argued elsewhere that the benefits of hatred are illusory and that the emotion is in fact self-defeating.[12] That argument is complicated, and I will not go into it in any detail here. But one problem with this emotion should be obvious, and it is a problem that Hobbes, in his initial definition of vainglory, actually picked out. The hateful pursuit of a high valuation is a strategy that is based on a *lie*. It is not the honest attempt to determine and accept what one's real valuation is, relative to others. It is, instead, the dishonest attempt to defy appearances and see the world as one wants it to appear, and the very dishonesty of the strategy undermines its effectiveness. The more I lie to myself about my high status relative to the person I want to see diminished, the more I find it hard to believe that he is high and I am low, and thus the more pressure I am under to *do* something to the other person to make it appear that our relative standings are as I wish.

Of course, a natural way of effecting these standings is through the use of violence. Aggression can be an effective way of showing superiority; if I harm, maim, or kill you I defeat you, and by defeating you I show that I am better than you in this struggle and thus higher than you on some ranking ladder that I would have us believe measures our value as persons. Such defeat can and frequently is pursued using means that are not physically violent (e.g., one may try to ruin another's career, steal her boyfriend away from her, humiliate her in front of others). However, violence is certainly one way of accomplishing the defeat, and it is a particularly appealing method for those who see physical prowess as a primary sign of value. (Hence King Saul sought to have David killed.)

So to the question, "Why do vainglorious people desire to hurt those who insult them?" we give the answer, "They strive to hurt insulters because the hurt is taken to represent a defeat for their insulters and a victory for them, resulting in their elevation and their insulters' diminishment in value."

IV. Glory-Seeking by Nations

This analysis of glory can, I believe, illuminate not only the conflicts of individual human beings but also the conflicts within and between nations. Leaders of rebellious factions in a political community may seek victory over a ruler primarily to achieve their own preeminence and their opponents' diminishment; rulers may decide to invade another country in order to exalt their reputations by achieving victory; officers of government may arrogantly usurp powers and responsibilities in order to appear glorious, and this can have serious national repercussions.

Hobbes too believed that the conflicts among the classes of his day were directly related to the pursuit of glory. Some of his critics even called him a "Leveller," the term used to describe radical egalitarians during the Civil War period, because, like them, he opposed the idea that there was a natural hierarchy of people. In the *Elements of Law*, he contends that

> the question, which is the better man, is determinable only in the estate of government and policy, though it be mistaken for a question of nature, not only by ignorant men, that think one man's blood better than another's by nature; but also by [Aristotle]. (part 1, chap. 17, sec. 1, p. 18)

And he goes on to argue in *Leviathan* that this belief promotes civil strife and sedition, causing people to fight over "trifles, as a word, a smile, a different opinion, and any other sign of undervalue" (chap. 13, par. 7, p. 62).

But Hobbes does not consider the way in which a nation's longing for glory can provoke war with other nations, and this gap in his discussion is explained, I believe, by the fact that his individualism prevented him from considering or theorizing about the psychology and behavior of groups. Yet I would argue that it is appropriate to say that nations long for glory too: recall Wally George's declaration that the USA is "number 1." This sentiment is very widespread in America, and very provocative to other vainglorious countries who want to see themselves with that ranking. It is also a wounding sentiment for smaller nations, who take offense at the dismissive treatment of them by the United States, prompted by this country's perception of them as low in ranking. Let me quote from a passage in *Leviathan*, substituting the word "nations" for the word "people" in the passage. With this substitution, the passage accurately describes the political tenor of the international scene, not only in Hobbes's day, but also in our own:

> The honour of great [nations], is to be valued for the beneficence, and the aydes they give to [nations] of inferiour rank, or not at all. And the violences, oppressions, and injuries they do, are not extenuated, but aggravated by the greatness of the [nations], because they have least need to commit them. The consequences of this partiality toward the great, proceed in this manner. Impunity means Insolence; Insolence Hatred; and Hatred, an Endeavour to pull down all oppressing and contumelious greatnesse. (chap. 30, par. 60, p. 180)

If Hobbes is right that a brazen proclamation of superiority will probably eventuate in violent strife (and given my analysis of hatred, I would argue that he is), then any country is simply asking for trouble if it behaves as if it is superior to others. The desire to

95

diminish a country that assumes such a stance can play a role in causing other nations to stockpile weapons, expand standing armies, and adopt saber-rattling policies.

But what do we do to stop vainglorious strife either between men or between nations? Should we attempt to cure human beings of their desire for glory, and so end both violent competition for excellence and hateful strife aimed at diminishment? Curing them would not, according to my analysis, mean that they would give up a desire for a high valuation, but only a desire for a high valuation understood according to a certain theory of human worth that defines value comparatively and competitively. Sometimes I think that such a cure is possible; other times I worry that it is not—that the pursuit of a high ranking is a biological and ineradicable remnant of our primate past, which we can only hope to control and not destroy.

Hobbes wrote as a political philosopher. How do his remarks on glory illuminate the nature and structure of our political system? Let me conclude by suggesting that the founders of the United States attempted both to eradicate and control the longing for glory.

Their attempts at eradication can be seen in their rhetoric. Like the Levellers, and like Hobbes, they insisted that no person's blood was better than another's and condemned aristocratic thinking. That "levelling fancy," as Hobbes's critics called it, has permeated the thinking of all Americans at the individual level. Yet as a nation, we persist in seeing ourselves as a kind of nobility in virtue of our achievements—a noble nation in a sea of inferior countries, or to use Wally George's phrase, the "number 1" country. Perhaps an "internationalist" Tom Paine will succeed in persuading us to take a leveling attitude not only toward one another but also toward nations, including our own, so that we come to renounce the idea of our comparative superiority in some kind of national competition for value.

Moreover, in addition to the rhetoric of democracy, the American founders bequeathed a government that limits the power of any one individual or group. Their design was not to eradicate but to control the pursuit of glory. Might some kind of international political structure be put into place that would curb the power of any one nation and thus limit or disallow any particular nation's potentially violent pursuit of glory until such time as that pursuit is destroyed in human beings? No such structures have been developed thus far, but I am inclined to think that their development may be both possible and necessary for peace. The comparative ambitions that are surely critical to the initial success of our species may well, if unchecked, be about to destroy it.

Eight

Mutually Acceptable Glory Rating among Nations in Hobbes

William Sacksteder

After demonstrating that the war of all against all results from human quarrel in the absence of civil power, Hobbes adds that kings and persons of sovereign authority "because of their independency" are in continual jealousies and stand in a "posture of war" respecting each other.[1] We are thus tempted to an enticing analogy between interaction among nations and the intricate and quasi-geometrical logic he has employed in depicting the natural condition of mankind. Yet analogies may mislead, and striking parallels—anticipated at first—may be disqualified by a more exact account of their suggestions.

Three headings, competition, diffidence, and glory, summarize the causes of quarrel among individual persons ungoverned by civil authority. The third of these is often neglected, as if it supplied no more than a rhetorical flourish. In international affairs, competition for goods and powers is the more apparent argument, along with diffidence, which I take to mean distrust and suspicious precaution against future strife. But I shall argue here that glory, although the more evanescent origin of conflict, is also the more insidious and destructive cause of quarrel among nations. Since glory gives voice to a nation's admiration for its own dignity, any detraction from it threatens to undo that stature on which rests communion with all other nations. Just so, recognition for glory is the beginning of cure for any previous affront. To underrate a nation's glory is to deny that it *is* a nation.

Let me begin with a few axioms that I shall suppose belong to a sort of "logic of glory," whether among nations or among individual persons. Each of them derives from Hobbes's analyses collectively entitled "Of Man," which comprise segments of his philosophy preliminary to his civil analysis. I do not as yet seek to distinguish glory as cause of quarrel among nations.

1. *Glorying is comparative.* That is, any reference to glory implicates a relative scale that rates *this* with respect to *that.* For this reason, I speak about demand for "the same rating," and about the insult found in "underrating." Elsewhere, Hobbes mentions a dog's "understanding of the rating of his master," that is, of the latter's relative approval or disapproval. Accordingly, I use the phrase "Rating among Nations" in my subtitle.

2. *Glory compares opinion only.* Questions of glory impinge on imaginings or opinions which are *thought,* that is, which are imputed to another or which are reputed concerning one by many others. I say "only" because such facts as superior bodily or military power are topics for glory solely so far as one believes in their superiority or can convince others to acknowledge them. Rating individuals or nations consists in what is *supposed* about them by themselves or by others.

3. *Persons, natural or artificial, are the subjects of glory.* Comparison is always between distinct units, although often or perhaps always it cites qualities and possessions, merely assuming fit units to which these adhere or to which they are attributed. The unit to which glory applies is ultimately either one human being, an "individual," as we say with a usage Hobbes avoids, or a group more or less civil for which there is one acknowledged "spokesperson." This latter verbal modernism is peculiarly suitable to Hobbes's discussion of persons and their authority, which topics I shall soon mention. Conversely, I employ no circumlocutions to soften his ubiquitous use of "man," seemingly chauvinist to us. For he means either "human being" or "artificial person" able to speak for several human beings. Each may be that subject which enjoys glory or worries about underrating by someone else. These, of either sex, are the units compared in glory. So also, seeming nations and corporate units may or may not be acknowledged to be persons in the relevant sense.

4. *The locus of quarrel is discrepant views of a subject's glory.* This is the simple point that quarrel is a notion interrelating two things. Comparison is made between diverse units, individual or national—between persons, as may be said with general reference. It takes two to quarrel. However, respecting glory as cause of quarrel, a hall of mirrors is disclosed. Somewhat after the manner of a novel

by Henry James, the issue is not merely what he thinks about her, and vice versa, but rather what he thinks *she* thinks about *him*, and vice versa, and so on. What two quarrel about is their respective opinions concerning each other.

5. *Signs of repute are words and actions.* This, again, I take to be obvious. It is also the reason, in all arguments of quarrel or reconciliation, for close and jealous scrutiny by both counterpart persons. Only through scorn or admiration found in things said and things done may relative esteem be assessed. The same provide excuse for retort or occasion inviting compliance or resentment.[2]

6. *Glory measures opinion of power.* To honor another is to value that person at a high rate. This worth in turn depends on the need and judgment the other places on the one in question. But power is present means to future apparent good, so that all evaluation of another looks to his relative power in comparison with our own powers, or rather in comparison between what we think two respective powers may be. For in addition to actual powers, Hobbes says, "Reputation of power *is* power" (p. 74).[3]

7. *The pursuit of glory is insatiable.* This assertion should be taken, not as an axiom, but rather as a theorem of sorts following from the preceding definitions. It can be demonstrated by two arguments. First, human felicity consists in continual progress of desire from one object to another, the purpose being to enjoy goods at one time and also to assure them for the future. Hence it is that the general inclination of all mankind is perpetual and restless desire of power after power. Glory—or opinion of our own powers—is one among them. Although "vain-glory," begotten by flattery, may serve as substitute, just confidence in one's own powers and ability is a joy that, presumably, each seeks to augment in perpetuity.[4]

Second, in quarrel over glory each compares his own opinion of his powers with the esteem in which he is held by another. For "every man looks that his companion should value him at the same rate he sets upon himself." I take it that the normal state of self-esteem and suspicion is such that no one can exact from any other merely natural signs adequate to the worth he sets—of necessity—on himself. Pathology and insecurity and dignities artificially induced may no doubt qualify or invert this natural expectation. But its free and honest and merely natural operation would seem to require disparity in opinions, one's own and another's. These, it would seem, are never sufficiently counterbalanced to match any one person's self-esteem.

8. *Reason obliges equal glory.* This last stipulation may seem misplaced among the remainder, which I have called quasi-geo-

metrical, and whose axiomatic character seems apt merely to "natural fact" as Hobbes understands it. For it introduces an obligation whose actual enforcement—we later find—depends on artificial powers. And moderns are disinclined to think geometrical reasoning can provide an "ought."[5] However, for Hobbes, laws of nature are also called theorems, they are "found out by reason," and reason itself is a natural capacity of mankind, necessarily discussed prior to establishing any community. In consequence, those obligations resultant from it, namely, the laws of nature, depend on human nature alone, irrespective of further need to secure their enforcement. Moreover, they may be regarded as theorems demonstrating, presumably, the conditions without which efforts to combine such units would be destructive of them.

In this way, however they may be enforced or even unenforceable, all obligations Hobbes cites arise from and apply to human units. Save for the subproviso of the first law, each law of nature stipulates those interconnections among human units that do not reduce to absurdity when applied to all. The first itself commands peace. This might be regarded as strict opposite to self-contradiction, that is, to construction of merely natural coexistence, which has been found to be geometrically impossible. The remainder prescribe preconditions in the absence of which peace is impossible. Each of these further laws, in my opinion, reduces to equal weighting in some respect, so that any disequilibrium in such balance destroys the very possibility of peace. Hence the summary metaphor picturing the pans of the old-fashioned scales in equilibrium. All laws of nature will seem reasonable when—"weighing the actions of other men with his own"—an intended action is exchanged with those in the opposite part of the balance.[6] As Hobbes's Introduction tells us, the analogue of reason in the commonwealth is "equity."[7] Obligation conformed to reason commands equalization among the units to be combined.

Hobbes's civil composition of individual humans into a commonwealth through these obligations is so familiar as to need no summary here. I insist only that it too is an idealized and quasigeometrical construction, as contrary to observable facts as is the inverse idealized case he found in reducing the natural condition to absurdity.[8] The power of both analyses is not in direct correspondence to fact, but rather in showing the consequences of two opposite sets of assumptions—in setting unhampered multiple units conflicting with each other against total commensuration under equalizing law. Actual facts, I presume, are always some mix of troubled events moving either toward reconciliation or toward dispute. Wisdom lies in knowing which is which and in considering whether prudence directs our precaution—and reason directs our obligation—toward this or toward that way of acting.

Pursuit of glory among individuals is controlled and redirected upon entry into the commonwealth. I am able to summarize this transformation in ways not as heterodox as my more general view of obligation in Hobbes. Under civil law and sovereign authority, all subjects are reduced to equality in two important ways. First, they are, as we say today, equal before the law. That is, the legal structure is their own, and it is justified by their consent. Hence all entry into litigation presupposes arbitration according to equity. Second, any disparity among subjects is reduced to nought when compared with the person of the commonwealth, that is, with the authority of that man or assembly of men who speaks for all of them or through whom they all speak. Once consent is granted to this governing power, the relative rating of all other subject powers is either derivative or equal. Their mutual evaluation is—or ought to be—the same and reciprocal. From their previous natural powers, subjects retain only those allowed or decreed by the sovereign or those made commensurable with all others—again by a sort of equality before the law.

Moreover, within a commonwealth, natural powers of individuals are not only redistributed. A new scheme of evaluation is superimposed. If distinctions are recognized by a sovereign authority, they cannot be gainsaid. These artificial ratings, Hobbes calls "dignities." They establish the public worth of a man, or the value set on him by the commonwealth.[9] Included among them are such distinctions as titles of honor, specific offices, and functions within the commonwealth. Public status may be enforced by civil powers, however mildly, and no matter what private grumblings continue.[10]

To whatever extent this new dispensation succeeds, the ill effects of pursuing glory are mitigated, as are those of competition and diffidence—or so we suppose. Any now legal disparities in rating are presumably backed up by civil powers. All others—those literally illegitimate—are prohibited and punishable by recourse to arbitration from which (I repeat) there is promise of equity or equalization of that sort we title "equality before the law." I have no doubt that man's natural inclination to look "that his companion should value him at the same rate he sets upon himself" will remain. Indeed, it must remain insatiable, as does all desire to enjoy and assure goods. But any effort outside the law to enforce that unlimited hope is actionable, and others are futile or reduce to frivolous ploys of social and domestic intercourse. "Invasion . . . for glory" is prohibited, and demands for reputation (or for the "trifles" Hobbes says signify it) are directed or moderated sufficiently that they no longer occasion the war of all against all.[11]

To the extent that enforcement by the commonwealth attains exact rating for each person by others on a comparative scale of evaluated powers and honors, pursuit of glory would obviously be far removed from the subtle psychology and pathology of human interplay. But a civil authority that scrutinized and regulated all the words and deeds of intercourse directed toward reputation would be as intolerable to Hobbes as, I think, to all of us. In addition, we know full well that in the give and take of human exchange, there is much trial and error directed toward both invidious distinction and cooperation. These moves are finally the instruments whereby such agreements as are possible among us are achieved and enhanced, just as they are also the instruments whereby degradation may be fended off and disagreements may be vented or rendered innocuous. When it does not degenerate to violence, dispute over glory among individuals is healthy competition, as we are wont to say currently. These endeavors after glory continue under a commonwealth, though presumably their destructive effects are lessened or redirected to useful ends.

For my title, I have coined the phrase "mutually acceptable glory" to indicate a degree of reciprocal esteem such that it is possible for *all* parties to dispute over rating to be willing to allow the same to every counterpart. It is that allotment whereby each is able to impute equal glory at once to himself and to those others with whom he engages himself, doing so in company with converse expectations from them. Assuming a perfected commonwealth, that standard is enforced on all subjects by their disparity from sovereign authority. Under its total government, violation of equality would be actionable in principle, though I think in practice only rarely and with intolerable scrutiny of signs employed in human discourse and interaction. Hobbes announces this redisposition of the causes of quarrel among private individuals—glory included—in a picture of the commonwealth no less idealized than his inverse analysis of the natural condition. Ill effects from the pursuit of reputation are prevented (or at least mitigated) through enforcement legitimated under a superior power. In a commonwealth, glory is made to be mutually acceptable by the ruling power, or so I shall pretend for my present argument.

But there is no ruling power among nations. Before I turn to this circumstance, and to its analogues (or lack of them) under the natural condition, I should like to list some ways in which something very like mutually acceptable glory is implicated even under incompletely civil conditions or along with the barest claim to legality.

a. Obligation to seek peace, as well as those prescriptions for mutual equality that are conditions of its preservation, hold prior to any civil agreements. Natural law is binding on all individuals, on every natural human being as such. Even the escape clause whereby the first law allows all means of preservation when peace is impossible is incumbent equally on all mankind, for this legislation is found out by reason, and it obliges each individual person, inside or outside the commonwealth.[12] According to the second clause of the first law, distrust or fear may trigger return to raw nature alone, just as assurance of peace may collapse. But everyone is bound equally to desire that the law of nature should prevail, though not to undertake each action it specifies.[13]

b. Both entrance into a legal order and continuation within it presuppose competence for undertaking contractual obligations, no matter that such origin may be implicit, coerced, or lost in history and biography. Subjects must first be *persons*, which is to say they must be competent to bespeak their consent, to act upon their contracts, and to acknowledge a corresponding integrity the same in others. Reciprocally recognized rating is a condition without which no civil undertaking is possible. Hence it is obliged before a commonwealth is formed, and it underlies any enforcement provided within one once established.

c. The same personal competence to consent among contracting agents is a condition for each agreement and enforcement undertaken within or according to a recognized legal order. Though equal rating is unenforceable in detail, all civil amenities require attributing it, if by fiction only, to each and every citizen as such. With respect to any limited transaction at hand, reciprocity between actions, consent, and expectations must be pretended, at least, by a sort of equalization at the point of agreement, no matter what other inequalities surround it. Each agreement imputes glory enough to rate the other as one person likewise competent to agree on stipulations, to carry out obligations, and to accept all parties as fellow contractors. No such mutually acceptable rating, no contract.

d. The image of mutually acceptable glory is present still within a functioning commonwealth in the equal respect of persons as such that any *rule under law* pretends. For individuals under a government, and despite aggressions usual in fact, that image is writ large in the supposition that a legitimate social order exists, and in the justifications (however flimsy in actuality) that invariably attend a functioning society. In promise, though that promise is rarely fulfilled, any legal order proposes equality of the sort we say is "before"

William Sacksteder

or "under the law." Within a society, when dignities and powers have been redistributed (or perhaps disparities legally sanctioned after the fact or enforced by violence), appeal is nevertheless made to a fiction of equal recourse and arbitration in principle and for all. Law poses as general rule over individual instances. With whatever success or failure, a legal order as such attempts to preserve that fiction. The prospect of such legal equality among persons is accepted as a premise, even in attempts to improve an existing order or to replace it with another by revolution.

I cite these implications of what might be called the moral logic of law for two reasons, both serving my inquiry into likenesses between international affairs and mankind under supposed natural conditions. First, to whatever extent one nation attains or proclaims for itself its internal legal and civil order, it professes also general adherence to those presumptions of equality that it is obliged to cite on behalf of its own stature and integrity. The very claim to be a nation projects before itself and toward other national units that model of balanced rating between personal agents. The logic of its own preconditions, obligations, and expectations is thus present, however much these implications may be belied in fact.

Second, in Hobbes's analysis of transition from natural to civil condition, the unit is the natural person, the individual as agent on his own behalf. Forming and maintaining a nation depends on personhood and its implications. In consequence, all claims among distinguishable national units are shaped according to their own like agency as artificial persons. Competence to be personal agents in this enlarged sense is announced for all national units to the extent that they invoke obligation, responsibility, and capacities for consent or opposition. Corresponding recognition for themselves is required from others—from friends and enemies alike.

Now my project here is to ask how far the analogues to glory as cause of quarrel may be extended to independent nations, each facing the other "in the posture of war." Pursuing the geometric methodology I attribute to Hobbes, I translate this inquiry into the question, How far do affairs among nations conform to the eight principles I count concerning pursuit of glory under the natural condition? For by hypothesis, there is no viable and secure commonwealth among nations. Rather, they confront each other neither according to enforceable law nor under jointly recognized power.

But, though nations may mutually adopt the "posture of gladiators," they need not be otherwise at war. Both playing field and players presumably differ from the interrelations supposed to prevail among hypothetical individuals trying (and failing) to survive in a

104

likewise hypothetical natural state. Though national groupings that are ill-defined may be fortified against neighbors across frontiers both dispute, these persons are yet quite different from natural individuals encountering each other face to face and also (so to speak) in passing and on occasion—randomly here and there or now and then. For in ways unavailable to natural persons, nations are able to claim a space and to pretend identity despite change of guard.

In my exercise in transposition, I confine my remarks to the pursuit of reputation for glory. I omit the remaining causes of quarrel, pretending for now that they are more readily subject to watchful control under granted but limited arrangements or else that it is clear to everyone that anarchy yet prevails concerning competition and diffidence. Regarding these, it may be true that no options remain between total war or submission to recognizable authorities keeping the peace, for it would seem that partial agreements are insecure without assured enforcement. Such at least is the view ordinarily imputed to Hobbes.[14] At present, I allow that competition and diffidence produce only fearful disjunction between total distrust and assured enforcement, though I think that local or passing agreements moderate extremes for both. Their resolution, in my opinion, depends on preconditions whose juncture is glory itself—commensurately recognized. Competition and diffidence, respectively, may enhance or ensure reputation. But they cannot be tamed, whether by limited and temporary mitigation or by international authority, without prior redisposition for correlate ratings that are mutually acceptable. Though glory is the more elusive cause of quarrel or hope for reconciliation among nations, it is also the more fundamental, so far as it is a condition for mutual recognition and further exchange. Hence I ask whether there remains any obligation to mutually acceptable glory when the incidence of these axioms I have called quasi-geometrical is upon existing nations lacking higher authority.

All but two of the stipulations about glory I have enumerated seem to transport readily to quarrel among nations, when it is supposed that they remain under uncivil conditions of nature respecting each other. That is, in this new application attention to glory is likewise (1) a comparative rating, (2) concerned with opinion only, (4) (skipping number 3) troubled by discrepant claims, (5) signified by speech and actions, (6) a measuring-rule for power or repute of power, and (7) insatiable. Applications analogous to these I shall assume to be obvious. I attend instead to the two questions that do not translate readily to the international context: (3) What distinct dispositions result when personal units are transposed from natural individuals to nations? And (8) in the absence of a ruling power, does there remain any force in reasoned obligation toward glory that is equal among these units?

More is hidden than revealed in calling the units concerned with mutual rating and glory "persons." For us, that word designates what Hobbes calls the "natural person." We cherish the word today, not only for its sexual neutrality, but for connotations indicating both that integrity we feel obliged to impute to each of our kind and that moral worth—beyond price—which may not be irrelevant to glory.[15] For Hobbes, the unlimited value we ought to respect in each natural person is located in the effort by each to preserve himself. Reciprocal recognition of that inherent and integral force is precisely the question of glory. The problem is that mutually acceptable rating may amount to nothing among nations, just as demanding it annihilates all persons in the natural condition.

Though his term "artificial persons" applies preeminently to the sovereign in a commonwealth, Hobbes is careful to prepare it in his preceding analysis "Of Man." The bases for it are the capacities and recognitions inherent in natural human beings. It indicates one unit (individual or assembly) who speaks for several with their authorization and agreement. They *speak through* him and as one, so that in all human intercourse, the unit is in some sense to be named a person, as I have stipulated.[16]

For internal purposes, and within a commonwealth, a true sovereign (man or assembly) speaks for *each* and legislates over *all*. This stipulated perfection I shall let pass, for now. The question at hand is whether and to what extent independent nations can or should be regarded as artificial persons in this extreme and mutually pretended or acknowledged sense. Any nation (a non-Hobbesian term I shall continue to use for convenience) claims also to interrelate as an artificial person with other nations. These in turn expect to be reputed correlate units. All nations profess to speak and act as one artificial person through representatives and by the authority of all their respective citizens. All attempt also to exact correlate recognition from friends and opponents alike. In international relations, *nationhood*, a word I use this once only, is on a par with *personhood*. Nations, too, pursue glory. But that pursuit is as yet untamed by any artificial civil order governing them.

Save for rhetorical purposes, no one believes that any nation, his own included, is in fact one person, being of one mind, and speaking with one voice in the sense required. Whatever is allowed for perfected political analysis, no nation functions exactly as one person, artificial or otherwise, when it faces other nations. Nor are the integrity and continuity and respect we anticipate (however vainly) in individual interaction ever to be counted upon in international affairs. Viable world government is in this respect utopian beyond measure, even were we to think it desirable or obligatory. The question of a rating mutually acceptable among nations is whether and how we are able to operate in a mixed condition intermediate between total warfare and assured peace.

These problems are exacerbated by claims to glory. The barest attempt to negotiate among nations, even any naked weapon pointed across a border, presupposes commonality between the one and the other, namely, the means to identify each and the means to distinguish each from others. Notice that in guerilla warfare or in any civil broils, identity and distinction are perpetually muddled, though insistence on group glory or on unified representation are diminished not a wit. Rather these claims are augmented the more, in inverse proportion to their visibility. But let me return, after this exaggerated detour into factuality, to my semilogistic discourse on glory.

Part, but only part, of what is at issue between nations, as among civil factions, is comparison and discrepancy in the evaluative opinions each holds respecting powers of many sorts possessed by the other. Moreover, this repute or reciprocal imputation is perpetually jealous of slight and never susceptible to full or assured satisfaction. Short at least of adequate joint consent by independent nations to a higher power, which is unlikely, Hobbes allows only two sorts of mitigation to warfare among nations, just as he does to the war of all against all. These are *counsels* of prudence, which may or may not be adopted, and *obligations* of reason, which alone are imperative, whether or not they are viable in the absence of an enforcing government. I attempt a brief status report for each.

I first discuss prudence apart from any obligations. For Hobbes, prudence is guidance for action derived from past associations. In this way, connections between causes and effects are accumulated from experience.[17] But these connections are temporal, rather than geometrical or scientific. Hence all recommendations from prudence are as yet uncorrected by scientific and definitive demonstration or by penetration to primary or inevitable principles. Though secondary to science, for Hobbes, prudence is far from negligible. I think we may equate it with what might otherwise be called street smarts or worldly wisdom. Both apply accumulated expectations to human behavior and to anticipated events. I submit that a fair degree of prudence that is sound in this sense may be anticipated in anyone who has participated with others of his species in any nursery, domesticity, office, elective process, boardroom, cocktail party, conference table, TV screen, negotiating team, game field, battlefield, or department meeting. However, I attend now only to counsels of prudence whereby nations rate each other, among which I list the following random few.

(1) Any nation attempts to augment its various powers respecting other nations, and therefore also to enhance its reputation of power in relative comparison. That is, it pursues glory. (2) Any nation looks fearfully and with care at all signs of other nations' opinions of its own relative rating, especially when friendship or enmity are contingent on opinions of worth or strength. (3) Any nation is highly indignant at each and every gross violation or detraction from the rating it professes for itself. (4) Any nation allows a certain discrepancy between value hoped for and actual rating, to the extent that differences in power are undeniable. Hence (5) the never-satiable demand for evaluation corresponding to one's own is set aside in practice.

So much seems fairly obvious. But let me return to indignation. (6) There is some flash point, never to be known in advance, at which verbal or active abuse of any nation's self-respect and demand for equal rating may erupt into retaliation entailing open warfare. Any devaluation beyond that point is war, however limited in scope and however reduced to minor irritants. Any signaled degradation (verbal or active) short of it is invitation to war, if not declaration of intent so to engage. However indeterminate that point of explosion may be, good sense prescribes that it ought to be approached or transgressed with lucid willingness either to retract or to embrace the consequences of not doing so. Wisdom requires awareness that each other nation has its own threshold of indignation. Prudence counsels diligent notice of that barrier.

The same advice against flirtation with danger informs the following considerations as well. (7) No nation ever is the integrated unit—"speaking through one person"—that it pretends to be. Hence to take sides with one internal faction in another professed nation approaches, however distantly, the indeterminate point threatening warfare. Prudence, as before, counsels caution or will to follow where actions lead.

(8) Every nation justifies its exploits and even its existence by a concoction of opinions and symbols we are inclined today to call an "ideology." This is always, I think, some mix of practical wisdom, professed science, historical rationalization, myth-making, self-congratulation, value-mongering, media hype, queasy philosophy, and sound platitudes. To whatever extent each such ingredient is valued, whether nationally or merely by internal factions, it shapes lively occasion for attack on ideology. To any nation, existing or anticipated, its ideology is the tie that binds. Hence both expression of scorn for it and effort to dispute it threaten self-rating and risk

indignant or belligerent declaration at the present threshold. Broadly, all counterideology is added irritant to glory.

(9) Nations are not equal. But wise courtesy, if not morality, has always dictated pretense that they are. The protocol for diplomacy, modes of communication, incidental arrangements (say, at a border crossing), and even declaration of war each presuppose—quite contrary to fact and opinion—that one nation addresses every other nation as a sovereign unit that shares equal status and represents a unified constituency. Nations presume ungrammatically but politely that *we* are *us*, and *they* are *them*. Etiquette requires mutual address between recognized civil persons. These niceties presume that each nation requires acknowledgment as if it were truly a nation, irrespective of an uneasy hold on such status. Though no nation can ever be perfectly a nation, that is still the glory each demands.

In each of the scattered cases I have mentioned, prudence counsels two fictions: that each several nation is one, and that they are equal. Public infringement of that polite presumption of nationhood is inglorious. It will be resented, whatever the powers for redress. Power-play in spite of it, like interference in internal dispute, must be kept under cover or subject to judicial neglect. Just because each proclaimed nation is anxious about its own unity and powers, it is jealous of its reputation in the opinion ascribed by "fellow nations," as—it is hoped—they will call each other. However minuscule the danger may be, every insult to glory among nations potentially deprives opponents of their claims to be a nation. Which detraction is war.

Moreover, each nation takes its stance from its own integrity as a nation. It stands on its own "dignity" as one civil person among others, I would say, were that not to violate Hobbes's terminology. Each nation presupposes its own national status, even in the course of scorning another nation or in using language detracting from that opponent's rating or reputation. It does so also in all acts of aggression, interference, and violation. Two opposed units are always presumed, even in declaring war, the extremity foreshadowed by each of these infringements in however muted a fashion. With this peculiarly reflexive twist, I overstep, as I think I must, the line separating wise counsels of prudence from reasoned moral obligation.

That transition is alluring for Hobbes, since accumulated experience, however worldly wise, ought to be realigned under strictly relational considerations prescribed by the laws of nature. After the first imperative commanding in disjunction either seeking peace or employing every art of war, all others point toward exact conditions of mutual acceptability that advance peace. Equality is the limit toward which they are projected. These laws do not overturn the advice of prudence so much as they shape it to exact and uncompromising reciprocity. In this sense, all advice for protocol I have just voiced is converted to imperative. That is, it commands so far as nations are to consider each other and are to consider themselves to be spokespersons for an integrated and worthy unit, for otherwise each nation retreats to its naked several powers, as occurs in all degeneration to warfare. The primary precondition of peace among nations is adherence as strict as possible to a fiction of intercourse between units such that each acknowledges correlate status and equal integrity in its opinions publicly rating the others. That is what I mean, in my title, by "mutually acceptable glory."

It is arguable that for Hobbes there is no strict obligation to that diplomatic nicety short of enforcement by a supernatural power, that is, no obligation this side of world government. Among natural persons, assurance that others can be forced to obey is a stipulation in the absence of which overt conformity to obligation should be self-destructive. Reason *does* oblige individuals, even under natural conditions. But it obliges only internally, in conscience, as we might say, or toward a will to mutual consent, and only so far as that may be assured. National units, too, it might be argued, can be informed by prudence only. They lack reasoned obligation whenever no power is able to assure reciprocity among other national units. I believe these arguments faulty, even for a strict Hobbesian, though I shall do no more than assert their contraries at present.

Applying either prudential advice or reasoned obligation as Hobbes understands them to national units depends on their analogy, likeness or difference in turn, to natural human units and to disputes or agreements among those human units. I submit that national units are more prone to *presumptive identity* than are individuals when we construe their interrelations strictly in a natural condition. That is, nations interrelated are such that we are better able to attribute to them equality, continuity, and responsibility, even when we are unable in practice to *enforce* the same. Merely natural encounters among individuals, short of symbolic aids to naming and spatial-temporal calculations, are never more than occasional: here and now. An encounter always occurs between just *this* or *these* combatants who turn up casually—without identity tags, so to speak. The next encounter is someone else, in another part of the forest, later, and armed with a more formidable weapon, or perhaps asleep or accompanied or hungrier.

Unlike the participants in more sporadic individual encounters, a national unit stays put, or else it pretends to do so with great effect. It defines—to its own satisfaction—its supposed boundaries; it fortifies them, if only symbolically; it takes umbrage if other nations

110

dispute them. Likewise, it claims a specific temporal continuity, as citizens die off and are born, and although new presidents or premiers are elected or semi-elected or even elevated by coups or replaced by civil strife. Any nation likewise pretends responsibility to obligation in forming alliances, in identifying enemies, and in the most minuscule encounter, whether formal diplomacy or border scuffle. Even fumbling to break treaties leads nations to concoct higher reasons and to persevere noisily in maintaining some semblance of identity through changed circumstances or through disturbed balances of power.

Finally, national units are spectacularly competent to identify themselves through all these linguistic and intellectual devices Hobbes calls collectively "speech." These include symbols of national integrity, as well as the ideologies I mentioned earlier. My lament for the absence of name tags in the state of nature was more than a passing joke. In analyzing mankind in that condition, Hobbes sets aside all accomplishments dependent on speech, including science and reasoned communication, along with naming and recognizable personal continuity, for all of these are artifices dependent on agreement. But nations name themselves unilaterally. They often perceive their identity in their language, and they are notorious for using every available verbal and symbolic device to enhance their glory. When they are unable to foist hopes for superiority on other nations, they fall back on proclaiming merely equal status with fanfare all the more blatant.

Now I have said nothing about the American Constitution. The little I shall say assumes that it is more Hobbesian in principle than is usually allowed. It may be regarded as an agreement, contractual, if you like, directed *toward* "a more perfect union." But it neither completes nor enforces a commonwealth in Hobbes's idealized or geometrical sense. Rather—with ambiguity I think happy—it occupies a middle region between merely natural interactions and total unity achieved, completed, and enforced. Whether by a giant step or a baby step, it advanced us forward from the one toward the other. It is not, as Hobbes might be thought—mistakenly—to require, a flip between extremes: total rule replacing anarchy.

Another ambiguity in the original Constitution, regarded as an agreement, was whether the units consenting to it were individuals or nation-states in my present sense. Happy or not, that tension—tested, realigned, and unresolved by a civil war—is with us yet. I hope that my Hobbesian interpretation differentiates these aspects and the distinct sort of reciprocity each presupposed, for the Constitution entails discrete courtesies and symbolic acknowledgements toward units of both sorts. For example, the House of

Representatives accommodates the idea of authorization by individuals; the Senate (with the original appointment process) accommodates that of authorization by distinct nations. The Electoral College and the Amendment Procedure muddle both demands. Likewise, the Preamble speaks ambiguously about hopes in a people not yet *"We, the* people," and about units roughly national seeking a union "more perfect" than (presumably) the Articles of Confederation.

Regarding either personal unit, individuals or nations, the Constitution presupposes and recognizes presumptive equality under the law, as must any mutual agreement or contract, however that precondition may be contrary to other and unequal considerations. To give consent, to assume responsibility, to require performance, and to be partners in a governing unity—each such action depends on a bare but reciprocal equality of rating underlying any remaining differences of degree. Otherwise, no membership in the greater unit is possible. Without a locus reducible to acceptable glory, no constitution. Only in accordance with that implicit reciprocity is law as such—civil, natural, or both—able to oblige mutually. On it, any law that constitutes us one must ultimately rest.

The balance among these compromises (or discrepancies) in our Constitution has been tipped over two centuries toward regarding ourselves as a unit nation. Thereby, my questions about "rating among nations" are largely transposed to external interactions and to a newly intensified sphere for international reciprocity or destruction.

I do not know whether the divergences between individual and national units I have cited in Hobbes's name intensify or moderate the dismal consequences that might attend analogies among nations to the natural condition. Nor am I sure that Hobbes would allow so much scope as I do to reasoned obligation among nations lacking superior enforcing power. However, I do think that the geographical, temporal, and linguistic increments to national identity just sketched intensify all senses in which friendship, enmity, or survival among nations presuppose reciprocal recognition of personhood for each national unit. Every nation announces its equal status loudly for itself, and each admits it for many others, if only for purposes of etiquette and convenient alliance and communication. Every nation, I think, employs presumptions of identity in naming other nations or even in scorning or fighting them. Each also cultivates its own correlate differentiation and recognition in story, ideology, and ex post facto justification. Prudence, at least, foresees risk whenever these claims are degraded; and bitter experience teaches that the cost of their complete denial is return to international sorts of incivility.

Symbolic identification, however insecure or malicious, names a unit. It presumes both some *one* who names and some other *one* named. And among persons natural and artificial, it attempts communion and recognition in some degree between diverse parties. Or else it is a supreme act of designation asking for recognition by all. In this way, all the language of national glorification trips over reason and its moral demand for reciprocity between equals and for mutual claims to recognition and corresponding status. By and large, that obligation may well be overlooked, and it often is. But no exchange between nations, not even war attacking more than a scattering of individuals, can be possible without language invoking claims to national status on both sides.

That these several claims ought to be weighed equally, this one in one pan of the scales balanced with that one in the other pan, is the further dictate of reason. Among nations, these obligations are presupposed for each party and they ought to command with or without powers of enforcement. Untrammeled pursuit of glory outruns that regulation, for no nation, just as no individual, can ask *less* than that others value him as he rates himself. But when shaped by reason, that demand is necessarily reciprocal. Whenever he or it listens to reason as well as to desire, the other too must be taken to be a self-valuing unit posing a like demand for recognition as such. By that conversion, "holding the other at the same rate he holds himself" can ask no *more* than that equal measure should be allowed to equal unit nations, if only by a fiction or with tongue in cheek. Though that commensuration may be demeaning, distressing, or dangerous, it alone is that glory mutually acceptable among nations.

Nine

Glory, Respect, and Violent Conflict

Andrew Altman

The human desires for respect and for glory are significant causes of interpersonal and international conflict. Perhaps some may think that such a point is so obvious that it is not worth making. They are wrong. It is worth making, and it is worth pondering. The two preceding contributions ponder the point and, in doing so, shed a good deal of light on the psychology of respect and glory and its connection to violent conflict. Professor Sacksteder is concerned to describe the outlines of an international order that harnesses in Hobbesian fashion the hankering after glory by nations and thereby contributes to the establishment of global tranquility. In part 1 of this essay, I will explore his contentions regarding such a system and argue that they run afoul of basic Hobbesian principles. In part 2, I will raise and examine an issue that underlies much of Sacksteder's discussion: whether the human population of the planet ought be organized into a system of sovereign nation-states. I will show how the theories of Sacksteder and of Hobbes are related to an influential view holding that such a mode of political organization is the one best calculated to generate global tranquility.

Professor Hampton's focus is on the individual rather than on the collectivity. She is concerned to elucidate the psychological subtleties that explain why the individual's desire for respect can lead to violence committed against those who display disrespect. But like Sacksteder, she aims to work within a basically Hobbesian framework in order to understand human psychology and its violent tendencies. In part 3, I will examine her account of the psychology of respect and violence and seek to show that it suffers from limitations deriving from its neglect of the malicious side of human nature. That side of human nature disrupts the rational regard for self-interest in terms of which both Hobbes and Hampton attempt to understand human life. I conclude with some summary remarks on the limitations of the Hobbesian framework within which Hampton and Sacksteder pursue their inquiries.

I. Mutually Acceptable Glory

Professor Sacksteder makes four principal points. First, the will to glory is an important cause of violent conflict among nations. Second, even in the absence of a global sovereign, there is a means for counteracting the tendency of the will to glory to give rise to international conflict. Third, the system he labels "mutually acceptable glory" is just such a means. Fourth, the system of mutually acceptable glory is consistent with the tenets of a Hobbesian understanding of human life.

The system of mutually acceptable glory consists of a set of practices wherein states treat each other as having equal claim to national glory. By one interpretation, Sacksteder can be seen to contend that such a system will in fact placate each state's will to glory just enough to prevent it from instigating violent conflict. This would be a straightforward empirical claim about international relations, although it would clearly have great normative import. Yet it may also be argued that he claims the system of mutually acceptable glory to be the one that is most fair, given the hankering for glory that all states have. On this second interpretation, the main point would be the normative one that nations are morally required to establish and abide by such a system, though their actual behavior may vary from what is required.

On either interpretation, Sacksteder runs afoul of Hobbesian principles. A radical departure from the Hobbesian framework is required for one to claim that Sacksteder's system is either empirically likely or morally required, given the absence of a world sovereign to enforce its arrangements.

The crux of Sacksteder's problem is that no nation capable of dominating other nations by means of its military or economic might has any Hobbesian reason to agree to a system of mutual and equal glory. Quite to the contrary, it has every Hobbesian reason for subjugating those states it is capable of dominating. If there were an effective world sovereign to which all nations consented and which decreed Sacksteder's system, then the situation would be radically different from a Hobbesian viewpoint. Nations would then be morally required to abide by the terms of the system. Yet in the absence of such a sovereign, the most fundamental principles of

Hobbes's political philosophy entail that powerful nations have no good reason of any kind to accord equal glory to the less powerful, and they certainly have no moral obligation to do so.

One of the critical premises in Hobbes's derivation of political society from the state of nature is that individuals are of roughly equal powers:

> Nature has made men so equal in the faculties of the body and mind as that, though there be found one man sometimes manifestly stronger in body or of quicker mind than another, yet when all is reckoned together, the difference between man and man is not so considerable as that one man can thereupon claim to himself any benefit to which another may not pretend as well as he.[1]

This rough equality of human beings is a major consideration in leading the individual to judge that he would be better off consenting to a sovereign than remaining in the state of nature and trying to subjugate his enemies. His enemies are too nearly equal in powers to him to expect that he could gain any lasting victory over enough of them to be secure for any reasonable length of time.

Relations among nations have never been characterized by a rough equality of power. Nations have been able to impose lasting forms of subjugation on other nations who may pose threats to their security or to their conception of their national destiny. Consider the Soviet Union in relation to Eastern Europe and to nations that were quite literally swallowed up by the Soviet empire. Or consider the United States in relation to the Native American nations.

In the absence of any rough equality of power across all nations, there is no Hobbesian reason to expect that Sacksteder's system of mutually acceptable glory could ever be established. And there is no Hobbesian reason to claim that such a system is morally required.

At one point, Sacksteder suggests that the current system of international relations and diplomacy is a very imperfect version of the practice of mutually acceptable glory. I believe that the suggestion has some merit to it. Of course, nations often do subjugate weaker ones, but sometimes they refrain, even when they could easily expand their territory and resources by doing so. Yet I do not think that this means that Sacksteder was correct after all in claiming that mutually acceptable glory is possible without a global sovereign, given Hobbesian premises. Instead, what it shows is that Hobbesian premises are not completely adequate to account for the behavior of contemporary nations. In the next section, I will examine the nation-state as a mode of political organization and suggest one important way in which certain contemporary nation-states depart from the Hobbesian model.

II. The Nation-State and Global Peace

In the centuries since the death of Hobbes, a striking transformation has occurred in human thinking about political organization. It is now widely (though not universally) taken for granted among political thinkers that the human population of the earth ought to be organized into a system of sovereign nation-states. No such assumption could be taken for granted in Hobbes's day. One had to argue for the superiority of the sovereign nation-state over competing modes of political organization, and Hobbes was one of the leading figures in a line of great thinkers who contributed to that argument.

In its most aggressive form, the argument for the proposition that the human population ought to be organized into a system of sovereign nation-states is an argument for three connected ideas. First, the territory of the earth should be divided up so that, for any given piece of it, there is one and only one state that exercises ultimate judgment and power over all human conduct that occurs there.[2] Second, there should be a plurality of such sovereign states, and thus there should be no single state whose territory covers every last inch of the planet to which humans have access. Third, each such state should recognize the sovereignty of the others within boundaries that all can agree to.

Hobbes argued vigorously for the first idea. A single sovereign over any given piece of territory was needed to end the war of all against all within that territory. For Hobbes this was a necessary truth, grounded in the nature of sovereignty and human life. On the other hand, although Hobbes accepted the second idea, within the framework of his theory its truth rested upon a conception of the limits of the technology of power in a way the truth of the first idea did not. In Hobbes's view, the possible technologies of social power simply did not allow for the establishment of a sovereign power over every part of the globe to which humans have access. If such a sovereign power were possible, it would clearly be the best Hobbesian solution to the war of all against all. It could establish peace and security for the whole human race over every part of the earth to which human conduct could penetrate. If it is not possible, however, then the next best Hobbesian solution is to establish a plurality of sovereigns, each of which can establish peace and security within some local portion of the globe. Other things being equal, such sovereigns should cover as large a territory as possible, that is, as is consistent with the effective exercise of sovereign power. If, in Hobbes's view, a world sovereign was too large to be feasible, the Aristotelian polis was too small to be desirable: peace and security could be extended to large stretches of territory by organizing political society on a scale larger than the defenders of the polis could have countenanced. The nation-state, of course, fit the bill: it was smaller than the infeasible world state but (typically) larger than the polis.

Hobbes believed, however, that domestic tranquility would have to exist side-by-side with international violence, since the nation-states would be in a state of nature with respect to each other. It remained for other proponents of the sovereign nation-state, such as Bentham, to argue that a system of nation-states was well-calculated to produce both domestic and international tranquility.[3] Their argument rested on the premise that it was a feasible arrangement for each sovereign state to recognize the sovereignty of the others within mutually agreed upon borders. Such thinkers thus proceeded to defend the third idea of the most aggressive argument for the nation-state system, namely, that each state should recognize the other's sovereignty over a territory that all could agree to.

If one's principal practical concern is to check international violence, then the idea of mutual recognition of sovereignty cuts closer to the heart of the matter than Sacksteder's notion of mutual and equal glory. The pursuit of national glory can take different forms, from cultivating the arts to promoting achievements in sports or science to preparing for victories on the field of battle. Not all such forms involve or carry the high probability of violence against other nations. Those forms that do implicate violence or the threat of it almost always involve a total or partial rejection of the sovereignty claimed by some other nation-states.

Sometimes the rejection of sovereignty concerns only a certain limited piece of territory that both nations claim as their own. Sometimes it concerns certain domestic or foreign policies that one of the states has adopted but the other seeks to have changed through violence or its threat. Sometimes it concerns the perceived illegitimacy of a certain state and the aim is to use violence to destroy it. Sometimes the rejection of sovereignty through violent means involves a mix of the above elements, and very often the motives behind the violence are a mixture of national glory with other components of national self-interest: economic, military, and the like. In fact, these other components are so intertwined with the pursuit of national glory that it may be difficult or impossible to separate them even as a conceptual matter.

In any event, the violent pursuit of national glory, as a rule, involves a challenge to another nation-state's sovereignty. The importance of this fact lies in its practical converse: to the extent that the mutual recognition of sovereignty over agreed upon territories can be made to prevail, the pursuit of national glory will have to be rechanneled along lines that do not involve violence or the threat of violence.

Moreover, the mutual recognition of sovereignty need not entail the mutual and equal recognition of glory, for there will still be spheres of human life—artistic, scientific, athletic, and so on—in which nations may regard themselves as having achieved a greater glory than other sovereign nation-states. Of course, there may come a point at which a nation rates itself so high in relative glory in these other spheres that its leaders and people are led to conclude that it can and should encroach on the sovereignty of other states. Perhaps Germany's brutal disregard for the sovereignty of other nations just prior to and during the Second World War was fueled by a dangerous combination of the humiliation of Germany represented by the Versailles Treaty along with the German sense that they were culturally superior to all other nations. Nonetheless, it is perfectly possible for certain states to rate themselves higher on the scale of national glory than other states and yet for every state to recognize the sovereignty of the others within borders to which all agree, and in such a situation international peace is likely to prevail. Contra Sacksteder, it is the mutual recognition of sovereignty rather than of equal glory that is of direct and vital importance in checking violent conflict between nation-states.

Yet one would have good reason to entertain serious doubts over whether the system of sovereign nation-states can really generate global tranquility. Indeed, it is a historical fact that the nation-state system as it has actually operated has failed spectacularly as a guarantor of global peace. One need know very little of human history during the nineteenth and twentieth centuries to know that the nation-state system has not only failed to prevent catastrophic global violence but has been partly responsible for it. Sovereign states have simply refused to respect the sovereignty of other states; the idea of mutual recognition of sovereignty has just not worked to pacify the planet. Hobbes would, of course, interpret such a historical record to confirm his claim that sovereign nation-states are necessarily in the state of nature with respect to each other. But how can those such as Bentham, with their decidedly more optimistic arguments in favor of the nation-state, construe such a historical record? After the failures represented by the two world wars of this century, one might have thought that no one in his right mind would argue that the nation-state system should be defended on grounds of its ability to secure international peace. The failure of the nation-state system in this regard has been at least as stunning as, for example, the failure of communism to generate the promised workers' paradise. Yet surprisingly few people are willing to draw the same conclusion that is widely drawn about communism, namely, that the system just does not work and should be junked.

One strategy for defending the nation-state is to argue that the problem has been, not with the nation-state system per se, but with the kinds of states that there have been: What is needed, the argument goes, is a system of liberal democratic nation-states. This Kantian view would interpret the international violence of the last several centuries as largely the product of sovereign states whose governments were not accountable to their populations through the institutions of representative democracy operating under the rule of law.[4] There is an important element of truth to this view, and I will explore it momentarily. But it seems to me that several points must be kept in mind when embracing the idea that a world system of liberal democratic nation-states could produce global tranquility. First, liberal democracy has always had great difficulty preserving itself in times of economic or social turmoil. The tendency to believe in a "Great Leader" who will pull us out of some mess still seems to be a powerful part of the human psychological constitution. Second, even in the absence of social turmoil, liberal democracy has had a very difficult time growing in certain cultural soils. Tocqueville remarked on the difficulty democracy had taking root in the authoritarian cultural soils of South America and Mexico, and although there is much optimistic talk of late about the victory of democracy in Latin America and the Philippines, for example, it remains to be seen whether such victories prove to be real and enduring liberal democratic achievements.[5] In addition, there are still vast regions of the planet where the ideology of liberal democracy is quite alien to the dominant ways of thinking.

It remains, however, a remarkable fact about recent human history that, for all its wars, virtually none of them have been between liberal democracies. Relations among the liberal democracies have been extraordinarily pacific. Michael Doyle has noted this striking aspect of the relations among liberal democracies: *"Even though liberal states have become involved in numerous wars with non-liberal states, constitutionally secure liberal states have yet to engage in war with one another."*[6] It seems to me that this fact is (in part) explained by the widespread acceptance within liberal democracies of a certain moral belief, the belief that liberal democratic states are morally legitimate because they rest on the voluntary consent of the governed. This belief leads the citizens and the officials of each liberal democracy to perceive that the other liberal democracies are, like their own, morally legitimate states. The mutual perception of legitimacy in turn motivates liberal democracies to avoid challenges to the sovereignty of other liberal democracies, and since such challenges are virtually always implicated in going to war against another state, it leads liberal states to avoid war with one another.[7]

The mutual perception of moral legitimacy among liberal states thus leads each of them to place limits on their pursuit of their national interests, including their pursuit of national glory. Moreover, these limits are observed without any supersovereign to enforce their terms. Liberal democratic states still do pursue national glory in science, athletics, and many other areas of human endeavor, and some such states do claim to have earned greater national glory than others. (Recall Hampton's example of the talk-show host in California whose banner proclaimed the USA to be "number 1"). But the pursuit of glory does not extend to violence against other liberal democracies owing to self-imposed limits that stem (in part) from the belief in the moral legitimacy of liberal democratic institutions. There is simply no room within the Hobbesian theoretical framework to allow for the possibility of such a belief leading a state to limit its pursuit of national self-interest, given the absence of a supersovereign.

III. The Psychology of Respect and Violence

Professor Hampton has posed the fascinating question of why it is that insults and demeaning behavior can move us to violence against those who show such disrespect toward us. The crux of her answer is that violence is a way in which a person who has some doubt about whether the disrespect was not really deserved can allay those doubts. The violent domination of the enemy provides us with evidence that we did not really merit the demeaning treatment at his hands. Hampton recognizes that such evidence would hardly be persuasive to the objective observer and likens the violent response to a one-sided effort to gather data in support of a preferred hypothesis. But she suggests that despite its tainted character, the evidence can be psychologically effective in allaying the self-doubts that emerge as a result of the demeaning treatment.

I think that there are two basic problems with Hampton's account of the connection between being victimized by demeaning behavior and a violent response against one's victimizer. First, the account claims that victims who do not experience any doubts about the unjustified character of their treatment are "beyond resentment" and so beyond violent response. This seems to me to be wrong. I do not question the claim that demeaning treatment can trigger self-doubt or that such a triggering might in some instances lead to a violent response as a way to allay the doubt and demonstrate that the treatment was not deserved. But persons who are beyond resentment and the inclination to violent response have a much more rare characteristic than merely being confident that the demeaning manner in which they were treated is unjustified. Many of us are confident that the disrespect we are shown is unjustified. Few of us are beyond resentment or beyond the inclination to violent response. Perhaps those few are sure of their own worth, but it is something more than that which enables them to face disrespect with equanimity. Indeed, I would suggest that sometimes persons respond violently precisely because they are so sure that they have been unjustly victimized. Moreover, persons who do experience self-doubt may well be more inclined to acquiescence and less inclined to violence than those who are sure that they have been wronged.

The second problem with Hampton's account is that it ignores a crucial fact: in almost all cases, the violent response, even if it successfully displays domination of the enemy, has virtually no logical connection to the claim that the demeaning treatment was unjustified. It is not simply one-sided evidence; it is no evidence at all with respect to the question of whether the treatment was warranted, and in many cases, one knows this full well but still feels the urge to violence.

In the early 1970s, Muhammad Ali and Joe Frazier fought each other in three boxing matches. Before one of their bouts, they were interviewed on television. Ali insulted Frazier, going through his usual routine in which he denigrated his opponent's boxing skills and predicted that he would "whup" the opponent, that the bout would be "no contest," and so on. Frazier took umbrage at these remarks and, in the television studio, jumped at Ali in an effort to pummel him then and there. Of course, this sort of thing is sometimes staged to promote interest in the bout, but in this case it seemed as though Frazier was actually moved to violence by Ali's insults. Yet Frazier knew full well, as did every boxing fan, that winning a street brawl is one thing; winning a boxing match quite another. Even if Frazier had "whupped" Ali then and there, it would have provided no evidence of Frazier's superior mastery of the sweet science of self-defense.

Most cases of insult are even further removed from the kind of direct and unregulated physical domination that is characteristic of violent outbursts against those who have demeaned one. I admit to feeling some tendency toward such an outburst in the aftermath of particularly demeaning treatment by some interviewers when I was looking for a teaching job not too long ago. In my view, they had denigrated my ability as a philosopher and had not given me a fair chance for a job I desperately wanted. I was furious. Punching them out obviously would not have provided evidence that I was really a good philosopher after all, and I hope it goes without saying that there was no chance that I would have actually been violent on that occasion. But I cannot honestly say that I was completely free of all violent inclinations toward those who had demeaned me.

Why did I have such inclinations? Why are people moved to violence when they know that it will not provide any grounds whatsoever that their demeaning treatment was not merited? Hampton's account is incapable of answering these questions. In order to answer them, we must begin with a point Hampton wholly ignores: we enjoy making those who have denigrated or humiliated us suffer, even if there is no benefit that we receive other than the simple pleasure of making them suffer.

Schopenhauer postulated that the desire to inflict pain on other creatures simply for the pleasure of making them suffer was the distinguishing mark of human beings. Man is not the rational animal, but the malicious one:

> To the boundless egoism of our nature there is joined more or less in every human breast a fund of hatred, anger, envy, rancour and malice, accumulated like the venom in a serpent's tooth, and waiting only for an opportunity of venting itself, and then, like a demon unchained, of storming and raging. . . . In the heart of every man there lies a wild beast which only waits for an opportunity to storm and rage, in its desire to inflict pain on others, or, if they stand in his way, to kill them. It is this which is the source of all the lust of war and battle.[8]

I believe that Schopenhauer's account of the malice that resides in the human breast, "accumulated like the venom in a serpent's tooth," as he puts it, is exaggerated in some important ways. As he portrays it, the human desire to inflict suffering is quite indiscriminate: any victim will do, as long as he, she, or it can feel pain. However, the desire to cause pain and the pleasure taken in being the agent of suffering are typically more focused: it hones in on certain individuals or groups for specific reasons. It hones in on those who are regarded as enemies, and although some persons have a rather expansive notion of the enemy, it is rarely as indiscriminate as Schopenhauer suggests. More typically, the urge to inflict pain for the pleasure of it focuses on those who we believe are in some way responsible for seriously wronging us or for harming someone or something we cherish. Victimizing us through insult or humiliation is a prime instance of the sort of wrongdoing that provokes the desire to strike back and the propensity to feel pleasure in the pain of the one who has victimized us.

Of course, when we are wronged the persons who are guilty may well deserve to have a serious loss imposed on them. Humans are masters of rationalizing their behavior in terms of the idea that they are giving people what they deserve, and such rationalizations are not always without foundation. People sometimes do horrible things that make them deserve to suffer some loss. However, this is not to say that they deserve to be the victims of physical violence. Nor is it to say that pleasure should be taken in the suffering imposed upon them. The human malice of which Schopenhauer writes is one that provokes physical violence against the perceived wrongdoer and takes pleasure in that violence. And the pleasure is all the greater when the one who feels the malice is the agent of the violence: there would be some pleasure simply to know that a third party had acted violently to make the perceived wrongdoer suffer; there would be more pleasure actually to see a third party inflict punishment; but the greatest pleasure, the pleasure toward which Schopenhauerian malice propels one most forcefully, is the pleasure of actually committing the violence oneself.

Thus, although Schopenhauer paints an excessively dark picture of human nature, I do not believe that we can understand our inclination to commit acts of violence against those who have degraded or demeaned us without giving some significant role to human malice. Moreover, the malicious impulses of humans can often be sufficiently powerful to override considerations of rational self-interest. At times such impulses provoke us to act in ways that not only harm the interests of the enemy but harm our own interests as well. The satisfaction of making someone who has humiliated us suffer sometimes proves so tempting that we act in ways that could not be countenanced by a rational regard for our own good.

There are two basic ways in which impulses such as malice can lead us to act in disregard of our own good. First, they can blind us to what is in fact in our own interests: the surges of hatred and enmity that accompany the desire to inflict pain on some enemy distorts our judgment of what serves our interests and what does not. Second, they can motivate us to act even in the face of our judgment that our interests would suffer from it. While a person's judgment is distorted in the first case, here in the second it is overpowered. It is likely that many cases involve some mix of the two mechanisms, distortion and overpowering. However, it is possible to have relatively pure forms of the one or the other.

Some of the points I have been making about malice can be illustrated if we turn to Shakespeare's infamous character Shylock.

Contrary to what Hampton's account would suggest, what drives Shylock is not doubts that he has about his self-worth. He is sure that Antonio's past treatment of him has been wholly unjustified. What drives him is the desire to inflict violent suffering on the one who has tormented him. He is propelled by Schopenhauerian malice. Moreover, he understands that the malice he feels does not reside only in the breasts of Jews; the venom can be found in good Christian breasts as well. And I believe that Shylock's craving to carve out the heart of Antonio does not so much distort his judgment of self-interest as overpower it: he seems to know that his rational self-interest will be little served by a pound of his enemy's flesh, and the malice and hatred he feels toward Antonio overpower that judgment. When asked what a pound of Antonio's flesh can possibly be good for, he replies:

> To bait fish withal. If it will feed nothing else, it will feed my revenge. He hath disgraced me, and hindered me half a million, laughed at my losses, mocked at my gains, scorned my nation, thwarted my bargains, cooled my friends, heated mine enemies; and what's his reason? I am a Jew. Hath not a Jew eyes? Hath not a Jew hands, organs, dimensions, senses, affections, passions? Fed with the same food, hurt with the same weapons, subject to the same diseases, healed by the same means, warmed and cooled by the same winter and summer, as a Christian is? If you prick us, do we not bleed? If you tickle us, do we not laugh? If you poison us, do we not die? And if you wrong us shall we not revenge? If we are like you in the rest, we will resemble you in that. (*Merchant of Venice* 3.1.50–64)

Once the good Christians of Venice and Belmont have Shylock within their power, they do not hesitate to act in a way that unwittingly confirms Shylock's point that Christians and Jews are no different when it comes to the craving for vengeance. Of course, Shylock makes the point by saying that Jews are no different from Christians in that regard. The Christians confirm it from the other direction, as it were, by showing through their actions that they are no different from the despised Jew, Shylock. They forcibly extract from Shylock a promise to convert to Christianity, a promise that no doubt satiates their thirst to humiliate him but that is otherwise as useless to them as Antonio's flesh would have been to Shylock. It is true that forcing Shylock to convert does not actually involve the direct physical violence of cutting out his heart (although such a forced conversion is as good a metaphorical case as one can imagine of carving out someone's heart). On such a basis one might argue that the malice of Antonio and his friends is more tame than the brutally violent, Schopenhauerian malice that Shylock feels toward

Antonio. Yet there is no reason to think that the good Christians of Venice and Belmont would be reluctant literally to carve out Shylock's heart if he should resist their efforts to humiliate him.

Hampton's failure to bring malice into her account is a product of her effort to stick as far as possible with the Hobbesian principle that we are egoists, but rational ones.[9] She has tried to show how the violent response of one who is demeaned can be the response of one who is a rational egoist, at least an imperfectly rational egoist. Malice throws a monkey wrench into rational egoism. It can incite conduct that is not only morally reprehensible but that makes no sense from the perspective of the rational pursuit of self-interest. The prospect of the pleasure of making an enemy suffer can be as powerful an enticement as the more notorious allure of sexual pleasure. Malice, no less than sexual desire, can provoke conduct in disregard of rational self-interest. Moreover, malice has this additional feature that makes it especially disruptive to the rational pursuit of self-interest: it provokes those persons on whom an individual vents his malice to return the favor as soon as they get the opportunity. Shylock may well have known that before he demanded the pound of Antonio's flesh, and he certainly knew it by the time the story was over.

In sum, there are many instances of the violent response to degrading or demeaning behavior that cannot be understood as some imperfect version of a rational strategy to secure evidence of one's self-worth or as any other rational strategy for the pursuit of one's own good. Rather, such responses are often rooted in the malicious and characteristically irrational human impulse to inflict suffering on those who are counted as enemies simply for the pleasure of making them suffer. It is malice, not rational self-interest, that explains much of the human reaction to those regarded as the enemy.

Hampton insightfully remarks at the beginning of her essay that Hobbes's argument for the establishment of a sovereign must downplay the pursuit of glory precisely because the desire for glory tends to provoke conduct that does not make sense for rational egoists. The Hobbesian argument, of course, is meant to appeal to rational self-interest, and it will be rendered problematic to the extent that humans are propelled by a nonrational will to glory. Hampton is not attempting to justify violence in response to insults or demeaning treatment, but she is trying to understand it in terms of the (imperfectly) rational pursuit of self-interest. And just as Hobbes had to downplay human impulses that disrupt the rational pursuit of self-interest, so must Hampton downplay the role played by malice in the human response to insult and degradation.

Malice is part of a side to human nature that is often downplayed or neglected in modern Western philosophy. Hobbes and Hampton are quite characteristic in that regard. Malice is difficult to fit into a picture of humans as either rational or moral. It is an element of human nature that seriously disrupts the rational pursuit of self-interest and that contributes generously to the fund of undeserved pain that persons suffer in this world. We should be dismayed by its power, but we should not underestimate it as Hobbes and Hampton have done.

IV. Conclusion

Both Hampton and Sacksteder have provided real illumination of the human psychology of respect and glory and its relation to violent confrontation. But the illumination extends only so far. I have tried to show that there are serious shortcomings in their accounts of respect and glory and that these problems stem from a failure to go sufficiently beyond the principles of Hobbesian thought. We humans are both better and worse than the picture Hobbes paints. We are better because we can sometimes act on moral grounds and show respect toward those whom we have the brute power to subjugate for our own benefit. The pacific relations among liberal democratic states is a manifestation of that side of human nature. We are worse because we sometimes inflict terrible pain on others for the pleasure of making them suffer. The malice that persons can exhibit in responding to those they regard as enemies is a manifestation of that other side of human nature. We are divine and we are satanic and we are something in between. Sometimes we act as Hobbes would have it. Sometimes we do much better. Sometimes we do much worse. If a just and secure peace among nations is our goal, as it ought to be, we must do much better.

Ten

The Viability
of Nonviolence
in Collective Life

Margaret Chatterjee

The theme that first suggested itself to me ran like this: "The viability of nonviolence in a Hobbesian world." I then began to wonder if we do in fact live in a Hobbesian world and decided to modify the title accordingly. Even as it stands now, my wicket is sticky indeed. It may seem almost impossible to avoid rhetoric on the one hand and ideology on the other, both of which we are bidden to eschew. Of course a case might be made out for nonpejorative uses of each of these. The persuasive element in speech is surely invoked by us all whenever we use arguments. Moreover, there is surely an innocuous sense in which all thinking about politics and morals moves within a formative framework of ideas. Bearing this in mind, I shall seek to be reasonably persuasive and deploy my nonviolent forces, such as they are, as innocuously as I can.

At the risk of trespassing on others' territory, I shall begin with a quick look at what Hobbes says about human nature, for so much of it reflects contemporary ways of thinking:

> For there is *no* such thing as perpetuall Tranquillity of mind, while we live here; because Life it selfe is but Motion, and can never be without Desire, nor without Feare, no more than without Sense.[1]

Human desires are difficult to curb, and we seem to be inexorably impelled by mechanisms within ourselves. So far, one might almost be listening to a Buddhist Jeremiah, were such an oddity possible. But unlike the Buddha or Patanjali or the author of the *Gita*, Hobbes does not think the attainment of perpetual tranquility of mind is possible, although the careful addition of the word "perpetual" suggests there might be occasional respites, analogous presumably to the way in which bodies can be momentarily at rest while forces do not actually impinge on them. The moral Hobbes draws is that, since human life is so precarious, it is incumbent on the state to preserve life,

> considering what values men are naturally apt to set upon themselves; what respect they look for from others; and how little they value other men; from whence continually arise amongst them, Emulation, Quarrells, Factions, and at last Warre, to the destroying of one another, and diminution of their strength against a common Enemy. (chap. 18, p. 139)

The way in which Hobbes links the whole argument in *Leviathan* to his "groundwork" analysis of human nature reflects the approach to human studies that extrapolates from the individual to the collective. This approach, however, is not much favored today. While critics of the organic theory of society or of the state did a great deal to undermine the analogy, a more basic question mark still attends how we understand human nature in the first place. While the retreating sea of faith may seem to take away with it a sense of radical iniquity, it may no less surely wash away the hope of redemption. In any case, I am not altogether sure that the sea of faith is retreating as much as some fear. But that is a theme for another day. Modern man is more likely to opt for a faith midway between Augustinianism and millennialist thinking. The concept of nonviolence probably belongs precisely here, as I shall try to show, enabling us to avoid too Hobbesian a view of human nature on the one hand, and too rosy-eyed a picture of the feasible on the other.

But how Hobbesian can we be said to be, situated as we are in the last quarter of the twentieth century? I refer now to our contemporary *Lebenswelt*. Hobbes's arguments in favor of government seem to point to the need for an international government. In the absence of such a government, anarchy is bound to prevail. But the extrapolation from the individual to the state and from the state to *inter*state relations becomes vulnerable at this point. What we find may not be a war of all against all, but a war of some against others, and this of course can show itself in more than one geographical region. I refer to the phenomenon of multiple isolated conflicts. Since Hobbes's time we are, moreover, familiar with the formation of blocs—another factor that could be said to mitigate the condition of a free-for-all state of anarchy. Furthermore, we now have a modicum of international bodies that mediate between governments, and also a corpus of international law. And yet, in spite of what appear as mitigating factors, the hard fact remains that now we live with the possibility of something worse than the anarchy that Hobbes envisaged for the single nation, the possibility of total destruction, something that is genuinely on the cards in virtue of the nature of modern weaponry. In other words, we now have a changed prospect of calamity beyond the confines of civil strife. The need for curbing national sovereignties and the structuring of international machinery for regulating the intercourse of states are all matters that Hobbes could not possibly anticipate.

We might at this point venture a little further in assessing whence we have come. While we may wish to modify in some ways the seventeenth-century mechanical model that Hobbes took for granted—I think here of quantum mechanics on the one hand and the apparently aleatory character of much of human affairs on the other—the fact remains that the element of *momentum* is still with us, most notably in the sphere of technological advance and economic life. Hobbes's apprehension of things going out of control has fresh warrant. Both of these types of momentum, in technology and in economics (and no doubt they are closely related), may serve to undermine contractual obligations. The twentieth-century steeplechase is strewn with not one, but several, scraps of paper.

We are familiar now with looking upon the state as an institution that can do either right or wrong but most often deploys itself in the grey area in between. Rebellion and revolt are now legitimized under conditions of the abuse of power, and in fact, it is in the context of the resistance against authority that the whole history of nonviolent political activity grew up.

The force of public opinion in democratic societies is one of the most hopeful factors that has developed since Hobbes's time. But this force is to be distinguished from the actions of the demos conceived as a mob, a demarcation that the concept of nonviolence can help to make clear. The health of a democracy, moreover, owes much to the voluntary institutions that are intermediate between the individual and the state, and it is these voluntary associations that have, since the seventeenth century, especially in the religious sphere, evolved techniques of nonviolent protest. In this connection, the role of nonconformist sects and organizations on both sides of the Atlantic is of historic importance. It would not be possible to overemphasize the contribution of this important stream of thought to the ethos of the founding fathers of the American Constitution. The concept of nonviolence jumped continents and centuries and surfaced in Gandhi's labors in South Africa and crossed the Atlantic once more, surfacing in Martin Luther King's work.[2] At its core lay a sturdy belief in the individual, a conception of human rights based on all that is inalienable in man, and at the same time a no less firm belief in the importance of *congregations* as foci of powers that exceed the combined individual strengths of their members. Such congregations acted as a leaven in society and, I venture to suggest, were arsenals of moral strength in times of civil discord.

What else has happened since Hobbes's time? I believe that the development of transnational associations is a very significant phenomenon to be noted in this regard. So much international contact is neither nasty nor brutish. Frontiers do not always prevent contact between the likeminded (they often do, of course). Ideas travel freely, although information sometimes may not. Contact apart, contemporary experience witnesses to myriad efforts in the pooling of points of view and the sharing of lifeworlds. We should not forget to mention also the way in which states often fund the comings and goings of people such as ourselves, even though the intellectual more often than not plays the role of the critic rather than that of the establishment voice. All such efforts, to my mind (and the colloquium for which this essay was first written surely illustrates this) operate as nonmechanical neutralizing forces in a plenum in which nonviolent strategies can well exert a subtle influence on the destabilizing forces in society. That a word like "destabilizing" should come to mind is perhaps significant. When Hobbes speaks of the "causes of quarrel," of "what disturbs the peace," he seems to presuppose an otherwise peaceful equilibrium on which considerations of competition, diffidence, and glory intrude. But if this is so, it hardly goes along with his initial analysis of human nature with its pushes and pulls of desire and aversion. The fact seems to be that human nature contains many contrary elements, some working toward tranquility and some working toward its opposite. It makes a difference, I suspect, whether we conceive the latter as restlessness per se, or as the sort of negativities/deadly sins frowned on in most religious traditions. A not-so-divine discontent may not be a bad thing, I tend to think, especially if it serves as the spur to a bettering of the human condition. But can a term like nonviolence cover both the idea of tranquility and the dynamism that a meliorist outlook requires? I shall explore this question next, assuming that we are now exploring a very different thought-world from that of Hobbes, but one that is strongly represented in the history of dissent, the framework of ideas that crossed the Atlantic and was eventually encapsulated in the lifeworld of the founding fathers of the American Constitution.

The ethic of nonviolence was carved out in the context of *resistance* to authority, and not, as in the case of Hobbes's *Leviathan*, in the context of the *legitimation* of authority. Looking at the history of nonviolent struggles in modern times, the following characteristics emerge. The protagonist of nonviolence is committed to an ethic of both responsibility and perfection, thereby combining categories that Max Weber distinguished. The ethic seems to cut across religious demarcations, although I myself find it, historically, present most of all in nonconformism. The nonviolent protagonist is committed to a gradual domestic decentralization of power, a decentralization that will—it is hoped—eventually obviate the necessity for a centralized political power (and that will in any case tolerate with difficulty the "individuality" of separate congregations), a power that certainly in modern times is bound to augment itself beyond national boundaries. This augmentation is evidenced amply by the way the market economy leads to colonialism and its latest counterparts in terms of spheres of influence, and so on. The protagonist of nonviolence propounds a logic of total peace that is the counterpart of the logic of total war. The latter is admittedly clearer to define, that is, a state of war in which, with the introduction of aerial bombardment, there is no distinction between the homefront and the battlelines. The advocates of nonviolence shift from considerations of space, that is to say, rival territorialities, to time, in the sense that only a logic of total peace can offer a viable future, or more simply, can hold out the prospect of survival. They aim not merely at a limitation of hostilities but at their dissolution.

Nonviolent resistance parallels "the rules of war" with its own rules. These include preparatory training to inculcate discipline; a prior exhausting of all other peaceful alternatives, such as petitions, negotiations, press campaigns; a staged embarking on nonviolent campaigns (illustrated, for example, in Gandhi's *satyagraha* campaigns or in the civil rights movement in the United States); and, within each campaign, selective targeting. Nonviolence has been used both by individuals and by collectivities. But in each case it is a last resort, when all other possibilities have been tried and found wanting. Those who are committed to nonviolence believe that therein lies a method of resisting subjugation without killing, that nonviolence does not itself incorporate any aggressive element. The psychological component of all this must not be missed. Nonviolent resistance is a method of overcoming a sense of helplessness. It shows what can be done by the humblest citizens in situations where the state power is heavily loaded against them.

Nonviolence as a policy clearly involves commitment to the use of an alternative weaponry, commitment to the moral equivalent of warfare. This expression was used by both William James and Gandhi, and I would like to recall the context in which, first of all, James used it. The year was 1906, and William James arrived in San Francisco booked to teach at Stanford from January until mid-May.

His famous speech on "the moral equivalent of war" was delivered on 25 February to the assembly of the entire university, although it was not published until 1910. He proclaimed:

> We inherit the warlike type; and for most of the capacities of heroism that the human race is full of we have to thank this cruel history.[3]

He did not, however, want to lose the warlike virtues of "intrepidity, contempt of softness, surrender of public interest, obedience to command."[4] The remedy was to find "moral equivalents," such as the conquest of nature or building a better society. He envisaged a canalizing of aggressive impulses and stoic attitudes of mind into "useful" attitudes. The possibility of taming nature might have received a setback in his mind when he witnessed an earthquake some months later and saw San Francisco in a shambles. But in an article written some weeks after the quake, he observed how the catastrophe had brought out the best in people, suppressing their selfishness and throwing up spontaneous leaders.[5] Putting together his experience of the earthquake and what Lutoslawski had written to him about Yoga, he subsequently explored the notion that most people have untapped energies that show themselves in times of calamity or when their willpower is called upon in an unusually demanding situation:

> We need a topography of the limits of human power, similar to the chart which oculists use of the field of human vision. We need also a study of the various types of human being with reference to the different ways in which their energy-reserves may be appealed to and set loose.[6]

James's scientific outlook inspired an objective analysis that was singularly free from moralizing. It may be worthwhile setting this analysis alongside the views of two other thinkers for whom the sense of human imperfection was more pronounced. James Madison wrote:

> As there is a degree of depravity in mankind which requires a certain degree of circumspection and distrust; so there are other qualities in human nature which justify a certain portion of esteem and confidence. Republican government presupposes the existence of these qualities in a higher degree than any other form.[7]

Madison's use of the term "distrust" compares in an intriguing way with Hobbes's use of the word "diffidence" and links up, moreover, with the contemporary use of diffidence in the connotation of self-doubt.

Margaret Chatterjee

Gandhi's analysis resembles James's and Madison's in varying degrees, although the overall picture he gives has its own characteristic contours. Looking back on his experiences in South Africa, he used the phrase "the moral equivalent of war" in an article in *Young India* of 5 November 1931. I am told that Gandhi knew a Bengali student who had audited William James's lectures at Harvard but have not been able to verify this, and in any case, James's famous lecture was delivered at Stanford and not at Harvard. The point, however, is that while Gandhi, like James, advocated a canalization of human aggressiveness, he thought this could be done most effectively through a technique of collective action he called *satyagraha*. Gandhi, moreover, did not think poorly of what others dubbed "monkish virtues," believing that collectivity needed to be leavened by qualities such as gentleness, forbearance, and the virtues listed in 1 Corinthians 13. That the path of nonviolence is the path of suffering was stressed by Gandhi again and again. As he wrote in the *Young India* article:

> Suffering is the law of human beings; war is the law of the jungle. But suffering is infinitely more powerful than the law of the jungle for converting the opponent and opening his ears, which are otherwise shut, to the voice of reason.[8]

Gandhi found that nonviolent resistance was a method that could be used not only by individuals but by collectivities: "It is a profound error to suppose that whilst the law [of life, nonviolence,] is good enough for individuals it is not for masses of mankind."[9] He was, moreover, well aware of the perfectionist bias in his own thinking but thought it vitally important to match the mechanistic analyses of man and society by an affirmation of a built-in teleology of the spirit that worked not only against the determinisms that dog us but against inertness, an Indian concept that can perhaps be set alongside the notion of acedia.[10]

Before we proceed to the nitty-gritty, let us see what Gandhi's advocacy of nonviolence as a tool for collective use amounts to in political terms. It seems to me that conceptually the ruling out of violence provides a ground of federation. But, as such, it provides a transcendental condition of an unusual kind. It provides a presuppositional framework for the neutralizing of a whole package of negativities—mistrust, unease, malaise, ignorance, misinformation, and misunderstanding. In calling it a "ground," I would like to point to its noncontractual character per se, but I would also suggest that it can be fertile for contracts, and not only for contracts, but for diverse forms of association and inventive social structures. If a nonviolent *Bewusstseinslage* is formal material in nature, as seems

134

to be the case, it can generate something midway between a *Gesinnungsethik* and an *Erfolgsethik*. If this were not the case, we should indeed be guilty of the sheerest rhetoric in discoursing on nonviolence.

In terms of political policy, as distinct from philosophical structure, nonviolence involves the following elements. First of all, it hinges on a radical pluralism that in James's case derived from the empiricist tradition and, in Gandhi's, from Jainism. The nonviolent protagonist tries to "neutralize" causes of quarrel, tackling economic and other grievances and at the same time embarking on what Gandhi called constructive work. This amounts to attacking areas of darkness in one's own backyard, a discipline reckoned to make the agents realize that all the darkness is not in the other camp. Gandhi, moreover, sees nonviolence involving the individual in the democratic process in a way that representative government by itself fails to do. A nonviolent strategy agreed on by a group resembles strategies stemming from covenant relationships in that it is carried out "in the presence of" some larger concern—in this case, in the presence of the public, a public that these days spans frontiers. Gandhi himself attached great importance to the lack of secrecy that attended his campaigns. On reflection one finds that the need for secrecy is connected most of all with defense, that is to say, with situations where the type and quantum of weaponry is crucial. One can also see how the necessary withholding of information that goes along with military strategy heightens a sense of "something going on behind the scenes," of "deals being made," and so on, all of which distance the electorate from the decision-makers.

As far as Gandhi was concerned, the supporting ethos that went along with nonviolence as a regulating principle, both within the state and between states, carried with it a stringent critique of technological civilization, on the grounds that the latter inevitably augments power at the center, thereby increasing the likelihood of conflict with others. Nonviolent protagonists believe that violence is never civilized, and so they exclude familiar concepts like "the just war," "limited conflicts," and "deterrents." They take an idiosyncratic view of success and failure, measuring success by collective well-being, where this is understood as involving both *Gesellschaft* and *Gemeinschaft*. That this is conceived as going beyond frontiers is made clear in Gandhi's "oceanic circle" model of political activity, the individual being at the center, but with increasing areas of involvement, there being no limit to the concentric circles generated by corporate activities. This could be contrasted with Clausewitz's understanding of war as in essence the clash of collective wills. On the oceanic circle model, there would be an expanding collective will for peace. Instead of competition, there would be a pooling of resources; instead of diffidence, trust; and instead of glory, value set on the welfare of the humblest of citizens. Gandhi did not work out in detail what kind of institutional framework all this would involve, but he was firm about the need to minimize state activity and about the importance of voluntary organizations as tools for mobilizing collectivities. In this respect, he was particularly aware of the factors that divide one community from another and the need for encouraging cross-sections of public opinion on issues that involve all in common. Above all, the nonviolent resource of resistance to authority when abused would give the community a sense of control over its own destiny, something that lies at the very core of the meaning of democracy.

We now come finally to the nitty-gritty problems arising in our minds, all those factors that tend to make us distrustful of what appears to be an ethic of perfectionism if not an ostrichlike disregard of political realities. The first difficulty arises over the extrapolation of what may be an admirable *Gesinnungsethik* for individuals into a policy for collectivities. I have already suggested that even at the individual level nonviolence is rather more than an "ethic of motive." It seems to bear a formal-material character if we examine the situations in which this counterforce has been deployed in many parts of the globe. As for the extrapolation from the individual to collectivities, and even more, from individuals to states, there are admittedly many nonparallels; for example, individuals may not imprison, compel obedience to rules, or declare war.

One may next ask whether nonviolent protagonists have fully understood the nature of the state, or whether, perhaps, they have understood it all too well. They see the state as essentially a focus of power, possessing a built-in violence that expresses itself, for example, in policing and taxing functions, and against which, even when the government is representative, individuals may often find themselves arrayed. In this connection, Gandhi himself said on many an occasion that it was impossible to defend by nonviolence what has been gained by violence. Following this argument through, it follows that states cannot pursue a policy of nonviolence. We seem to be driven to this conclusion *malgré nous*. But are there any mitigating factors to take the sting out of this conclusion? I think there are.

First, the machinery of representative government, with its attendant checks and balances, along with the attendant network of associations that bridge the gap between the individual and the center, provides, or should provide, avenues for the expression of the will of the people. Second, the evolution of political institutions in the free world in this century has made of states today (I hope I am not too optimistic about this) not only foci of power but in some sense vehicles of culture. We come back at this point to the old, but not out of date, concept of ethos, which takes a recognizable *national* shape and which in countries with constitutions is reflected, often paradigmatically, therein. It will always be good for the state to have critics, and this is where the nonviolent strategies of collectivities, those intermediate bodies of whose importance Rousseau was so convinced, can exert an invaluable influence on public policy. The moralizing of politics, to my mind, can only take place in this apparently roundabout way, but it is a way that makes the people themselves, rather than any other agency, the guardians. If such a degree of participation, whether by way of criticism or cooperation, were truly operative, it would be possible to say that citizens were *responsible* for the acts of their governments.

Let us raise a further question. Are there duties across frontiers? Do leaders not have a prime duty to their own people? Contemporary moral sensitivity, in many quarters, recognizes the reprehensibility of "letting die," just as it intuits something very wrong in damaging the genetic structure of the unborn. These new sensitivities in our own time, to my mind, serve to foster an awareness of duty beyond national boundaries. The adherent of nonviolence, one might venture to say, is more likely to detect the concomitant but unintended violence to others involved in policies that do not eschew military alternatives. Contemporary "diffidence," it seems to me, is not grounded on skepticism concerning knowledge, but on fundamental uncertainties, especially regarding "what the others may do first."

In our own day, and this is where we differ from Hobbes and his contemporaries, we are haunted not so much by the threat of civil war as by the possibility of a flying apart at the seams stemming from ethnic diversity, regional disparities, urban guerilla activity, and terrorism. While these challenge the body politic, their impact cuts across national boundaries. No matter how excellent a constitution may be, it cannot provide a therapy for them. The therapeutic stance ties in with the philosophic, both requiring a diagnostic eye and generating a search for a way of dealing with the effects set in train by such causal factors. In liberal societies, the diagnostic eye demands a convergence of conscience and consciousness that the founders of the American Constitution believed democracy would foster.

Somewhere along the way, the seventeenth-century intuitions of radical human defect and hope of redemption have been replaced by a complex of attitudes that includes a sense of dismay at the

frightening acceleration principle of many processes we have ourselves set in motion. Hobbes would have found this familiar. But
the very mechanism of democratic procedures seems to provide sav-
ing factors, a means of self-correction that owes as much to individual initiative as it does to collective agency. The concept of
resource can provide a valuable antidote to mechanism. And somewhere among the resources is a history of nonviolent ways of bringing about meliorist change, a history that spans frontiers and
continents. As Gandhi knew only too well, the potentiality of the
moral equivalent of warfare has yet to be fully explored. Let us recall
Madison's words once more:

> There are other qualities in human nature which justify a certain
> portion of esteem and confidence. Republican Government pre-
> supposes the existence of these qualities in a higher degree than
> any other form.

Eleven

Reflections on Hobbes: Anarchy and Human Nature

Charles Landesman

I

Hobbes was born more than four hundred years ago. How long ago that really was can be brought home by his brief and passing remarks on the nature of tyranny. He recognizes that the commonwealth that is established by the social contract may assume three different forms, which he calls monarchy, democracy, and aristocracy. He then points out that "there be other names of Government, in the Histories and books of Policy; as *Tyranny*, and *Oligarchy.*"[1] How do these other names fit into his basic threefold classification? Is tyranny a different form of commonwealth? He rejects that possibility. These extra names "are not the names of other Formes of Government, but of the same Formes misliked. For they that are discontented under *Monarchy*, call it *Tyranny*" (p. 240).

In an earlier part of *Leviathan*, Hobbes presented a discussion of words and speech in the course of which he classified as words of *"inconstant* signification" those "names of such things as affect us, that is, which please, and displease us, because all men be not alike affected with the same thing, nor the same man at all times" (p. 109). Those who are pleased by a form of government in which the sovereignty is in an individual ruler will call it monarchy; those who are displeased—and there will be some who will be displeased, particularly those who are excluded from power but whose desire for power is great—will call it tyranny. "For though the nature of what we conceive, be the same; yet the diversity of our reception of it, in respect of different constitutions of body, and prejudices of opinion, gives everything a tincture of our different passions" (p.

109). The term "tyranny" differs from "monarchy" not necessarily in respect to differences in the thing itself that is named but in respect to the differences in the passions of those who use the names.

As usual, Hobbes has an important insight to communicate here. He realizes that political discourse is often used ideologically as a device to arouse our passions in order to further the political ambitions of an individual or a faction. This he thinks is the standard use of such negatively evaluative terms as "tyranny," "oligarchy," and "anarchy." The correct, philosophical use of political concepts is to provide us with an impartial understanding of the origin, nature, and worth of the commonwealth, of whatever form it assumes on the stage of human history. Used philosophically, such terms would not be of inconstant signification, for the intent of such discourse is not to arouse our passions but to produce understanding.

Hobbes's motive in his discussion of "tyranny" and other political terms of inconstant signification is not only to uncover the rhetorical impediments to correct understanding but also to disarm the critics of existing established forms of sovereignty. The fact that a form of government displeases us for some reason or other is not reason for denying it legitimacy and obedience. Critics of established governments are either those who are seeking power for themselves and thus wish to discredit the incumbent or those who fail to perceive the necessity of unlimited sovereign power to maintain peace and security.

Hobbes considers two objections to his political principle that the sovereign in a commonwealth shall have unlimited power. According to the first, "men may fancy many evil consequences," but he replies that "the consequences of the want of it, which is perpetual warre of every man against his neighbor, are much worse" (p. 260). We should not expect to have political order "without inconvenience" (p. 260). Such is the nature of human life and circumstances. Moreover, many of the "evil consequences" of absolute monarchy are only fancied, that is, exaggerated by critics whose motives are questionable. In his reply, Hobbes allows us only two alternatives: either absolute sovereignty or the war of all against all. His perspective was limited. We can see what he could not, that governments that are based upon divided sovereignty—such as ours—can be stable and enduring and do not inevitably produce a war of all against all.

In the second objection that he considers, Hobbes implicitly concedes that there are governments whose sovereignty is not unlimited. This is "the greatest objection," and it is based upon actual practice: "where, and, when, such Power has by Subjects been acknowledged" (pp. 260–61). According to this objection, people in general do not institute the type of sovereignty that Hobbes recommends. So perhaps his analysis is irrelevant to the actual issues facing subjects. In reply, he asks "when, or where has there been a Kingdome long free from Sedition and Civill Warre?" (p. 261). Hobbes thinks that an argument based upon the actual practices of humankind is invalid: "For though in all places of the world, men should lay the foundation of their houses on sand, it could not thence be inferred, that so it ought to be" (p. 261). We can see from this response that his theory of the commonwealth is not intended as a description of actual practice but as a prescription for reducing civil conflict and sustaining peace over a prolonged period of time. Only an unlimited sovereign can produce long-term political stability. And since the major inconveniences that stem from absolute sovereignty are caused by the disobedience of subjects (p. 260) and disputations about political authority (p. 261), the subjects also have a lesson to learn from Hobbes's theory.

The time and events that separate us historically from Hobbes have provided us with the opportunity to learn that the term "inconvenience" is too moderate a description of the "many evil consequences" that have flowed from the sovereign power of the modern nation-state. Hobbes's use of "inconvenience" is itself tinctured with a certain passion, namely, with the desire to trivialize the criticisms of established sovereign power. But because he lived at the beginning of the modern nation-state and did not have the opportunity to observe its long-range tendencies, there were several matters that he missed. First, he could not see that the enormous military power of the nation-state—sustained by progress in science and technology—would enable political leaders to initiate and sustain wars of unspeakable horror. Second, he could not see that a particular combination of political ideology along with cruelty, ambition, lust for power, envy, racial, religious, and class hostility would motivate sovereigns to unleash death and destruction upon their own citizens. With the example of twentieth-century governments before our eyes, we cannot recommend Hobbesian obedience as the sole solution for domestic and international disorder. Nor can we agree that the evils of disobedience are always greater than the evils of obedience. In our own times, there have been political regimes whose behavior has made it morally absurd to describe tyranny merely as a legitimate form of government that is "misliked."

II

There are many points of view that one can adopt in reflecting upon the course of modern history. One of them is to interpret the historical record as a series of experiments with a variety of institutions and practices. As Hume pointed out, a priori, anything can cause anything. It is only through experience that facts reveal their consequences. That is why political philosophy rests in part upon empirical premises. The career of the modern nation-state, a career that was just getting started in Hobbes's time, has in its maturity manifested certain characteristics that make us wonder whether the state is an experiment that has failed. The actions of the states have produced enough in the way of evil consequences to justify a certain lack of enthusiasm in our evaluation of them.

John Rawls has recommended that the way to consider whether a political principle is justified is to place ourselves behind a veil of ignorance whose purpose is to conceal our identities in order to foster impartiality in our deliberations. Suppose we place ourselves behind a veil of ignorance in order to appraise impartially the value of the modern nation-state. Those who live in commonwealths that are relatively beneficent and successful do not know that they do so. Those who live under regimes that are wicked or inefficient or incompetent or corrupt have this information suppressed as well. Suppose also that the veil does not conceal the course of modern history in all its woeful detail. We can observe everything that has happened to everyone, but we are kept from knowing whether we are among the beneficiaries or victims. If we could start all over again, would we choose the nation-state as the vehicle for protecting our security and providing the conditions of a contented life? If the course of modern history were presented to us as a possible world, would we choose to make it actual? Upon reflection, we would soon realize that the career of the nation-state has produced enough victims so that the probability that any one of us would be found among the victims once the veil has been lifted is not insignificant. So our first response would be to hesitate. Our second should be to ask, What is the alternative? There is one alternative for which Hobbes had a name, "anarchy," that designates the condition of the absence of any political authority whatever. Under anarchy, there are no nation-states, no city-states, no states of any sort. Anarchy is a circumstance in which neither Hobbes's absolute sovereign exists nor does the divided sovereignty of certain democratic states. It is the condition in which the victims, whoever they are and however they came to be victims, are not the victims of any state.

The fact that political authority is absent in anarchy does not imply that no one has any authority of any other kind. As Hobbes has taught us, the use of coercion and the threat of force are essential and distinctive ways by which the state produces results. Political authority is backed up by force; it attempts to achieve a monopoly of the instruments of coercion within its sphere of operation. In a condition of anarchy, on the other hand, there can, in theory at least, be cooperative ventures in which certain individuals or groups are assigned leadership roles and function as authorities. In anarchic communities, however, subordination to authority is voluntary and temporary; and authority is awarded on grounds of proven competence for the task at hand.

Should we choose anarchy over the state? From the perspective of an experimental approach to social organization, it is difficult to know how to answer this question. All of us have lived under political regimes. Even our voluntary cooperative endeavors have proceeded under the shelter of the nation-state. We have had little direct experience of anarchy—and the few cases in which we have had the opportunity to observe anarchy in practice have been in places where the political structures have weakened and broken down; in these cases, anarchy has not been particularly inviting. The mainstream of Western political philosophy has argued, for the most part, against anarchy and in favor of political authority and of the citizen's obligation to obey, under normal conditions, the rules and commands of constituted authority. Political authority has been perceived to be necessary for social peace, and peace necessary for survival and well-being. The most famous and influential version of this argument has been provided by Hobbes himself. Although his argument is extraordinarily complex and many-sided, certain of its central premises are spelled out in the famous chapter 13 of *Leviathan*. As we remain behind the veil of ignorance, perhaps a consideration of what Hobbes argued in this chapter will help us to clarify the issues.

III

In chapter 13, Hobbes reflects upon the state of nature, that condition in which there is no political authority to keep the peace. It is a state of anarchy and, as Hobbes eloquently argues, a state of "warre, as is of every man, against every man" (p. 185). It is a condition in which all are "apt to invade, and destroy one another" (p. 186). As a result, everyone lives an insecure life of bare subsistence. In Hobbes's famous words, "the life of man, [is] solitary, poore, nasty, brutish, and short" (p. 186).

Breaking with the Aristotelian tradition, Hobbes asserts that humans in the state of nature are roughly equal in ability, and that each has the right "to use his own power, as he will himself, for the preservation of his own Nature" (p. 189). Under such conditions, human beings inevitably find themselves in a state of war. The fault, says Hobbes, lies in human nature: "In the nature of man, we find three principall causes of quarrell. First, Competition; Secondly, Diffidence; Thirdly, Glory." Let us consider these causes of quarrel one at a time to see if Hobbes is correct in his judgment of their inevitability. First, diffidence or distrust.

Diffidence. Diffidence plays a special role in Hobbes's argument because it is the source of preemptive aggression or "anticipation" in the state of nature. "And from this diffidence of one another, there is no way for any man to secure himself, so reasonable, as Anticipation; that is, by force, or wiles, to master the persons of all men he can, so long, till he see no power great enough to endanger him" (p. 184). Because all individuals have reason to expect aggression from every other, the most reasonable strategy is to strike first. Since all know this and act upon this knowledge, the state of nature quickly becomes a state of war. Thus behavior that is reasonable for each to pursue produces a result that is harmful to all. According to Hobbes, the only way out of the difficulty is to establish a coercive power strong enough to make anticipation too costly a strategy to pursue. This is one of his major arguments against the anarchy of the state of nature.

Although Hobbes asserts that diffidence lies in "the nature of man," his actual account of its origin fails to support the claim that it is an innate propensity. He tells us that human beings *learn* to distrust one another because of the aggression that stems from competition (p. 184). Each person comes to distrust all others because of the *experience* of their belligerence; we are not born believing that others are a threat to our survival. The very young child's dependence upon others and need for the company of others defeats the hypothesis of innate and universal distrust. Human survival would be threatened if diffidence were instinctual. Imagine the infant fleeing from its mother's breast. Thus the major source of the reasonableness of anticipation in Hobbes's argument must lie in competition. So let us consider that cause of quarrel in "the nature of man."

Competition. All individuals have goals and adopt means to realize them. Because of their approximate equality of ability, they will endeavor to satisfy their desires with roughly the same intensity. "And therefore, if any two men desire the same thing, which nevertheless they cannot both enjoy, they become enemies; and in the way to their End, (which is principally their owne conservation, and sometimes their delectation only,) endeavour to destroy, or subdue one another" (p. 184). Competition consists of two or more individuals desiring the same thing, which they cannot both possess. What prevents them from both enjoying it is that when one enjoys or consumes it, nothing remains for the other—after consumption, the consumed good ceases to exist as a desirable object.

Let us call such goods "exclusive goods." Why must we become enemies when competing for an exclusive good? Presumably, the argument goes as follows. When I consume it, you believe that your life or comfort or pleasure are thereby threatened. Because you and I are equal in ability and in natural rights, you will realize that you have just as much right to the good as I and that you have no reason to subordinate your needs to mine. You will see me as depriving you of something that you have a right to, and you will learn to hate me and to desire my death. I become an obstruction to your satisfactions. Realizing that I believe the same of you, you will adopt anticipation as a strategy. So will I. Thus the war of all against all.

Not all goods are exclusive. Some can be jointly enjoyed, for example, watching a sunset. But many are, and these are the most important for survival. However, conceptual caution is required at just this point. Goods are not intrinsically exclusive or nonexclusive. How they are to be classified depends upon how we slice them up. For example, the air we breathe is nonexclusive—we may all breathe it. And yet the portion of air that I am here and now breathing is exclusive; once I have breathed it, I have used up its beneficial qualities, and none remain for you. A good conceived as a whole may be nonexclusive even though particular consumed portions of it are exclusive. Exclusivity is a matter of perspective. It is not built into the nature of every type of good as such.

Let us now imagine two individuals, Cain and Abel, in the state of nature, both simultaneously spying an apple on a tree. Both are hungry; both want to eat the apple. Each wants the other not to have that apple. Does that mean that they must become enemies as Hobbes asserts? Hobbes's argument assumes that only one course of action is rational for each—to try to capture the whole apple. On that assumption, Hobbes is right: Cain and Abel will become enemies. The loser will hate the winner. But our discussion of exclusivity shows that another course of action is available to them. The apple is, as such, neither an exclusive good nor a nonexclusive one. There are various ways of dividing it up—there are apple parts as well as apples. Cain and Abel may well agree to divide it in half, and each may be contented with his share. In that case, they have no reason to become enemies; they have not learned, as yet, to distrust one another.

So there are two possibilities; let us call the first "selfish" and the second "cooperative." Which is the more reasonable? Hobbes seems to suppose that it is usually the first. And if eating that whole apple is the only thing that stands between survival on the one hand and death by starvation on the other, then, clearly, the selfish course is the best. Selfishness, by producing anticipation, increases the probability of death; but Cain and Abel are, we suppose, faced with certain death if they are cooperative. If the resources of the state of nature are so confined and restricted as to make the selfish alternative the most reasonable one, then introducing the commonwealth would not be a solution anyhow, since the parties cannot benefit by cooperation.

For Hobbes's argument for the commonwealth to work, the state of nature must be a condition of only moderate scarcity. There is enough for all to survive, but some effort is required in order to obtain goods—the state of nature is not a golden age. In that case, cooperation would be rational, for it would allow individuals to enjoy their possessions in peace and security, and it would enable them to increase their stock of possessions. In such circumstances, neither Cain nor Abel need the whole apple in order to survive. They can afford to cut it in half. Cooperation is more rational than selfishness in the state of nature because it allows survival without the great costs of war of all against all. Because goods are not usually intrinsically exclusive, cooperation is usually available as an alternative. When it is, people, being rational and not yet having learned to distrust one another, will realize that they can survive without war provided that they are willing to negotiate with each other over the division of consumable goods. Because of the availability of this alternative, we no longer have a situation in which the course that is most rational for each is a disaster for all. So an external coercive authority whose function it is to make anticipation more costly than cooperation is not required; cooperation is already less costly than selfishness in the state of nature. Thus reasonable individuals, in the state of nature, will cooperate rather than compete. Competition as a cause of quarrel has not been shown to be an innate or inescapable feature of human nature.

Glory. For Hobbes, glory is the third cause of quarrel in human nature. "For every man looketh that his companion should value him, at the same rate he sets upon himself: And upon all signes of contempt, or undervaluing, naturally endeavours, as far as he dares (which amongst them that have no common power, to keep them quiet, is far enough to make them destroy each other,) to extort a greater value from his contemners, by dommage; and from others, by the example" (p. 185). The problem is that people have a tendency to undervalue one another and value themselves more than they deserve, "from whence continually arise amongst them, Emulation, Quarrells, Factions, and at last Warre" (p. 235).

In the Introduction to *Leviathan*, Hobbes points out that self-observation is the basis of the political philosopher's knowledge of human nature (p. 82). "Read thyself" is a saying that he endorses. Hobbes must have discovered the murderous effects of glory in his own heart. Later, in describing the rights of the sovereign that are produced by the social contract, he argues that the sovereign shall have the power "to give titles of Honour; and to appoint what Order of place, and dignity, each man shall hold; and what signes of respect, in publique or private meetings, they shall give to one another" (p. 236). Hobbes likely had in mind here the problem of ameliorating the rivalries among the nobility and members of the ruling factions for fame and recognition. These were people that Hobbes knew well from personal experience. He was probably present at numerous conversations in which malicious gossip and rumor were used to destroy the reputations of rivals. Those of us who are members of academic communities will also recognize this phenomenon. Hobbes accepted the duel as a method by which men could punish others for their contempt (p. 349).

However, in the state of nature, there is no nobility; there are no ruling factions; there are no ambitious intellectuals. The preoccupation with reputation and the willingness to kill those who undervalue one would appear to be dispositions that are products of certain cultures rather than unvarying traits of human nature. Even if it is a part of human nature to dislike being undervalued, it does not follow that it is rational to kill or maim others for that reason. What is the benefit?

Suppose that Abel values Cain at a rate much lower than Cain values himself. Either Abel is correct in his estimation of Cain's worth or he is not. If Abel is correct, then Cain's attacking Abel will not change Cain's actual merits or Abel's opinion of them. And if Abel is mistaken, Cain's attacking him will not change his opinion (unless, of course, Abel's opinion concerns Cain's courage or retaliatory prowess); it will, at best, influence Abel's expression of contempt. In the state of nature, whether or not one goes to war is supposed to depend upon a cost-benefit analysis on the part of each individual. That is why, in the case of competition, Hobbes thought that anticipation was a reasonable individual strategy that unfortunately led to the war of all against all. But striking out at those who undervalue us does not appear to be a reasonable strategy. It accomplishes little, and produces retaliation in response.

IV

I conclude that this part of Hobbes's case against anarchy fails. The state of nature does not inevitably produce the war of all against all.

War is not the inevitable result of human nature placed in circumstances of moderate scarcity without a coercive power to keep the peace. Cooperation is a reasonable strategy in the state of nature for individuals to adopt, until they are faced with actual examples of aggression. As far as Hobbes's arguments show, anarchy is a viable theoretical alternative. What shall we make of this? Can a case actually be made for anarchy?

The term "anarchy" represents a family of social ideals all of which have in common the rejection of coercion and violence as a method of producing social peace and cooperation. All things being equal, anarchic methods are preferable to political ones just because political procedures involve a particular cost that is absent under anarchy. If we could return to the state of nature able to choose either to form a commonwealth, knowing what commonwealths have wrought, or alternatively, to devise noncoercive methods, we would have every reason to experiment further with anarchy before entering into the trials and tribulations of political history.

However, we are no longer in the state of nature. We are in the midst of these very trials and tribulations. Modern history for us is a fact, not just a future possibility. The nation-state is well-entrenched and things are seldom equal. Even if I could liquidate the current political regime by a simple movement of a finger, I would not do so for fear that another regime, much worse than this, would take over. It is the nation-state that now makes the nation-state indispensable.

Nevertheless, political ideals do not cease to be valid just because they are not practically realizable in the foreseeable future. As an ideal, anarchy and related libertarian traditions provide a point of view by which to evaluate and criticize the policies and tendencies of current political regimes. They also generate a research program and a field of social experimentation. They pose the problem of discovering noncoercive procedures of producing peace and cooperation in every area of human life. Even in the midst of political regimes, we can create and experiment with pockets of anarchy.

Hobbes says: "For by Art is created that great LEVIATHAN called a COMMONWEALTH, or STATE." And perhaps by art that "great LEVIATHAN" may gradually be dismantled.

Twelve

Two Types of Philosophical Approach to the Problem of War and Peace

Peter Henrici

Reflecting about war and peace, the philosopher must pose questions and suggest answers that are not just empirical: they must go beyond the concerns of what war is; how it happens; what its political, economic, social, and psychological causes are; and how it might actually and eventually be prevented. Philosophers have to inquire as well about the very essence, and that means about the necessity, of the phenomena of war and peace. Is quarrel so inherent in human nature and in the nature of human societies that war is inevitable? Is war perhaps a good thing, has it a positive function in regulating international life? Is peace, on the contrary, more congenial to humankind, so that war (even if it fills up most of human history) is to be considered an exceptional condition, which naturally should (and therefore could) be overcome? In what consists the real essence of peace: is it just absence of war or something else? And if peace is deeply rooted in human nature—at least as a necessary end of human striving—why then do wars happen at all?

To these philosophical questions about war and peace, two types of answers have been given. The one may seem more realistic, and therefore pessimistic; the other is more optimistic, and one would therefore call it idealist. But we can also label these two types of answers historically, as the modern and the medieval ones.

I

The modern type of answer starts from reflecting on human history as it really happened and as it is still going on. History was the primary object of philosophical reflection for Hegel, and he is indeed the most representative thinker of this first approach. Hegel's philosophy tries to understand what has happened in history, grasping by the "concept" its eternal necessity. "Philosophy is its own time apprehended in thoughts."[1] From this, Hegel develops in the *Philosophy of Right* a theory of war that is, to say the least, disappointing. War, according to him, is essential for the well-being of human society. Hegel's principal saying on the benefits of war is well known and perhaps too often quoted:

> War has the higher significance that by its agency, as I have remarked elsewhere, "the ethical health of peoples is preserved in their indifference to the stabilization of finite institutions; just as the blowing of the winds preserves the sea from the foulness which would be the result of a prolonged calm, so also corruption in nations would be the product of prolonged peace." (sec. 324)

This might be understood as a simple and spontaneous recognition of the virtue of courage that war brings about and of its civic effects. Hegel, then, might simply have repeated what Kant had already written in his *Critique of Judgment*. Presenting the warrior's courage as an example of the kind of "sublime" human quality all human persons spontaneously admire, Kant concludes: "Hence whatever disputes there may be about the superiority of the respect which is to be accorded them, in the comparison of a statesman and a general, the aesthetical judgment decides for the latter." He then adds:

> War itself, if it is carried on with order and with a sacred respect for the rights of citizens, has something sublime in it, and makes the disposition of the people who carry it on thus only the more sublime, the more numerous are the dangers to which they are exposed and in respect of which they behave with courage. On the other hand, a long peace generally brings about a predominant commercial spirit and, along with it, low selfishness, cowardice, and effeminacy, and debases the disposition of the people.[3]

A similar esteem for the warrior's virtue we find of course in Nietzsche and in all kinds of fascism.[4] It would be easy to write the history of two and a half millennia of misunderstanding of Heraclitus's "war is the father of all," in the sense of an exaltation of war and of its virtues.[5] But this was not Hegel's thought. His positive appraisal of war is integrated in his overall theory of human society.

As it is known, Hegel distinguishes three levels of social organization: the family, civil society or *bürgerliche Gesellschaft,* and the state. "Civil society"—a new interpretation Hegel gives to an old term—is the organization of human sociability that is brought about by merely economic factors: human needs, interests, productivity, and exchange of merchandise. That kind of organization took independent and permanent shape only in modern times, so that only the modern state—which is not simply a gathering of families or individuals, but a legal and therefore rational overarching and transformation of the fundamentally irrational and anarchic civic society—represents for Hegel the full development of human sociability and its inherent rationality. In this conception of the state, "civil society" (which should be more appropriately translated as "bourgeois society") therefore represents a necessary, yet negative, moment. It is the caricature of true society, since its members behave strictly as individuals and since it is linked, paradoxically, by private interests. Both individuality and private interests must be overcome in the state, and in this lies the positive function of war. War is the negation of the negativity that "bourgeois society" represents. In war, public interest overrules private interest; private property is endangered and even destroyed; individuals have to sacrifice their well-being and even their lives for the conservation of the state. With his usual sarcastic charge against pietism, Hegel notes:

> To be sure, war produces insecurity of property, but this insecurity of things is nothing but their transience—which is inevitable. We hear plenty of sermons from the pulpit about the insecurity, vanity, and instability of temporal things, but everyone thinks, however much he is moved by what he hears, that he at least will be able to retain his own. But if this insecurity now comes on the scene in the form of hussars with shining sabres and they actualize in real earnest what the preachers have said, then the moving and the edifying discourses which foretold all these events turn into curses against the invader. (sec. 324, add.)

As an empirical confirmation of his theory, Hegel points to the fact that external wars tend to strengthen the internal coherence of a state—a phenomenon that could be observed in most of the belligerent and even neutral states during World War II.

Positively, then, war brings about courage and even a particular "class" (*Stand*) characterized by courage: the standing army that, along with the other states, completes the organic and rational articulation of society (sec. 326). Courage, however, is for Hegel a virtue only with regard to its end, which is in this case the conservation of sovereignty—a universal principle that should be promoted by universal means and not so much by individual courage. Hence, Hegel argues, the invention of modern armaments, which "has transformed the individual form of courage into a more abstract one," is altogether rational. It follows from the inner logic of historical development according to which the enemy tends to be less personalized and is replaced by a "hostile group" (sec. 328). The invention of guns is not to be ascribed, as Bacon suggested, to a mere accident of history. The history of the development of missiles and nuclear weapons seems to confirm this view of Hegel's.

War as such is seen by Hegel, in metahistorical perspective, as a necessary moment in the dialectic of rational construction of reality. Wars, however—that is, concrete, historical wars—remain altogether contingent; and Hegel shows, in a concluding section of the *Philosophy of Right* on international relationships between states, the necessity of such contingency (secs. 330–40). He rejects the Kantian construct of a federation of nations that would be able to grant "eternal peace," and he sees war as the only way to decide quarrels between states—since every state in its turn is an individual and there is no intrahistorical universal principle (i.e., reason) that could overcome the states' particularities (secs. 332–34). The causes of war therefore are always particular (secs. 335–37, 340). Reason, however, postulates that in war itself the possibility of concluding peace is preserved and the established international customary rules of wars are observed (secs. 338–39). Thus, above all, reason is still sovereign over all historical contingencies. It is the metahistorical "World Spirit," from the viewpoint of which the rise and fall of empires are regulated by an inner logic of historical development— "progress in the consciousness of freedom" (secs. 340–58).

Hegel's theory represents the most successful attempt at a philosophical justification of war—not an apology for war, but a demonstration that war, be it utterly contingent and disastrous, still has its rational necessity, and therefore intelligibility, for the constitution of human social life. Hegel's demonstration, like the rest of his philosophy, is guided by two fundamental insights. The first is the well-known rationality of the real, as expressed in the preface to his *Philosophy of Right*. This often abused principle merely enunciates that neither in nature nor in history is anything so contingent and purely factual that it is not based on some underlying necessity and hence intelligibility, which rational thought may discover and which constitutes the phenomenon's very essence. This argument, Hegel says, is not only fundamental for Platonic thought, but even more for the Christian religion, which understands history as a history of salvation. Hegel's second insight, therefore, is that philosophy has to start from theological principles, which it transforms into philosophical, rational concepts. The ultimate rationality of history, indeed, is theological by its very nature, and Hegel's "World Spirit" probably cannot be understood otherwise than as a rationalization of divine providence or, more precisely, of Pauline "mystery." War therefore receives from Hegel quasi-theological accreditation.

Now, if from these general Hegelian insights we come back to his particular theory of war, we notice that it includes some supplementary assumptions that Hegel has in common with most modern thinkers. First of all, it is assumed that a negative element is ineliminable from human nature and from human history, indeed it is their dominating and determining element. Human beings by their very nature are "radically evil," as Kant, systematizing Rousseau's thought, pointed out in his *Religion within the Limits of Reason Alone*. At a more concrete level, the same thinkers conceive of society as made up of individuals and thus as bringing them together in their individually wicked natures, exasperating them and leading to conflict. War therefore is seen as the normal and natural condition of humankind, and peace as the exception—which accordingly is negatively defined as "absence of war." Nevertheless, peace is possible, for the evil side of man's nature can be overcome, indeed the evil itself may in a certain way lead to the good. The means to overcome evil is reason, which in some way perceives the good, proposes it to human choice, and is essentially (if not always actually) able to overcome the wickedness of human nature.

The history of modern social philosophy shows a progressive deepening and widening of this role of reason as salvation: Machiavelli finds reason concentrated in the Prince, who by his "virtue" and by force and ruse has to bring his subjects to reason and thus restore the corrupted Republic. For Hobbes it is reason that persuades all individuals to form a Commonwealth by social contract, in order to overcome the evils of their natural condition. This social contract, for Rousseau, is not only a work of reason, it is reason itself, re-emerging from the evils of the associated state of humankind in the assembly of all reasonable beings. Yet the actual French "National Assembly" disappointed these optimistic expectations, ending in the Terror—and it was this disappointment that led Hegel to his theory of the "cunning of Reason," which combines pragmatic pessimism with metahistorical optimism.

As for other points of his social philosophy, Hegel's "cunning of Reason" had a forerunner in the Kant's less aprioristic philosophy of history, repeatedly exposed the latter's popular writings. Kant's is, in my opinion, the most credible modern theory on war and peace. Whereas the earlier theorists focused on individuals coming together to form a society with their strivings, desires, and reasoning, Kant considers human societies in themselves. In his first work on this topic, in 1784, he shows that nature not only leads humankind in states and under political authorities, but it will lead the states themselves to join in a cosmopolitical "Society of Nations," precisely in order to prevent war. This will happen because the growing international economic links will make war so disastrous that it must be avoided by all possible means.

> In the end, even war gradually becomes not only a very artificial undertaking, so uncertain for both sides in its outcome, but also a very dubious one, given the aftermath that the nation suffers by way of an evergrowing burden of debt (a new invention) whose repayment becomes inconceivable. At the same time, the effect that any national upheaval has on all the other nations of our continent, where they are all so closely linked by trade, is so noticeable that these other nations feel compelled, though without legal authority to do so, to offer themselves as arbiters, and thus they indirectly prepare the way for the great body politic (*Staatskörper*) of the future, a body politic for which antiquity provides no example. Although this body politic presently exists only in very rough outline, a feeling seems nonetheless to be already stirring among all its members who have an interest in the preservation of the whole, and this gives rise to the hope that, finally, after many revolutions of reform, nature's supreme objective—a universal *cosmopolitan state*, the womb in which all of the human species' original capacities will be developed—will at last come to be realized.[6]

Ten years later in his essay *Perpetual Peace*, Kant draws up the fundamental articles of an international law on which such an everlasting peace could and should rest. Finally, in 1798, referring to the experiences of the French Revolution—America is, for Kant, still far away—he sees in the introduction of republican constitutions in all states the means to remove the very possibility of war.

> The idea of a constitution in harmony with the natural right of man, one namely in which the citizens obedient to the law, besides being united, ought also to be legislative, lies at the basis of all political forms; and the body politic which, conceived in conformity to it by virtue of pure concepts of reason, signifies a Platonic Ideal (*respublica noumenon*), is not an empty chimera, but rather an eternal norm for all civil organizations in general, and averts all war. A civil society organized conformably to this ideal is the representation of it in agreement with the laws of freedom by means of an example in our experience (*respublica phaenomenon*) and can only be painfully acquired after multifarious hostilities and wars; but its constitution, once won on a large scale, is qualified as the best among all others to banish war, the destroyer of everything good. Consequently, it is a duty to enter into such a system of government.[7]

This text shows us the intricate epistemological status of Kant's assertions. He is reasoning on three different levels. On the level of pure reason, a republican constitution is a necessary idea, which as such is no object of human (empirical) knowledge. In his first writing on this topic, Kant calls it an "end of Nature," which we cannot know or assert but have to assume, yet it regulates human behavior. Hence, on a second level, striving toward such a constitution is not only possible, but a moral obligation, which will produce (and is already producing), on a third level, its empirically verifiable effects:[8]

> Gradually violence on the part of the powers will diminish and obedience to the laws will increase. There will arise in the body politic perhaps more charity and less strife in lawsuits, more reliability in keeping one's word, etc., partly out of love of honor, partly out of well-understood self-interest. And eventually this will also extend to nations in their external relations toward one another up to the realization of the cosmopolitan society.[9]

However, these good effects for Kant are *only* empirical, nothing but a better external behavior, without any inner moral improvement: "Not an ever-growing quantity of morality with regard to intention, but an increase of the products of legality in dutiful actions whatever their motives. That is, the profit [result] of man's striving toward the better can be assumed to reside alone in the good deeds of men."[10] Notwithstanding his ideal of a cosmopolitical, peaceful commonwealth of nations, Kant is still reasoning along the guidelines of the modern type of approach, based on the wickedness of human nature, that sees in peace nothing more than the absence of war and therefore expects the coming of peace from a mechanism of the self-destruction of war.

II

To counter this perspective another kind of metaphysics is wanted, according to which the end, the ideal, is not only a norm for moral obligation, but an active and effective reality. Medieval Christian metaphysics, which combined Platonic and Aristotelian insights with Christian eschatology, was such a perspective. Indeed, Kant's "eternal peace" as its very name indicates, is also an eschatological concept, and so is Hegel's conception of universal history as universal judgment ("Die Weltgeschichte ist das Weltgericht," the history of the world is the world's court of judgment) (sec. 340). As for reaching "eternal peace," the most we can expect is an asymptotic approximation of this end; Christian eschatology, on the contrary, speaks about what is actually real but not manifest, the true essence

155

of reality. Such was the final cause, the *entelecheia*, for Aristotelian metaphysics: it is directing and stimulating the whole process of becoming—which is less real than the final end insofar as it is only becoming. That means that the true condition of a being is its final one; the laws of nature therefore have to be understood teleologically and not mechanically; and with regard to human striving, the end is not only an ideal proposed to reason and for the choice of free will, but it represents an actually and continually effective force.

Such teleologic metaphysics leads then to a specific anthropology. Whereas for Kant, as for most modern thinkers, humankind is to be conceived as a composition of good reason and bad striving, the medieval Christian philosophy admits also, and most of all, good strivings in human beings. Reason itself is, in this conception, not a neutral faculty of right judgment, but a spiritual striving toward the true and hence the good. Thanks to these actively striving faculties, the good, which is their object, actively influences and determines our choices and behavior. We need not be forced to choose the good by the misfits of the evil; the good itself attracts us—even beyond and above our eventually wicked wills.

It is in the framework of these metaphysical and anthropological assumptions that we can understand the single most influential Christian theory on peace: that which Saint Augustine proposed in his *De Civitate Dei*.[11] The other opinion leader in Christian thought, Thomas Aquinas, took the Augustinian theory as a base. Let us then briefly summarize it.

Peace for Augustine is first of all an eschatological good, nay, *the* eschatological good. "On earth we are happy, after a fashion, when we enjoy the peace, little as it is, which a good life brings; but such happiness compared with the beatitude which is our end in eternity is, in point of fact, misery," for in that end "there will be a peace so good that no peace could be better, a peace so great that a greater would be impossible" (chap. 10). These are obviously theological assertions, but in following chapters, Augustine supports them with philosophical considerations. He first notes that "peace is so universally loved that its very name falls sweetly on the ear" (chap. 11). He then explains the universal striving for peace by a kind of phenomenology, considering borderline cases where at first sight one would not expect to find a longing for peace.

The most obvious of these cases is war, more specifically, "men who are bent on war." However, "what they want is to win, that is to say, their battles are but bridges to glory and to peace. The whole point of victory is to bring opponents to their knees—this done, peace ensues. Peace, then, is the purpose of waging war; and this is true even of men who have a passion for the exercise of military prowess as rulers and commanders" (chap. 12). The confirmation of this is the fact that "even while waging a war every man wants peace, whereas no one wants war while he is making peace. And even when men are plotting to disturb the peace, it is merely to fashion a new peace nearer to the heart's desire; it is not because they dislike peace as such" (chap. 12). The same is confirmed by the other fact, that even a man given thoroughly to war, "a robber so powerful that he dispenses with partnership"—we remember Hobbes's description of the natural condition of humankind[12]—"certainly in his own home wants to be at peace with his wife and children and any other members of his household" (chap. 12).

In order to reach the very limits of possible negation of the universal striving for peace, Augustine imagines "a being so wild and antisocial that it was better to call him half-human than fully a man": Cacus (the wicked) of Greek and Latin poetry and mythology. After all, his "injustice, greed and savagery were merely means of self-preservation," and all he looked for was to be secure from outside aggressions and to quiet his bodily needs and appetites, "procuring peace within himself and in his cave" (chap. 12). Reflecting on this imaginary borderline case, Augustine discovers the search for peace as a universal law of nature that applies to wild beasts, which "meet and mate, foster and feed their young"; to the union of body and soul, which will not be disintegrated even in an unnatural position (i.e., hanging upside down) "that disturbs the peace of the body and is therefore painful"; indeed, to the inanimate body itself, "its weight . . . crying out for a place where it can rest" (we recognize the Aristotelian theory of falling bodies striving to their "natural place"); and, to conclude, even to putrefaction:

> Even when tiny bacteria spring from the corpse of a larger animal, it is by the same law of the Creator that all these minute bodies serve in peace the organic wholes of which they are parts. Even when the flesh of dead animals is eaten by other animals, there is no change in the universal laws which are meant for the common good of every kind of life, the common good that is effected by bringing the like into peace with the like. (chap. 12)

It follows that the gathering of humanity in peace has to be seen as an effect of the same law of nature. "By the very laws of his nature [man] seems, so to speak, forced into fellowship and, as far as in him lies, into peace with every man" (chap. 12).

From this phenomenology of striving for peace, Augustine draws his definition of peace by a kind of induction. In all cases, what is searched for is a kind of "ordered harmony" or "ordered equilibrium," from which peace flows. Therefore, "peace, in its final sense, is the calm that comes of order" (*tranquillitas ordinis*), order being "an arrangement of like and unlike things, whereby each of them is disposed in its proper place" (chap. 13). This definition finally allows Augustine to give two a priori arguments for peace as a positive and universal reality. Both arguments rely on the logic of privation (*steresis*), a shortcoming that reaffirms the positive reality on the basis of which it is constituted as a shortcoming.

The first argument applies directly to war. "Notice that there can be life without pain, but no pain without some kind of life. In the same way, there can be peace without any kind of war, but no war that does not suppose some kind of peace. This does not mean that war as war involves peace; but war, insofar as those who wage it or have it waged upon them are beings with organic natures, involves peace—for the simple reason that to be organic means to be ordered and, therefore, to be, in some sense, at peace" (chap. 13). The argument is perhaps more impressive than really convincing, for it implies (in contrast to the example of life and pain) a leap from one reality to another, from war to the warriors.

The second argument, then, is the really convincing one, and I would call it transcendental in the Kantian sense of this term. It argues that "anyone who grieves over the loss of peace to his nature does so out of some remnant of peace wherewith his nature loves itself," because, first, "there can be no nature completely devoid of good" and more specifically "if there were no good left, there would be no one to lament the good that has been lost" (chap. 13). In other terms, a loss of calming order is felt only thanks to and in contrast with a remnant of such order, that is, peace.

In his *Summa Theologica*, Thomas Aquinas adopts Augustine's definition of peace as *tranquillitas ordinis* and adds an important specification. Peace consists not only in harmony or concord between different persons, but it presupposes also an equilibrium between the appetites of a single person. As he explains: "For there is no real peace where a man comes to an agreement with another not freely and of his own will, but forced into it by fear. In such a case the proper order of things, where both sides come to agreement is not kept but is disturbed by some one bringing fear to bear. This is why Augustine says previously that *peace is the tranquility of order*, the tranquility consisting in the fact that all the movements of man's appetite are in harmony with each other."[13]

From this explanation, Thomas draws a supplementary a priori argument that all things desire peace. All men indeed (and even animals and inanimate things) "desire to obtain what they desire, and consequently, the removal of anything that stands in the way of his doing so. Now such an obstacle, in the form of a contrary desire, can come either from oneself, or from another, and in both cases it is through peace, as we have shown, that the obstacle is removed. Hence it must needs be that everything that desires tranquility and without hindrance to obtain its object, which is the very meaning of peace" (art. 2c). And he makes immediate application to the case of war:

> Even those who are bent on wars and dissensions are really only desiring a peace, which, in their eyes, they do not possess. For, as we have said, it is not peace if a man agrees with another against what he himself prefers. And so by war people try to upset such agreement, for they find the peace somehow defective, and their intention is to arrive at a peace in which nothing that conflicts with their own desires will be found. This is why a people at war seek by war to arrive at a peace which will be more perfect than before. (art. 2, add. 2)

We notice that in these arguments Thomas relativizes Augustine's conception of peace as an absolute end. Peace is for him an indispensable object of desire insofar as it is a means or condition to obtain the very end of human appetites. In this, Thomas's view is less eschatological, more realistic than Augustine's, who was led by his theological insight of peace as the supreme good to overstrain his philosophical arguments. Both authors, however, agree that to foster peace the double commandment of loving God and loving one's neighbor is the most potent help. Indeed, Thomas argues:

> As already noted, peace implies two kinds of union: one, a bringing of all one's own desires to an ordered unity; the other, union between one's own desires and those of another person. In both cases it is charity that brings it about. In the first case, since charity means that we love God with our whole heart by referring everything to him, all our desires become focused on one object. Likewise with the other kind of union; for loving our neighbour as ourselves makes us want to do his will even as our own. (art. 3c)

Augustine adds in chapter 14 of *De Civitate Dei* that this commandment implies "first, that he harm no one, and second, that he help whomever he can"—a positive promotion of peace that goes far beyond sheer avoidance of quarrel and war.

III

We are now able to confront this medieval Christian conception of peace with the modern one we have seen before. At a first glance, peace as a law of nature seems to rejoin Hobbes's fundamental law of nature "that every man ought to endeavour peace, as far as he has hope of obtaining it" (chap. 14). The difference between the two conceptions lies in the little word "ought." Natural law, according to the medievals, explains an order that *exists*; it therefore indicates what all beings are actually doing or striving for—even if this striving or doing will not always gain its end or show its effect. According to this conception, a law of nature has therefore unconditioned and unlimited validity, whereas Hobbes's obligation to strive for peace is only valid "as far as" one has hope of success and is limited by the immediately following clause: "and when he cannot obtain it, that he may seek, and use, all helps and advantages of war" (chap. 14). This means that peace differs in the two conceptions, not only in its positive (as "tranquility of order") as opposed to its merely negative definition (as absence of war and quarrel), but also in that according to the medieval conception peace is an absolute and un-limited good, while according to the moderns it is only a relative and limited one.

According to the medieval conception, then, there is more hope of actually achieving peace than in the modern perspective. Striving for peace, according to the medievals, pertains to the very nature of humankind and therefore can never be totally absent or overcome, whereas for the moderns it always remains exposed to the hazard of an "ought"—most explicitly in Kant's "finality of Nature."[14] At the basis of these two conceptions there are indeed two different theological theories on human nature. For the medievals, though corrupted by original sin, human nature remains fundamentally good, and from that very root, therefore (especially as it is healed by grace), the good will spring. For the moderns, on the contrary, wickedness is the mark of our (fallen) nature; it is and remains intrinsically corrupted (even when God shows mercy on it); therefore the good is always only an end proposed to free choice.

So far, so good. But is not the medieval conception utterly uto-pian? And do not utopian conceptions, in public life, lead to fanat-icism and to violence? Moreover, is the medieval conception fitting at all for public use—is it not limited to individuals, and unfit to illuminate political and international life? It is true that this kind of approach inspired Thomas More's *Utopia*, which was probably written as a response to Machiavelli's *Prince*. Utopian views lead to fanaticism and to violence only when one takes them as an end that ought to be realized. And we have seen that peace, according to the medievals, is rather a good to be hoped for than a work to be achieved. It is, it is true, especially in its eschatological meaning, more a fulfillment of individual longings than a structure of political and international life. However, we have seen the medievals dis-puting about war, and we know that the moderns (except Hegel) build their political theories on an anthropology of individuals. What, then, makes the medieval theories on peace look so strange to us? It is not their chronological distance (Thomas Aquinas is closer to us than he was to Augustine!), it is their way of reasoning and of looking at things that have become unfamiliar to the modern mind. We are used to looking at empirical facts and to interpreting them, if at all possible, mechanically. Hobbes is a good example of this kind of worldview—although his reasoning is perhaps less purely empirical than it may seem. Medievals were worried about the metaempirical essence, and that means about the very end and meaning of things. The two approaches, as one can see, are not exclusive of each other. And perhaps it may be useful to conduct empirical research about war and peace with the metaphysical insights of the medievals. It may help us to understand *why* men consider the search for peace a high priority and peace one of the most precious goods. It may give us hope that such universal and indeed connatural longing is not necessarily vain.[15] It may help us, in particular, to understand the pacifist movement—and to correct it at the same time. This growing movement is understandable when we recognize that the longing for peace forms part of our very nature. But if this is true, then pacifism is wrong when it bases its dynamism mainly on the fear of (nuclear) destruction and when it centers its action on fighting against armament and military force. There are deeper and more human motives for searching after peace, and there are more effective means to promote it than just the prevention of war. We could learn these by meditating afresh on the medieval, Christian approach to the philosophical problem of peace.

Thirteen

The Light at the End of the Tunnel and the Light in Which We May Walk: Two Concepts of Peace

Gray Cox

The two concepts of peace on which I will focus are best understood in the context of two very different cultural paradigms, two different networks of beliefs, practices, and institutions. The first conceives of peace the way Hobbes did in the *Leviathan*, as a condition of stasis or equilibrium distinguished by the absence of war, confrontation, or other forms of conflict. The second conceives of peace as a process distinguished by the presence of activities aimed at cultivating genuine, voluntary commitments to shared expressions, projects, and practices. One useful statement of this second notion is found in R. G. Collingwood's *The New Leviathan:*

> Peace is a dynamic thing; a strenuous thing; the detection, even the forestalling, of occasions for quarrels; the checking of the process by which non-agreements thus constantly generated harden into disagreements; the promotion of a counter-process by which disagreements (not without the use of force) are softened into non-agreements; and the dialectical labor whereby occasions of non-agreement are converted into occasions of agreement.[1]

The first conception of peace (as a "static absence") is dominant in our culture. The second conception (the "active presence" notion) forms part of an emerging cultural matrix or paradigm that is transforming our culture. Questions about the differences between—and relative merits of—these two networks of beliefs, practices, and in-

stitutions pose a host of important philosophical issues. They concern a shift in our view of social reality that is as profound as the shift in the understanding of physical reality that Galileo discussed in his *Dialogue Concerning the Two Chief World Systems.*

I

Peace is usually defined the way death, irrationality, crime, and killing are. It is usually defined in a static, negative, derivative, morally neutral way—the way Hobbes defined it. As you will recall, Hobbes said: "the nature of war consisteth not in actual fighting, but in the known disposition thereto, during all the time there is no assurance to the contrary. All other time is PEACE."[2] For Hobbes—like Kenneth Boulding and a host of others—peace is the state or condition in which war is absent.[3]

Here the activities of warring are used to define the state of war the way the activities of living are used to define life. But peace is defined as a state in which warring—or the "known disposition thereto"—is absent, just as death is defined as the absence of living and life. Our grammar reflects the widespread use of this static notion of peace. While we use "war" as a verb we do not use "peace" as a verb. People can be said to be "warring" but they cannot be said to be "peacing"—any more than corpses can be said to be "deathing."

Notice also that Hobbes's definition is logically negative or exclusive, the way a definition of "*ir*rationality" would be. Just as irrationality is distinguished by what it is not, by what is absent (rationality), peace is distinguished by what it is not, by what is absent (war). Hobbes had peace among nations in mind, the same "light at the end of the tunnel" that Richard Nixon repeatedly claimed to see during the Vietnam conflict. And when people speak of peace between races, social classes, family members, or different impulses in a single person, they usually define peace in the same way, namely, as a state in which there are *not* riots, quarrels, or other types of conflict.

This makes the concept of peace derivative the way the notion of crime is. Crime can only be defined in terms of the more primary notion of the law it violates. Similarly, peace is here defined in terms of the more primary notion of the warring that is absent.

The words "conflict" and "war" have negative emotive charges for most people because conflict and war can make life nasty, brutish, and short. But peace can make life a boring, lifeless, rut in which people accept oppression or even extermination. In that sense, as Wladyslaw Strozewski has noted, "peace can be either good or bad"—depending on whether it brings freedom from pain and death or the continuation of oppression and injustice.[4]

II

What accounts for the widespread use of the static absence notion of peace? There are a number of seemingly excellent justifications—reasons that all provide independent warrant for a world view that makes it difficult to conceive of peace in any other way.

The central doctrine of this world view is that conflict is an essential element of human life—the way hydrogen is an essential element of water. Notice that if we want to remove all the hydrogen from a person's body, we must remove all the water, because to have water is to have hydrogen. Now if conflict is essential to life, then to have life is to have conflict. This means that to reduce or eliminate the amount of conflict in a person's experience, we must reduce or eliminate the amount of life she experiences.

Now it seems as though peace involves, at a minimum, the absence of conflict. But if a reduction or elimination of conflict requires a reduction or elimination of life, then peace can involve, at a maximum, nothing more than the absence of conflict. As things become increasingly peaceful, they become decreasingly lively until you reach a state of total peace in which there is a total absence of life—the "peace" in which the dead are said to rest—and there is nothing left over for peace to *be*.

So if we adopt a world view that holds that conflict is an essential element of life, then it is hard to conceive of peace as anything other than a static absence.

There are indeed many widely adopted views that might lead us to suppose conflict is essential to human life. Some are so familiar a single phrase suffices to bring them to mind: the Augustinian doctrine of original sin, the Hobbesian state of nature, the Darwinian struggle for survival, the Hegelian dialectic of history, the Marxist theory of class conflict, the Sartrean existentialist doctrine that "Hell is other people," and the Freudian Oedipus complex.

A further set of conflict-centered assumptions is perhaps more influential—though the nature of its influence is perhaps also less obvious. The assumptions concern the nature of reason, social research, and rational action. They spring from the Anglo-Saxon (Hobbesian) tradition that culminated in logical positivism. They are entrenched in contemporary practices of legal debate, social science, and policy analysis. They include these views: meaning comes in atomic propositions, truth consists in a correspondence to reality that is governed by the law of the excluded middle, emotion is a nonrational passion, the reasoner is a Cartesian mind, social science should be modeled on natural science as conceived by the early Hempel, and rational action is the instrumental manipulation of causes to achieve subjectively preferred ends. These assumptions may seem to have little to do with our view of the role of conflict in life and our conception of peace. Yet they lead to an eristic notion of reasoning and a scientific world view that makes conflict essential to human activity.

Briefly put, the doctrines concerning meaning, truth, emotion, and the self give us a picture of reasoning as a process in which individual sentences are used by critical reasoners to stake out and defend claims in arguments. The goal of rational argument is to defeat opposed views and achieve victory. Reasoning is, in essence, a kind of strife or "eris"—a state of nature in which it is "every man for himself" and emotions enter in only as betrayals of personal weakness and irrationality. As George Lakoff and Mark Johnson have noted:

> It is important to see that we don't just *talk* about arguments in terms of war. We can actually win or lose arguments. We see the person we are arguing with as an opponent. We attack his positions and we defend our own. We gain and lose ground. We plan and use strategies. If we find a position indefensible, we can abandon it and take a new line of attack. Many of the things we *do* in arguing are partially structured by the concept of war. . . . It is in this sense that we live by the ARGUMENT IS WAR metaphor in this culture; it structures the actions we perform in arguing.[5]

In a different way, widely employed methods in social science and policy analysis lead us to adopt the "rational action is war" metaphor. How? We are lead to assume, first, that objective knowledge of social reality is acquired by a "value-free" or "value-neutral" study of the efficient causes of social events—and to assume, second, that rational action consists in the instrumental manipulation of these efficient causes in order to achieve the effects that maximize our subjective "utility."

The connection between these familiar notions and the static absence view of peace is this: Because objective knowledge is "value-free," disputes over values cannot be rationally adjudicated. Social science claims to tell us what are the most effective and efficient means to achieve our goals—and reminds us each person's utility preference curves should be self-consistent in order to meet the minimum requirements of rationality. But when two or more individuals' preferences differ (as they do with frequency) and when resources are scarce (as they are with frequency) and when the circumstances of one person's actions affect others' experience (as ecology tells us they all do), then conflict becomes an inevitable, pervasive, and ineliminable aspect of social reality.

So we find, for example, that social scientists attempting to construct theories of peace base their models on accounts of conflict and its resolution. The work of Walter Isard is representative. In an article that attempts to provide "a definition of peace science" viewed as "the queen of the social sciences," Isard tries to crystallize theory with a "step-by-step development of a broad conceptual framework," and he introduces his construction in this way: "Begin with a basic production subsystem, with simple conflict among two participants over the joint action."[6] There's social reality for you. Two islanders, one coconut, and a dispute over who gets it. All the rest—politics, diplomacy, religion, art, culture—is nuance added to this basic model. It is a model rooted in a cultural tradition that leads us to view conflict as essential to human life and that leaves us with a static absence notion of peace. Yet that notion of peace has important flaws. To begin to see why, reflect for a moment on the motto mentioned earlier.

III

If we think of peace as the absence of war and we seek peace, should we prepare for war by deploying offensive weapon systems like tanks and stealth bombers? The answer, based on game theory and the historical record, is an unequivocal no. Offensive weapons do not deter attack. They threaten the opponent's security and give her an incentive to strike first, preemptively, as Israel did at the start of the 1967 war.

Should we build defensive antitank installations and antiaircraft systems? Yes. Purely defensive weapons raise the opponent's expected cost in attacking and yet offer no incentive for preemptive strikes. This strategy was used with success by Switzerland in World War II.

In general, a rational policy of war deterrence calls for the creation of an incentive system in which would-be attackers find their expected profits are maximized by not attacking, by living in peace rather than initiating war. Only one half of this incentive system can be adequately analyzed using the static absence notion of peace, namely, the costs of war. We can clarify a variety of ways of imposing expected costs—through civilian-based defense, international political sanctions, and economic embargoes, as well as military defenses.

But incentives for peace cannot be clarified because the static absence notion does not tell us what peace is.

IV

The definition is negative in a way that violates one of the oldest rules of logic—Aristotle's rule that requires a definition explain what a thing *is* rather than simply what it is *not*. Further, like most negative definitions, this one has the additional flaw of being too broad. If nuclear winter set in and all life forms on earth became extinct, there would be a condition of the absence of war. But it would be wrong—or at least extremely bizarre—to include this as an example of peace. Peace, we would like to say, requires more than the mere absence of war. It requires the presence of living *homo sapiens.*

But living how? Suppose, for example, that there are two communities of people living on islands near each other, but they are unaware of each other's existence. We might say they are "at peace" with each other, but this would be misleading—because, isolated as they are, the two communities are not really "at" anything at all with each other. For them to be at peace in a more meaningful way, they must establish some contact. They must visit one another and cultivate enough of a common language to make discussion possible.

There is a continuum of relations of increasing peace as we move from (1) mere absence of war between isolated communities to (2) communities in contact and "at peace" to (3) communities that interact and cooperate in a host of ways and are "living together in peace." For a fuller and richer kind of peacefulness, greater interaction and cooperation in more meaningful ways is required. The communities may, for example, share experiences of daily survival, adventures into the beyond, or rituals of celebration. Or they may make exchange of goods, services, ideas, or people (in intermarriages, for instance).

Insofar as the two groups have different beliefs and practices, such sharing and exchange will be the constant occasion of questions: What sorts of interactions should take place? How should they proceed? These questions may be treated either as statements of opposition that pose conflicts to be fought out or as shared problems that call for shared inquiry. It would be most natural to say that the two communities are living together more peacefully insofar as they opt for the second approach and cooperate in inquiry and negotiation rather than compete in conflicts for victory.

To live together in peace they should, in other words, find ways of reaching specific "understandings" or agreements that enable them to share in joint projects and practices. To do this, they must be able to achieve a more general kind of background understanding of each others' words and deeds.

Notice, then, that the motto associated with the static absence notion of peace—"If you want peace, prepare for war"—turns out to be only half true. It should read: "If you want peace, then prepare defensive weapons and other disincentives to dissuade your opponent from attack *and* provide positive incentives to persuade your opponent that peace is more profitable." Further, reflection on these positive incentives in which we "prepare for peace" lead us to adopt an "active presence" notion—conceiving of peace as an activity of living together with people whom we study to understand and with whom we negotiate in order to reach agreements.

But what is involved when people agree? The victims of an oppressive social system may be "pacified" by being kept ignorant of what is happening to them and what their alternatives really are. The victim of a rape may, with the gun at her head, submit to orders imposed on her. But neither case is the same thing as agreeing to an offer proposed to them. Genuine agreements require mutual understanding and voluntary consent. The increasingly popular notion of "positive peace" or "peace with justice" is motivated by this concern. True peace, peace in the strong and full sense of the term, requires the cultivation of genuine, voluntary agreements.[8]

V

Now if my last remarks make sense, then notice something very strange. The doctrines concerning reason, social science, and rational action reviewed earlier seemed to imply that conflict is essential to human life and that it would not be possible to conceive of peace as anything more than a static absence. And yet we seem to have done just that: we have a concept of peace as the activity of cultivating genuine, voluntary agreements. This suggests that those doctrines themselves may be flawed.

I believe that they are flawed, although I lack the space to demonstrate that here. I believe, in fact, that contemporary philosophers have shown that we should revise—and largely reject—the eristic notion of reasoning, the positivist method of social science, and the game theorist's instrumentalist model of rational action. Instead, we should adopt a maieutic notion of reasoning, a critical participatory method in social research, and a theory of rational activity rooted in an account of organic human practices. But rather than rehearse these arguments, I will simply tell you a story that may help to direct our discussion toward the epistemological and metaphysical issue at stake in the emerging cultural paradigm that adopts the active presence concept of peace.

> Once there were two islanders and one coconut. Both wanted it. They bargained and threatened and conciliated and finally compromised and split it in half. The first took his portion and scooped out the meat to eat it. The second scooped out his and made the shell into a cup with which to drink. Each threw away what was left over.

In playing to win and accepting a toss up, they assumed conflict was a constitutive feature of their situation—when, in fact, there was no necessary conflict at all. Conflict is not essential to human life. Conflict is a language game, a way of interpreting social reality. If we interpret situations in terms of problems and their solutions, we can avoid using conflict categories entirely. In that sense, we can completely eliminate conflict—not the way smallpox was eliminated with inoculation programs but the way games once played by Aztecs were eliminated once no one played them any more.

Suppose there are two sisters and one orange, and each wants it. Is there a conflict yet? Not necessarily. If one wants the pulp to squeeze juice and the other wants the rind to make frosting, they simply have a problem: how can they best separate the rind and pulp? But what if each wants the whole orange, rind, seeds, and all. Still there need not be a conflict. In such situations, we may choose to view ourselves as simply facing a shared problem: How do we get another orange?

But then, when *do* we have a conflict? The answer: As soon as the sisters start playing some version of the language game of conflict by viewing each other as opponents competing for victories that are mutually exclusive. Either sister may opt to play it, but neither can compel the other to play—because each always has the option of viewing the situation as presenting a problem that calls for inquiry and solution in terms of objective standards of truth, justice, and happiness. Conflict is thus an *optional interpretation* of social reality, not an essential element of it. We are free at any time to stop playing conflict and start performing the activity of peace. We do not need to wait for the light at the end of the tunnel in order to "walk in the light" of peace.

Fourteen

On the Causes of Quarrel: Postures of War and Possibilities of Peace

Peter Caws

Atque metum tantum concepit tunc mea mater,
Ut pareret geminos, meque metumque simul.
Hinc est, ut credo, patrios quod abominor hostes,
Pacem amo cum musis, et faciles socios.

(And such fear did my mother then conceive that she gave birth
to twins, I and fear together. From this, as I believe, [comes the
fact] that I hate my ancestral enemies, [and] love peace, with
study, and good-natured companions.)

—*T. Hobbes Malmesburiensis Vita*

Thus Hobbes, looking back on his life in 1772 from the age of eighty-four, describes the unquiet time that preceded his birth, the effect of the rumors of the Armada that reached Malmesbury, the evil that he felt had been born with him (*mecum tot quoque nata mala*). So he grew up hating Spaniards, as my generation of English children grew up hating Germans. We may suppose, though, that by the time of the *Vita* the hatred had perhaps become less personal; the apposition of *abominor hostes* and *pacem amo* suggests a hatred of war itself, and the disturbance of the peaceful and studious life that accompanies it, rather than of enemies.

In Hobbes's lifetime, most of the disturbance came not from foreign but from civil war. Whatever its source, it is as a threat that it impresses itself upon him, as a disposition, an agitation that needs to be quieted. Many of our contemporaries in this age of uneasy global peace (by which I mean only the absence of global war) feel the twinship of fear, and sense the threat beneath the surface. I am reminded of the Academy for Peace Research, to which I referred in the Introduction, for whose members the threat seems to be embodied in the globe itself: if only, they say, they could quiet Earth's magnetic field! There are two Latin words for peace—not only *pax*, meaning settled agreements, but also *quies quietus*, meaning repose or calm, and the derivatives of the two are often used in apposition: peace and quiet. The basic idea of the latter is rest, stay, suspension, inactivity, passivity; opposed to it are work, motion, engagement, activity, which under control are certainly admirable, but out of control may blindly produce just the unfortunate consequences the quest for peace seeks to avert.

The basic asymmetry here is between doing things and stopping or refraining from doing them—not even actually doing them, but being willing to do them. "All other time is PEACE": so Hobbes too defines peace negatively, as the absence of armed conflict or the "known disposition thereto."[1] By this criterion, there has been no true American peace since the Monroe Doctrine. On the face of it, the very concept of a standing army is obviously incompatible with peace in this sense, and was so understood by the Founders. Article 1, section 8, of the Constitution says that "the Congress shall have Power [among other things] To raise and support Armies, but no Appropriation of Money to that Use shall be for a longer term than two Years." According to Hamilton, in *Federalist* 26, "the people of America may be said to have derived [from the Glorious Revolution of 1688, in which the right of the Crown to maintain standing armies without the consent of Parliament was abolished] an hereditary impression of danger to liberty from standing armies in time of peace."[2] Hamilton expected that the two-year provision would effectively prevent this danger: "The legislature of the United States will be *obliged* by this provision, once at least in every two years, to deliberate upon the propriety of keeping a military force on foot; to come to a new resolution on the point; and to declare their sense of the matter by a formal vote in the face of their constituents."[3]

The means of quarrel and the disposition to use them are among its causes; thus standing armies are among the causes of war. A lively awareness of what leaders are equipped and willing to do seems to me of great importance for our present purposes, for war (among other things) is *a willingness to use death as an instrument of policy*—primarily and preferably the death of the enemy, but there obviously has to be a willingness to use the death of one's own people also. (Death as such may not be the "other means" referred to by Clausewitz in his celebrated remark, but he would certainly have agreed happily enough that it was implied: in his cameo appearance in *War and Peace*, Tolstoy has him remark that "since the aim is to wear out the enemy, one cannot, of course, take into account damage and injury suffered by private persons."]⁴

There are several distinct cases of the willingness to use death in this manner, and the progression through them marks the development of war, in recent times, from the civilized to the barbaric (a reversal of what we piously take to be the usual sequence): first, the deliberate killing or allowing to be killed of designated persons, usually members of the armed forces; next, the accidental killing of anyone, including civilians; finally, the deliberate killing of civilians. There is to be added to this a concomitant progress from small to very large numbers. The willingness to do any of these things (without the permission of the victims) is a willingness to be immoral, an equation expressed in the second formulation of the Kantian categorical imperative—categorical because Kant couldn't see, and most of us can't either, how it could possibly be contradicted, or in other words, how there could possibly be a hypothetical on which it might conditionally depend—according to which humanity, whether in one's own person or in that of another, should *never* be treated as a means only, but always as an end. For some reason it provokes in me an echo of a much older and half-remembered text that says of somebody's God that he was "unwilling to cause the death of a sinner." No doubt one of the functions of the idea of God is to recall to humankind what ought to be its own humanity.

I put all this in the stark terms of death rather than of, for example, violence because violence, unless controlled in a cold-blooded way (as in the case of torture), implies an acceptance of the risk of death. Large forces in small spaces are always liable to get out of hand. Violence is from *vis*, "force," and it is worth noting that originally this meant natural force, of horses, of rivers (*equorum, fluminis*), whereas its opposite, "gentle," is from *gens* and therefore essentially human. Violence, in other words, is not in the end a fully or maturely human means of achieving ends—it is to be grown out of. Violence in fact is to be considered a characteristic of the state of nature, not a feature of society; it is found in each of us severally, and the extent to which we individually rise above it in ourselves is the extent to which we leave nature for society. If there is a "human nature" at the primitive level, it still must be said that "becoming human" means transcending it.

This ambiguity as to what it is that constitutes human nature—whether it is what human beings naturally have in common, which would include a tendency to violence, or whether it is what individual humans are capable of rising to, which might include the renunciation of violence—arises out of the fact that the term "human nature" can be used both descriptively and normatively. It has been recognized since Aristotle, who attributes the idea to Evenus in the *Nicomachaean Ethics* (1152a32), that human nature can change, what is habitual becoming natural ("second nature"), so that nothing precludes the eventual emergence of a peaceable second nature. However, such a second nature would presumably always be underlain by its corresponding first, and it is Hobbes's virtue to have recognized the universality of the latter, although he does not put it in these terms. The two levels are asymmetrical: it is certainly possible to have the first nature (or just "nature") without the second (or "humanity"), but the reverse is not plausible and to assume it would be dangerous.

War, to repeat, involves a willingness to use violence and its risk of death as instruments of policy. Who formulates and sanctions the policy? Who carries it out? Who actually exerts violence? Who inflicts death? And to what degree are the immediate agents of these things aware of what they are doing? There is, for example, a kind of remoteness in high-technology death, as was brought home to me forcibly by an explosion or sudden fire that I once observed, in Nebraska or thereabouts, from a plane in which I was traveling from one coast to the other. The puff of smoke was distant and tidy, thirty thousand feet below; and I thought that if I had caused it, by skillful bombardment, for example, I might have been proud of its precision, no matter how many tiny people might at that moment have been dying in agony in it. It would be a charitable (perhaps undeservedly charitable) interpretation of the warlike posture of some statesmen to say that they are really only willing to use the death of tiny people as an instrument of policy. But they don't like to be reminded that in their "policies" the victims are real, and large, and have names (in this awkward fact lies the uncanny effectiveness of the Vietnam war memorial).

It is important, I think, to insist here on the individual, in spite of the impression, especially in the international case, that there are collective agents. For of course there really aren't collective agents, only individual agents of collectivities, a point made elegantly by Kierkegaard in his discussion of the assassination of Mucius Scaevola when he remarked that "the crowd had no hands." It is a matter of real individuals and their responsibilities throughout, whether at the top or at the bottom. And among other things what must be confronted is the phenomenon of the hero in combat, the individual taste for risk and death, the willingness—quite apart from questions of policy—to kill *and to be killed,* on which war feeds. This human disposition is deeply rooted, as psychoanalysis insists, and is not easy to eliminate. Yeats, in "An Irish Airman Foresees His Death," shows that it need have nothing whatever to do with the outcome of the war:

> I know that I shall meet my fate
> Somewhere among the clouds above;
> Those that I fight I do not hate;
> Those that I guard I do not love;
> My country is Kiltartan Cross,
> My countrymen Kiltartan's poor,
> No likely end could bring them loss
> Or leave them happier than before.
> Nor law, nor duty bade me fight,
> Nor public men, nor cheering crowds,
> A lonely impulse of delight
> Drove to this tumult in the clouds;
> I balanced all, brought all to mind,
> The years to come seemed waste of breath,
> A waste of breath the years behind
> In balance with this life, this death.[5]

In warfare, we may say, death is generally inflicted by people who have no personal interest in inflicting it, acting under orders. That, of course, was Eichmann's defense; it is no excuse, but it does shift the locus of the inquiry. Who gives the orders to kill, and why? What is the structure of command—and more important, that of countermand? Command lies, we may suppose, with policymakers and strategists, and it is they who maintain the posture of war: "kings, and persons of sovereign authority," in their "continual jealousies."[6] It is important here to distinguish willingness to kill, which is primitive and impetuous, from willingness to use death as an instrument of policy, which is cultivated and reflective. A special problem arises if policy itself is in the hands of primitives, which may happen in special cases—terrorist groups, for example, or even (for reasons to be specified) democracies. For the moment, I assume a distance between the makers and the executors of the policies of death, and suppose that the former exploit the primitive appetites of the latter, noting parenthetically the heavy moral responsibility that they thereby assume.

Now it is true, as Tolstoy was fond of pointing out, that command may be illusory—the generals think they are determining the outcome of the campaign, when actually it is history or nature or chance. However, there is an asymmetry here too: the same cannot be said of countermand. It is possible, in principle, for a statesman or general to avert or stop a war by suitable countermand at a suitable moment. Who is in a position to do this? normally only a person higher in rank than the person commanded can do so, that is, in the last resort, the commander-in-chief. War, then, is a posture of those in the highest positions. In earlier times, it could sometimes "break out," but everyone now agrees that there have to be safeguards against this. The language of war, over time, has progressed from "breaks out" to "is declared"—for the latter it has seemed possible to impose safeguards (parliamentary or congressional approval, etc). But in the nuclear case, we are afraid again of war's "breaking out." How? It may "break out" by escalation, by the need for rapid decisions that may be taken unreflectively. By whom will those decisions be made, by persons with what qualities of mind? Can they be counted on to have the courage to countermand when common survival calls for that?

One thing it might seem reasonable to expect is that the ascent of the chain of command would at the same time be a movement away from the warlike state of nature in the direction of a reflective humanity. Yeats's airman, it is to be hoped at any rate, would not, if promoted to commander-in-chief, feel free to gamble romantically with the lives of his countrymen or with the fate of humankind, however stimulated he might have been by purely personal risk; having a weakness for romantic gambling of this sort might properly be a disqualification for command. The fact that high-ranking officers normally have to survive the scrutiny of their superiors during the long sequential process of promotion through the lower ranks probably means that some of the more primitive traits of character are in effect filtered out.

But in the Western democracies at least, a complication arises, namely, that because of the principle of civilian control of the military, the commander-in-chief, of all people, may be just the person who has *not* had to come up through the ranks. In parliamentary democracies, the person with the effective power (discounting constitutional figureheads) will probably have had to come up through the *political* ranks, but when the election of the chief executive takes place independently, and by popular suffrage, the normal filter is not in place. This is not to say that the normal filter eliminates all primitive modes of thinking, since some of them may be shared all the way up the hierarchy; but the filters through which candidates for elective office have to pass may eliminate no mode of thinking, as such (although their practical effect may be to eliminate *all* serious modes of thinking above the primitive). This is not, I feel obliged to add, an argument against civilian control of the military; peace cannot be left solely to those whose professional competence lies in war, though they have their own interest in peaceful outcomes. It is, though, a comment on the structure of leadership in popular democracies, a point to which I shall return.

The causal chain that leads to quarrel passes through the commander-in-chief, in the sense at least that a break in the chain at that point would abort the quarrel. If the positions of commander-in-chief on both sides of a global conflict were occupied by humane and learned persons, each would surely countermand any order arising from below that would seriously threaten the continued existence of the race, and both would presumably insist on a continuing and open dialogue aimed at the resolution of the conflict by peaceful means. If there were a global conflict and this did not happen, that might be because either, or both, of the commanders-in-chief was, or were, not sufficiently humane or not sufficiently learned or both; or because either assumed that the other fell short in these respects; or perhaps because the office of commander-in-chief in one case or the other was deceptively so called, in that its holder did not in fact have the real power of countermand; or perhaps because, while this power was real, exercising it was too risky for the comfort or ambition of the commander-in-chief in view of the precariousness of his or her tenure of office.

Any of these problems might arise on either side of the present political divide between the world powers. In Hobbesian terms, the operative causes of quarrel in this case will usually turn out to be either diffidence or glory, whether private or public, since the failure of learning required to believe that competition, using nuclear weapons, is a viable option would surely have to be monumental. (It is not, alas, altogether ruled out—for example, a commander's hands might be tied by an inherited commitment to a competitive stance, though a strong leader would have to know how and when to break such a commitment.) Everything, then, would seem to hinge on the character of the commander-in-chief, and on his or her security, both in the esteem of subordinates and in the power of office. And these in turn depend on dominant values, and on political structures and the mode of election (or selection) of national leaders. With respect to diffidence and political structure, there is the question not only of knowing what the other person will want to do but of trusting his or her resolution and ability to do it. As we have seen, it is one of the very meanings of "peace" that things are settled or agreed upon, so that uncertainty and apprehension, with their attendant risks of preemptive hostility, are not compatible with it. And with respect to dominant values and glory, there is the question of maturity, whether the persons involved have grown out of what Virginia Woolf calls "the stage of human existence where there are 'sides,' and it is necessary for one side to beat another side, and of the utmost importance to walk up to a platform and receive from the hands of the Headmaster himself a highly ornamental pot."[7]

Unfortunately the structure of power and access to power, in the United States at least, leads to vulnerability on both counts. On the one hand, the electorate and the press are feared by officeholders, who may vacillate or dissemble in response to popular desires or criticisms; what Tocqueville said of the legislative is true today, *mutatis mutandis*, of the executive also (because of popular elections unmediated, in practice, by the body of electors originally supposed to protect it, and because of its being largely staffed by appointees unscreened by any formal process): "The social power thus centralized is constantly changing hands, because it is subordinate to the power of the people. It often forgets the maxims of wisdom and foresight."[8] If an administration cannot be clear and honest at home, it will hardly be perceived as reliable abroad. On the other hand, and for similar reasons, anyone realistically eligible to the position of chief executive has to share, if only for appearances' sake—and the bad faith involved in appearing to share them while really believing something else would weaken the office in another way—the relatively primitive aggressive and patriotic passions of the crowd. A leader who would lead the world to peace would have to be strong and charismatic enough to carry those passions into unfamiliar channels of humility and restraint. No such leader seems to be available (though if, by the time this text is published, such a person should *per impossibile* have been found and perhaps elected, I shall be only too happy to abjure my own pessimism).

It is worth noting that war, whose absence if sufficiently certain and general would surely amount to a kind of peace, has itself two different sets of connotations, just as peace does. The Latin equivalent of the term (the counterpart of peace as covenant or fixed disposition), stresses the absence of agreement between opponents, the fact that there are two sides, two combatants, hence one victor (if any) to carry off the ornamental pot: *bellum* is derived from *duellum*. But its Germanic root (the counterpart of peace as quiet) stresses the absence of stability and calm, the fact that everything is stirred up and chaotic: the English word "war" and the French *guerre* are cognate with the archaic German form *wirren*, to confuse or perplex (we get "worse" from this root as well). Even if the two-sided character of war were to become obsolete, globally speaking— if as suggested above no leader of a major power could be so ignorant as to believe a nuclear war worth fighting under any circumstances— still its character as perpetual unrest might survive, partly because technological resources formerly commanded only by the great powers are now available to small ones or even to terrorist and guerrilla organizations. Global wars might escalate into impossibility, only to be replaced by local ones with global reach—indeed, something like this has already happened. It sometimes seems that *the* technological question is the nuclear one; and it is true that in the absence of that question, the problem of war and peace in our time would look altogether different—and in some respects even less tractable, as proponents of deterrence theory would argue. But the level of power available to violence has increased everywhere because of improvements—or perhaps I should just say developments—in the technology of other weapons systems.

Oddly enough, the limit case of technological power, that of nuclear weapons themselves, may be an exception to what seems to be a general rule, namely, that greater intelligence is needed for the responsible command of deadlier force. For even a very slow-witted person might see that the end of everything, including him- or herself, was an undesirable outcome and one to be avoided, although something short of the final holocaust still seemed a plausible risk. Reflection on the wise disposition of power suggests a measure that I will call the I/T ratio, where I stands for the intelligence and insight and integrity of a commander and T stands for the level of technological resources available to him or her. There is reason to fear high T, but double reason to fear it when it is accompanied by low I. And it seems to me that the I/T ratio is dropping everywhere. The effect of this is that more and more command is out of control. Hence the proliferation of small and futile wars, terrorist attacks, and so on. Of course, here too the immediate provocation is seen in confrontational terms; war as *wirren*, it might be argued, reduces to many local cases of war as *duellum*—and yet one might want to say that the condition of war existed generally, without wishing to dignify each small episode with that name.

Among the causes of quarrel, then, must be counted leaders of limited wisdom in command of an almost unlimited technology of violence. Still the exception referred to above may yet save the situation, as far as the major threat is concerned. The two levels of war, conventional and nuclear, are conceptually asymmetrical at least in this sense: that the avoidance of nuclear war is a precondition that must be met if human beings are after all to have the chance to design a world in which conventional war is unnecessary. Might peace in the limited sense of freedom from mutual annihilation descend on us in spite of ourselves, without anyone's heroically leading us to it, simply because of a lack of positive resolution toward war on the part of world leaders, whose disinclination to global risk might come in time to have the practical effect of countermand even if not given that form explicitly? This is a tenuous, though perhaps our only, hope, one that might be realized if (and this is a perilous "if") the necessary time were in fact allowed it.

Let me revert for the last time to the point that war involves a willingness to use death as an instrument of policy. With local setbacks (for example, in the United States), there has been an increasing unwillingness to use death as an instrument of domestic policy, in the form of capital punishment. Might that ever extend to international policy? Here the United States is again the most obvious case to begin with, in view of the history of protest against the war in Vietnam. The passion of that movement is now only a memory, though it might be revived if there were a new adventure that required a draft. At all events, it seems clear that there are many people who do not want war. Surely if world leaders do not lead their people into nuclear confrontation, and if pressure is kept up not only for the negotiated settlement of minor disagreements but also for the removal of the injustices that provoke them, there might over the long run be a gradual reduction in the level of quarrel worldwide.

Unfortunately, not wanting war is not the same as wanting peace as a settled state. What obstacles arise and what advantages belong to peace so understood? It would involve in the end a practical refusal, not only on the part of draft resisters but on the part of policymakers as well, to use death as an instrument of *any* policy, with everything that that entails. And it is here that some of the subtler causes of quarrel emerge, in the form of pressures to keep alive, for reasons having nothing to do with any desire for quarrel as such, the conditions that minister to it. Thus the first thing peace in this strong sense would entail would be the realization of the possibility envisaged by Hamilton, in the passage from the *Federalist* quoted above, that the standing army might be disbanded.

Against this possibility, however remote, there will at once be marshaled formidable objections. Some of them were anticipated in President Eisenhower's farewell address, which in the light of the recent creation of a cabinet-level Department of Veterans' Affairs— thus building into the very structure of government a permanent resignation to the continued existence of the military over the long term—seems like an echo from a more innocent age. What has happened to the peaceable intentions of the American founders, or even of their successors who, in designing the Pentagon, made provision for its easy conversion into a hospital when the need for it had passed? Eisenhower's fear was that industry would come to depend irreversibly on military appropriations, and in some sectors this has already happened—sectors not merely of industry but of the country, so that the very congressional representatives on whom Hamilton counted to weigh the issue impartially have acquired (given their strong desires to be reelected as well as, if not instead of, governing wisely) a vested interest in an outcome favorable to the maintenance of a standing army.

Of course, the army is needed for defense. Here much might be said about the means that are used to keep alive fears of foreign aggression, but I will content myself with a citation from an ancient source, the *Peace Manual* issued by the American Peace Society in 1847. The *Manual* cites a inquiry into the actual causes of war, carried out in 1825 by the Peace Society of Massachusetts, which

> besides a multitude of petty ancient wars, and of those waged by Christian nations against tribes of savages, ascertained 286 wars of magnitude to have had the following origin:—22 for plunder or tribute; 44 for the extension of territory; 24 for retaliation or revenge; 6 about disputed boundaries; 8 respecting points of honor or prerogative; 5 for the protection or extension of commerce; 55 civil wars; 41 about contested titles to crowns; 30 under pretense of assisting allies; 23 from mere jealousy of rival greatness; 28 religious wars, including the crusades;—*not one for defense alone!*[9]

There is obviously something dubious about this source, especially in its attitude toward "tribes of savages"; and for every aggressor there will have been one or more defenders. But it suggests a second thought about warlike postures of defense: How serious is the threat, really? How much firepower is needed to counter it? Since the people have a constitutional right to bear arms as potential members of a "well regulated Militia" might this not be enough to discourage the invader, without the need to maintain a standing army?

There is a third form of objection that would obviously arise, not from economic interests or national fears of vulnerability but from the persons most immediately affected by the dissolution of the army, namely, its own personnel. Even if peace were to be established—especially if peace were to be established—the military life would be passionately defended. For along with the expensive machinery that enables Yeats's airman to indulge, in time of war, his taste for the risk of death, there go, in time of peace, the privileges of the mess. Nobody has expressed better than Tolstoy the seduction of the armed forces between engagements:

> Our moral nature is such that we are unable to be idle and at peace. A secret voice warns that for us idleness is a sin. If it were possible for a man to discover a mode of existence in which he could feel that, though idle, he was of use to the world and fulfilling his duty, he would have attained to one facet of primeval bliss. And such a state of obligatory and unimpeachable idleness is enjoyed by a whole section of society—the military class. It is just this compulsory and irreproachable idleness which has always constituted, and will constitute, the chief attraction of military service.[10]

Of course today nobody could accuse the military of idleness—officers are always bustling about, like the grand old Duke of York in the song, who marched ten thousand men to the top of the hill and marched them down again. The army is not just an economic and political but a cultural fact of life, and it has been so in almost every civilization in history. There are a few exceptions—one thinks of Costa Rica, and of postwar Japan, though in the latter case the absence of a military establishment was imposed rather than chosen (and yet this seems, in economic terms, to have been a blessing rather than a hardship; military expenditures do not seem to be necessary for the health of industry, a point that is worth bearing in mind in discussions of the eventual possibility of peace).

A more obvious and more significant case, though one that is liable to be overlooked, is that of the early United States. While there seem always to have been armed forces of some sort at the disposal of the War Department, these were authorized only for a year at a time, and there were significant periods during which they were minimal, consisting of little more than a handful of officers under commission and enough recruits to man a fort or two and patrol the territories not yet organized as states. For one night, that of 2 June, 1784, the United States had no army at all. The American grain was originally antimilitaristic; indeed, it might be said that the country was on the whole a reluctant military power up until the Second World War. Inconceivable as the dismantling of the military establishment now seems, it is in fact much closer to us, both historically and conceptually, than is the case for any other major power.

It is an idea whose time, if the world is fortunate enough, will come again. Whether it will do so, and how soon, depends on the relative pace at which certain necessary changes proceed: the correction of economic and political injustice, the reduction of the population burden of the globe, the elimination of religious fundamentalism, an increase in the availability and acceptance of education. Worldwide, many of these indicators seem to be in decline, and given the history of the race so far, it is natural (but still in the primitive sense of natural) to respond to the resulting conflict by escalating armaments. However, as I have tried to show, human beings need not be at the mercy of their first, or primitive, nature, and in privileged and technologically advanced societies there is no excuse for remaining in that condition.

The United States is such a society. Unfortunately, as was parenthetically remarked above, some of the indicators in question are moving in the wrong direction here too. The death penalty has been resuscitated and is currently practiced in a number of states. American leaders not only insist publicly on the need for arms but have been found to trade in them privately, and not always for worthy ends. Of course unilateral total disarmament in the face of raging and fully armed hostility everywhere would be imprudent; the trouble is that the gravity of this condition is too easy to exaggerate, and it is too often taken to preclude entirely any discussion as to the possibility of genuine peace. And yet the United States, more than any other society in the history of the world, is in a position, or could be if it would, to show the rest of humankind what the constitutive benefits of peace are. They are exactly what the United States was explicitly founded to establish and preserve, namely, every individual's ability—the civil conditions, the material resources, the accessibility of information and instruction—to do what he or she has a mind to do, free of coercion or interference. And the familiar name for this is, simply, liberty.

Clearly peace is not to obtained everywhere overnight. But the vision of it is to hand, and if leaders could be found who allowed themselves to entertain that vision, not as a concession to utopian thinking but as a matter of practice and resolve, renouncing postures of war and insisting on possibilities of peace, the world would move with them. Slowly, to be sure: the process has to be stepwise—slightly more intelligent leaders, small reductions in the arms level, modest exercises of trust—but in each case persistent and cumulative. A beginning might be made by opening a debate on Hamilton's topic, "the propriety of keeping a military force on foot," without for once taking its outcome to be a foregone conclusion. Some political leader, some day, will have the sense to acknowledge the justice of Virgil's remark that "there is not enough reason in arms," the ingenuity to devise instruments for the carrying out of political relations by *other* means, and the courage to convince the rest of the world that it can have confidence in those instruments rather than diffidence, appealing to the human capacity to acquire the necessary second nature. This is a hope we should be unwilling to abandon and an end toward which we should be always willing to work.

Fifteen

A Positive Concept of Peace

Steven Lee

Peace has been an elusive goal. The causes of quarrel are many, and means developed for its avoidance have too often proved inadequate. A strong desire for peace and the willingness to work hard for it are not enough. We must, as Aristotle says, know that at which we aim. Achieving peace requires having an adequate concept of what peace is. If our concept is inadequate, peace may elude us, despite the vigor of our efforts. An inadequate concept of peace may be part of the reason that enduring peace has eluded us for so long. Many of those concerned about peace have recognized the importance of understanding the nature of peace and have attributed our failure to achieve peace to a lack of this understanding. Genuine peace, it is often said, is not merely the absence of a clash of arms between nations, but the presence of a measure of justice in their relationship. More generally, the claim is that the proper concept of peace is positive, not negative, in the sense that it involves the presence of certain features in the relations among nations, not merely the absence of violent conflict. This is the claim that I will explore in this essay.

This claim raises three questions. First, is it true? What are the arguments for and against our adopting a concept of peace that is positive. Second, if the proper concept of peace is positive, which positive concept should we adopt? What is the nature of peace understood positively? Third, what is the special relevance, if any, of the positive concept of peace to our situation of potential nuclear belligerency? The first and second questions can best be addressed together, and I will discuss them by considering the proposals for a positive concept of peace offered by Gray Cox and Peter Caws elsewhere in this volume.

Peace is, at the minimum, the absence of violent conflict. Those who argue for a positive concept of peace claim that there is more to the concept than merely this negative notion. In his discussion of pleasure in the *Republic*, Plato suggests that if we imagine a mid-point between pleasure and pain, we can see that what most people regard as pleasure, namely, bodily pleasure, is really only the process of removing the pain of bodily deprivation, that is, the process of moving from pain to the absence of pain at the mid-point. But pain soon returns. In contrast, intellectual pleasure is a truer and more enduring form of pleasure, because it does not arise out of a state of pain, but is a process of movement beginning at the mid-point and rising to a full state of pleasure. We might refer to this as Plato's positive concept of pleasure. Analogously, what most people regard as peace is the cessation of violent conflict, but this is followed invariably by the resumption of such conflict, as satiation is followed by hunger. If we regard pleasure merely as the absence of pain, we will never know true, enduring pleasure. Likewise, if we regard peace merely as the absence of violent conflict, we will never know true, enduring peace. So, our concept of peace, like our concept of pleasure, should be positive.

This suggests that the problem of whether we should adopt a positive concept of peace is a *practical* one, namely, the problem of how violent conflict is to be kept from returning. We can hope to achieve enduring peace, only if we regard peace as something more than merely the absence of violent conflict. This is to argue for adopting a positive concept of peace based on our practical concerns. For Plato, there is an identification of the enduring with the true, such that the correct formulation of a concept, such as pleasure, is one under which the state to which it refers is enduring. But his metaphysical assumptions are not ours. We often treat concepts as tools, allowing our purposes in using them to determine how they are characterized. Our interest that peace be enduring is the basis for claiming that it is appropriate to regard peace as more than the absence of violent conflict. We need to know how to wage peace successfully, and defining peace negatively gives little indication of how this is to be done.

Does this practical justification for adopting a positive concept of peace give any indication of what the concept should be? Gray Cox proposes that peace be seen not merely as the absence of violent conflict, but as the presence of cooperation. We wage peace by actively cooperating with those with whom we might otherwise be in conflict. Given the practical concern for achieving an enduring peace, however, Cox's proposal is inadequate. Cox adopts an overly simplistic dichotomy between conflict and cooperation. He seems to see peace as involving the absence of conflict in general (rather than specifically violent conflict), and in seeking a positive concept of peace, he seeks to characterize this absence positively. Since relations that are not conflictual are cooperative, peace involves the presence of cooperation. In this vein, Cox criticizes those who claim that conflict is essential to social life. He suggests that conflict results from the adoption of an optional language game. But scarcity of resources makes conflict inevitable in social life, and Cox recognizes this, though he refers to disagreements about resource allocation as "problems" rather than conflicts. He claims that problems, not conflicts, are resolved by cooperation, thus preserving peace. But this way of putting things obscures the positive characterization of peace that can better guide us to an enduring peace.

A more adequate approach is to recognize that peace involves the absence, not of all conflict, but only of violent conflict. We cannot avoid all conflict, but peace requires only the avoidance of conflict that is violent. In order for conflict not to become violent, it must be resolved short of violence. The proper positive characterization is that peace is the nonviolent resolution of conflict. Cooperation is one species of the nonviolent resolution of conflict, but it is not the only one. It is a good thing for the possibility of enduring peace that it is not, for cooperation will often fail, despite our best efforts. The other means of nonviolently resolving conflict is adjudication, the third-party, authoritative disposition of matters in dispute between two parties. Adjudication is one of the primary functions of government, and it makes large-scale social life possible. This is an aspect of the positive concept of peace missing from Cox's account.

Cox's failure to include adjudication in his concept of peace is not a mere oversight. He blames our inadequate concept of peace, in part, on the view that "argument is war," that is, the view that reasoning involves a conflict between differing points of view, and he mentions the procedure of the law courts as one of the manifestations of this view. But the law courts are a paradigm example of adjudication working to preserve social peace, and their conflictual character is essential to their task of giving a hearing to both sides in cases where cooperative efforts to resolve disputes have failed.

Adjudication works to preserve peace by dispensing justice, both formal and substantive. When the adjudication procedure is perceived as just, when each of the disputants perceives that he or she has been fairly dealt with, adjudication is most effective at keeping conflicts from becoming violent. Thus another way to put our criticism is to say that Cox fails to recognize that the positive concept of peace should include the presence of justice. The role of the notion of justice in a positive concept of peace has been expressed recently as follows:

> Positive peace is a concept which refers not just to the absence of physical violence but also to the presence of those conditions without which people cannot achieve their full potential. Of particular concern here are social justice and human rights.[1]

To achieve their potential, people must have freedom of action and access to resources. Justice, in a broad sense, serves this end by securing fairness in the distribution of rights and resources. Distributive justice will ensure that no person lacks important legal rights and a resource base with which to develop his or her capabilities. Thus, beyond adjudication in the narrow sense, the kind of formal dispute settlement that goes on in a courtroom, this aspect of positive peace involves the workings of the complex and often informal sets of rules and judgments by which society assigns legal rights and distributes resources.

The importance of this aspect of positive peace was recognized by Peter Caws in the colloquium presentation on which his essay is based. Peace, he remarked, is the availability to each person of the resources needed to further his or her own ends. This remark too may be seen as an implicit reference to the role of justice in securing peace. Thus Caws supplies the aspect of positive peace that Cox's account lacks. But we need to add cooperation, the aspect emphasized by Cox. Caws does not propose that peace requires that the ends people pursue need be of any particular kind. But for peace to be maintained, at least some of the ends people pursue must be cooperative ends. Unless people are willing to cooperate some of the time, social mechanisms for administering justice will not be sufficient to keep conflicts from becoming violent. The two methods of resolving conflict nonviolently are both required if conflict is to be contained short of violence. We need the administration of justice because cooperation is not strong enough to defuse all conflicts, but at the same time, we need cooperation because without it there would be too much work for the administration of justice. For example, we recognize the importance of law in society, but we recognize also that there is a danger when it is asked to do too much, as is evident in the widespread concern that American society is becoming too litigious.

Finally, to provide a positive concept of peace among nations, we must apply to the international sphere these same two aspects of peace. Positive international peace requires the existence among nations of substantial measures of cooperation and mechanisms for securing formal and substantive justice.

Now that we have some sense of what an adequate positive concept of peace might look like, we may return again to the question of whether or not we should adopt a positive concept of peace. Apart from the practical argument offered earlier, are there any other arguments for or against adopting a positive concept of peace? A logical argument against defining peace in a negative way would be nice, but we are unlikely to find an argument showing that a negative concept of peace leads to contradiction or incoherence. There seems to be nothing wrong in general with defining concepts in a negative way. Indeed, some concepts seem to be inherently negative, in that they are parasitic on other concepts. One example, cited by Cox, is death, which can only be defined as the absence of life. In addition, the attempt to derive absurd conclusions from the negative concept of peace does not seem to succeed. Cox suggests that defining peace as the absence of violent conflict leads to the absurd conclusion that the extinction of life on earth would represent the truest form of peace. But it is easy to avoid such conclusions by formulating the negative definition more carefully, for example, by stipulating that peace involves the absence of violent conflict among existing human societies.

Ronald Glossop argues against a positive concept of peace on two grounds. First, a positive concept of peace "seems not to be faithful to our normal use of the term."[2] Second, a positive concept of peace "actually interferes with our thinking clearly about the issues of peace and justice and their interrelations," such that, "we would be forced to overlook certain distinctions which must be made if we are to understand the problems involved in creating an ideal society."[3] The first point is that a positive concept of peace is not descriptively adequate, that the negative concept, peace merely as the absence of violent conflict, best fits actual usage. But is this so? The United States and the Soviet Union are said to be in a state of "cold war," a bit of ordinary usage that implies that the absence of violent conflict does not necessarily signify peace. True peace would presumably involve positive relations between the nations, which would ameliorate the hostility and suspicion that could lead to violent conflict. But whatever ordinary usage may be, our chief interest is in prescribing, not describing.

Glossop's second point is that lumping the absence of violent conflict and the presence of justice under a single concept interferes with our thinking clearly about alternative social situations. This is, in effect, a criticism of the practical justification for adopting a positive concept of peace, for it suggests that a positive concept would interfere with our clarity of thought, and so impede rather than assist our efforts to achieve a better world. Glossop observes that, while the degree of injustice between nations is sometimes great enough that violence would be a justified response, as in some cases of outright aggression (the basis of justifiable wars in just-war theory), often it is not, owing to the just-war requirement of proportionality.[4] Glossop's argument seems to be that, while cases in which injustice justifies war and cases in which it does not are distinct, both morally and prudentially, the positive concept of peace does not allow us to make this distinction, since we would not then be able to assess the cases in terms of justice separately from categorizing them in terms of the concept of peace.

But this is a spurious concern. That two situations fall under the same category, whether the category is that of war, peace, or a lack of peace, does not impede our ability to rank the two situations, either morally or prudentially, even when the criterion of ranking is part of the definition of the category in question. For example, two situations of war can be morally or prudentially ranked in terms of the degree of violence involved, even though the presence of violent conflict is part of the concept of war. The positive concept of peace still allows us to determine that a situation of violent conflict is morally or prudentially worse than an unjust situation in which there is not violent conflict, or vice versa, even though neither situation counts as a state of peace.

There is another objection to adopting a positive concept of peace alluded to by both Caws and Glossop.[5] The question whether justice obtains, unlike the question whether violent conflict obtains, is not ideologically neutral. Justice means different things in the East and in the West. So the positive concept of peace would make the pursuit of East/West peace more difficult, since there would then be disagreement about what counts as peace. The checkered history of the notion of peaceful coexistence and the factors that undermined detente in the 1970s are illustrations of this. Two points may be made in response. First, an answer to the question whether violent conflict obtains may not itself be ideologically neutral. Marxists, for example, may regard the bourgeoisie under capitalism as being at constant war with the proletariat, perpetrating economic violence against them. Second, an ideological divide on the nature of peace would not at all preclude mutual recognition that armed conflict must be avoided, since each side would see the avoidance of such conflict as a necessary precondition for the achievement of peace in either sense. Moreover, if it is true that measures of justice and cooperation, however hard they may be to achieve between ideological opponents, are necessary for the enduring absence of armed conflict, it would be of great value to adopt the positive concept of peace in order to keep this truth manifest.

There remains, then, the practical justification in favor of adopting a positive concept of peace. Consider the following conditions that might hold among nations: (1) violent conflict, (2) no violent conflict and little justice and cooperation, and (3) no violent conflict but a substantial measure of justice and cooperation. The first is war and the third is peace, but what of the second?[6] Our argument is that since the concern is to avoid condition 1 permanently rather than temporarily, we should understand the pursuit of peace as a pursuit of condition 3 rather than of condition 2. This argument is not based on the intrinsic desirability of justice and cooperation, but rather on their instrumental value in avoiding the resort to violent conflict. As mentioned earlier, there is support for this in ordinary usage, where, in regard to East/West relations, condition 1 is referred to as a "shooting war" and condition 2 is referred to as a "cold war." This suggests that the divide between war and peace falls between conditions 2 and 3 rather than between conditions 1 and 2.

Hobbes, it seems, would endorse this. According to him, "the nature of war consists not in actual fighting but in the known disposition thereto during all the time there is no assurance to the contrary. All other time is PEACE."[7] For Hobbes, there is no social peace outside of the legal regime imposed by a sovereign. In our terms, there is no international peace without the kind of cooperation and justice typically, though perhaps not exclusively, found within a social order under a sovereign. We recognize, with Hobbes, that what is important about peace is not merely that one is not at the moment subject to violent attack, but that one has reasonable assurances of not being subject to violent attack in the future.

Despite all that has been said, however, the debate over whether to adopt a positive or negative concept of peace remains largely a verbal dispute. Our discussion has revealed the important truth that the likelihood of avoiding violent conflict between nations can be eliminated or greatly reduced only if substantial measures of cooperation and justice are introduced into their relationship. But this truth can be recognized whatever concept of peace one adopts, even though it may be more apparent when one's concept is positive. Nevertheless, the debate is still of value. It may at least be taken as a roundabout way of emphasizing this truth. Beyond that, the discussion of positive and negative concepts of peace has a special relevance to the problem of war and peace in the nuclear age. This brings us to the third question.

The condition of mutual assured destruction existing between the United States and the Soviet Union is historically unique. Nuclear weapons are powerful, plentiful, easily deliverable, and relatively invulnerable to attack, to the extent that each side is capable of destroying the society of the other even after being hit by a surprise attack. For the first time in history, a great-power war could result in both sides being completely destroyed. This puts a special premium on guaranteeing that great-power violent conflict never recurs. This would seem to give special importance to the positive concept of peace. On the contrary, however, mutual assured destruction seems to create a situation in which both the possibility of positive peace is *excluded* and the need for a positive peace is *transcended*. It seems that positive peace is excluded because mutual assured destruction makes it unrealizable. At the same time, the need for a positive peace seems to be transcended, in the sense that mutual assured destruction appears to provide a basis for an enduring absence of violent conflict *without* the measures of justice and cooperation that positive peace encompasses.

The nuclear situation seems to make a positive peace unrealizable, because nuclear weapons forestall efforts to achieve substantial levels of cooperation and justice between the superpowers. As Dan Farrell points out elsewhere in this volume, nuclear weapons make international relations more like a Hobbesian state of nature, because there is a kind of equality of power between nations or alliances, each of which has a capacity for assured destruction against the other. They are equals, even if their arsenals are different in size, in that each can destroy the other. Each believes that violent conflict can be avoided only by its maintaining a threat of annihilation against the other, and the resulting fear and suspicion make it unlikely that cooperation and a shared commitment to justice will develop very far between them. The vulnerability of each to utter destruction by the other and each side's belief that it is preserved from destruction only by its own apocalyptic threats against the other create a climate in which enmity is seen as inescapable and lawlessness is seen as avoidable only through such threats.

To put the point another way, in a Hobbesian state of nature, positive peace is possible only through the institution of a sovereign; so to the extent that nuclear weapons make international relations like a Hobbesian state of nature, a positive peace becomes possible only through a world sovereign. Thus a positive peace is possible only if a world sovereign is possible. But the creation of a world sovereign appears to be a practical impossibility. To the extent that this is correct, nuclear weapons exclude the possibility of a positive peace. Does this show that a positive peace in the nuclear age, whether through a world government or by other means, is impossible? This may put the point too strongly. But it does show, at least, that a positive peace will be more difficult to achieve now than it has been in the past, and it has always been difficult.

At the same time, it seems that the need for a positive peace is transcended, in the sense that nuclear deterrence provides a way of ensuring that great-power violent conflict will not recur without the great powers having to develop substantial measures of cooperation and justice in their relations. This is one important way in which international relations are, today, unlike a Hobbesian state of nature. Nuclear weapons seem to create the kind of security found under a sovereign without the need for one. This is because the capacity for assured destruction is mutual. Each side can, even from the grave, administer capital punishment to an aggressor, so a world sovereign is not necessary to guarantee that even murderous aggression will be punished. Under a sovereign, peace is achieved, in part, by the deterrent threats of punishment of a legal system; but under the regime of mutual assured destruction, such deterrence can be achieved without a sovereign or a legal system. In addition, the punishment that is threatened, annihilation, is grossly disproportionate to whatever an aggressor might hope to achieve. Thus, under nuclear deterrence, a nation will never have a sufficient reason to start a war, and the absence of violent conflict will endure. Nuclear weapons appear to realize, at last, the hope that was born with the application of industrial technology to war, namely, that war could be made so horrible that it would never again happen.

Unfortunately, the argument that a policy of nuclear deterrence transcends the need for a positive peace fails. The situation of mutual assured destruction may guarantee that, short of madness, neither superpower will ever deliberately start a war. But wars do not always start as a result of cool deliberation. There is the possibility of accidental nuclear war. Though this possibility may be small, it is, given short ballistic-missile flight times, probably greater than it was prior to the nuclear age.

But more important is the possibility of escalation to nuclear war growing out of some relatively minor incident between the superpowers, their alliance partners, or their Third World clients. A decision to use nuclear weapons in such a case could be made in the heat of the moment, without the opportunity for level-headed decisions. Of course, decisions made in the heat of the moment are still influenced by the perception of likely outcomes. But the possibility of escalation to nuclear war cannot be made completely negligible, because decisions under stress may be less influenced by likely outcomes than decisions resulting from more careful deliberation. In addition, there are strong tendencies in the nuclear arms race that work against reducing the probability of nuclear war through escalation, namely, counterforce weapons systems that could in a crisis make each side fear that the other side perceives a first-strike to be to its advantage. Thus the appearance that the need for a positive peace is transcended under the regime of mutual assured destruction is an illusion. In the nuclear age, as previously, only a genuinely positive peace will provide assurance that the absence of violent conflict will endure.

Nuclear weapons thus create a severe and unprecedented practical problem. First, they make the enduring absence of violent conflict much more imperative than before. Second, nuclear weapons seem to exclude the possibility of a positive peace. A positive peace, the enduring absence of violent conflict, is now more necessary, but the conditions for its establishment are more difficult, if not impossible, to achieve. Third, the need for a positive peace appears to be transcended, but in reality it is not. As a result, many may now wrongly believe that a positive peace is no longer necessary to achieve an enduring absence of violent conflict, so that the motivation to work for substantial measures of cooperation and justice in the relations between the superpowers is seriously undercut. Now, more than ever, we must adopt a positive concept of peace. Only by emphasizing the need to base relations between the superpowers, and among all nations, on substantial measures of cooperation and justice can our civilization have a real hope of survival.[8]

Notes

Chapter One

1. Peter Caws, *Two Centuries of Philosophy in America* (Oxford: Basil Blackwell, 1980).

2. Frank M. Coleman, *Hobbes and America: Exploring the Constitutional Foundations* (Toronto: University of Toronto Press, 1977), p. 129.

3. Jean-Jacques Rousseau, *The Social Contract* trans. Maurice Cranston (Harmondsworth: Penguin Books, 1968), p. 49.

4. Thomas Hobbes, *Leviathan,* ed. C. B. Macpherson (Harmondsworth: Penguin Books, 1968), p. 82. All citations in the text are to this edition.

5. The positive argument for Hobbes, rather than Locke, as the ancestor of the founding documents cannot be rehearsed here, but it can be found not only in Coleman's *Hobbes and America* but also in George Mace's *Locke, Hobbes, and the Federalist Papers: An Essay on the Genesis of the American Political Heritage* (Carbondale: Southern Illinois University Press, 1979).

6. Reinhold Niebuhr, *Moral Man and Immoral Society* (New York: Charles Scribner's Sons, 1932), xx.

Chapter Two

1. Jay F. Rosenberg, *The Practice of Philosophy* (Englewood Cliffs, N.J.: Prentice-Hall, 1978), p. 8.

2. Ibid., p. 10.

3. Heraclitus, frag. B72, in *Die Fragmente der Vorsokratiker,* 10th ed. Hermann Diels and Walther Kranz (Berlin, 1953); reprinted in Jonathan Barnes, *Early Greek Philosophy* (Harmondsworth: Penguin Books, 1987) p. 125. Norman Angell, *The Great Illusion* (London, 1910) is quoted in J. Glenn Gray, *The Warriors: Reflections on Men in Battle* (New York: Harper and Row, 1959), p. 232.

4. Hans Morgenthau, *In Defense of the National Interest* (New York: Alfred A. Knopf, 1951), p. 242.

5. *The Prince,* chap. 15, in *The Portable Machiavelli,* trans. P. Bondanella and M. Musa (Harmondsworth: Penguin Books, 1979), p. 127.

6. Stephen Rasner, *International Regimes,* a special issue of *International Organization* 32, no. 2 (1982): 186.

7. Thomas Hobbes, *Leviathan* (Indianapolis: Bobbs-Merrill, 1958), pp. 86–87.

8. R. V. Sampson, *The Discovery of Peace* (New York: Pantheon Books, 1973), p. 197.

9. See Tolstoy's *War and Peace*, trans. Aylmer Maude (London, 1943), p. 1327; Sampson, *Discovery of Peace*, p. 165.

10. Gene Sharp, *The Politics of Non-Violent Action* (Boston: Porter Sargent Publishers, 1973).

11. Tolstoy, "Love the Supreme Law," in *The Morality of Peace and War*, ed. Martin T. Woods and Robert Buckenmeyer (Santa Barbara, Cal.: Intelman Books, 1974), p. 385.

12. Sampson, *Discovery of Peace*, pp. 177–78.

13. Ibid., p. 200.

14. In addition to the works cited above, see Hannah Arendt, *Crises of the Republic* (New York: Harcourt Brace Jovanovich, 1972), and *Eichmann in Jerusalem: A Report on the Banality of Evil* (New York: Viking Press, 1964); Albert Camus, *The Rebel*, trans. Anthony Bower (New York: Alfred A. Knopf, 1956); Elias Canetti, *Crowds and Power*, trans. Carol Stewart (New York: Viking, 1962); Mohandas Karamchand Gandhi, *An Autobiography; or, The Story of My Experiments with Truth*, trans. Mahadev Desai (Amedabad: Navajivan Publishing House, 1969), and *Non-Violent Resistance* (New York: Schocken Books, 1951); Martin Luther King, Jr., *A Testament of Hope: The Essential Writings of Martin Luther King, Jr.*, ed. James M. Washington (San Francisco: Harper and Row, 1986); and Simone Weil, "The *Iliad*, or The Poem of Force," in *Simone Weil: An Anthology*, ed. Sian Miles (London: Virago, 1988).

Chapter Three

1. *The Laws of Plato*, trans. T. Pangle (New York: Basic Books, 1980), p. 100.

2. Thomas Hobbes, *Leviathan*, ed. C. B. Macpherson (Baltimore: Penguin Books, 1972), chap. 13, p. 185. All further citations from the *Leviathan* are from this edition, and page numbers are included in the text. My brief remarks about Hobbes are based solely on this text of Hobbes, and do not pretend to present anything like a thorough discussion of the relevant points of the *Leviathan*.

3. *The Republic of Plato*, trans. A. Bloom (New York: Basic Books, 1968), p. 49. I note that in using the term "Platonic" in this essay I am allowing for the possibility that Plato's teaching may be considerably more complex and subtle than the views I have labeled "Platonic." These views are stated in Plato's dialogues and have often been taken to represent Plato's teaching, and reference to them suffices for the purposes of this essay. But I strongly suspect that a more detailed study of the dialogues (for which this is not the place) would yield a different interpretation.

4. That Hobbes's claim that death is the *summum malum* is a moral judgment rather than an empirical description has been argued by L. Strauss

in *The Political Philosophy of Hobbes,* trans. E. M. Sinclair (Chicago: University of Chicago Press, 1973), chap. 2. Strauss points out the Hobbes "could not have maintained his thesis that death is the greatest and supreme evil but for the conviction vouched for by his natural science that the soul is not immortal" (p. 167). Since that conviction is key to many religions (especially revealed religions), Hobbes's claim about the *summum malum* seems at odds with religion so understood. It thus becomes unclear how Hobbesian premises could solve the problem of religious war.

5. John Locke, *The Second Treatise of Government,* ed. T. P. Peardon (Indianapolis: Bobbs-Merrill, 1976), pp. 50–52 (pars. 90–92).

6. See Thomas Jefferson's letter to John Adams of 5 July 1814; Adams's letters to Jefferson of 3 Feb. 1812, 28 June 1812, 16 July 1814 (all available in volume 2 of *The Adams-Jefferson Letters,* ed. L. J. Cappon, 2 vols. [Chapel Hill: University of North Carolina Press, 1959]). Also revealing is Jefferson's letter to W. Short of 4 Aug. 1820, in *Thomas Jefferson: Writings,* ed. M. Peterson (New York: Library of America, 1984), pp. 1436–37.

7. One such community, "Nashoba," was established and lasted for a short while. See also Wright's *A Plan for the Gradual Abolition of Slavery in the United States without Danger or Loss to the Citizens of the South* (1825).

8. Madison writes in that letter, "In cases where portions of time have been allotted to slaves, as among the Spaniards, with a view to their working out their freedom, it is believed that but few have availed themselves of the opportunity, by a voluntary industry; And such a result could be less relied on in a case where each individual would feel that the fruit of his exertions would be shared by others whether equally or unequally making them; and that the exertions of others would equally avail him, notwithstanding a deficiency in his own. Skillful arrangements might palliate this tendency, but it would be difficult to counteract it effectually." (*Sources of the Political Thought of James Madison,* rev. ed., ed. M. Meyers [Hanover: Brandeis University Press, 1981], p. 330).

9. See Madison's letter to N. P. Trist, 29 Jan. 1828 (Meyers, *Sources,* p. 356). Madison's commentary continues as follows: "His enterprise is, nevertheless, an interesting one. It will throw light on the maximum to which the force of education and habit can be carried; and, like Helvetius's attempt to show that all men come from the hand of nature perfectly equal, and owe every intellectual and moral difference to the education of circumstances, though failing of its entire object, that of proving the means to be all-sufficient, will lead to a fuller sense of their great importance."

10. See R. Hofstadter's "The Founding Fathers: An Age of Realism," in *Moral Foundations of the American Republic,* 2d ed., ed. R. H. Horwitz (Charlottesville: University of Virginia Press, 1979), pp. 73–85; F. M. Coleman's *Hobbes and America: Exploring the Constitutional Foundations* (Toronto: University of Toronto Press, 1977).

11. R. Dworkin, *Taking Rights Seriously* (Cambridge: Harvard University Press, 1978), p. 188.

12. *Federalist Papers,* ed. C. Rossiter (New York: New American Li-

brary, 1961), p. 322. Consider also Madison's statement in *Federalist* no. 55: "As there is a degree of depravity in mankind which requires a certain degree of circumspection and distrust, so there are other qualities in human nature which justify a certain portion of esteem and confidence. Republican government presupposes the existence of these qualities in a higher degree than any other form. Were the pictures which have been drawn by the political jealousy of some among us faithful likenesses of the human character, the inference would be that there is not sufficient virtue among men for self-government; and that nothing less than the chains of despotism can restrain them from destroying and devouring one another" (p. 346). Similarly, consider Hamilton's assertion in *Federalist* no. 76: "The supposition of universal venality in human nature is little less an error in political reasoning than the supposition of universal rectitude. The institution of delegated power implies that there is a portion of virtue and honor among mankind, which may be a reasonable foundation of confidence. And experience justifies the theory" (p. 458).

13. Madison's "Universal Peace" was published originally in the *National Gazette*, 2 Feb. 1792; it is reprinted in Meyers, *Sources*, pp. 192–93.

14. See Madison's "Memorial and Remonstrance against Religious Assessments" (1785), in ibid., p. 11.

15. Adam Smith, *Wealth of Nations*, book 5, chap. 1, part 3, art. 3, p. 793 (volume 2 of the Liberty Classics edition [Indianapolis: Liberty Press, 1981]).

16. Jefferson, "Statute for Establishing Religious Freedom," in *Writings*, pp. 346–47.

17. See Meyers, *Sources*, pp. 7, 8–9.

18. See David Little's "Religion and Civil Virtue in America," in *The Virginia Statute for Religious Freedom: Its Evolution and Consequences in American History*, ed. M. D. Peterson and R. C. Vaughan (Cambridge: Cambridge University Press, 1988), p. 249.

19. This "motivational" issue is referred to by Jefferson in the context of his reflections on slavery: "And can the liberties of a nation be thought secure when we have removed their only firm basis, a conviction in the minds of the people that these liberties are of the gift of God? That they are not to be violated but with his wrath?" The context makes it fairly clear that Jefferson thinks the answers to both questions are negative (*Notes on the State of Virginia*, query 18, in *Writings*, p. 289).

20. See Karl Popper's *The Open Society and Its Enemies*, 5th ed. (Princeton: Princeton University Press, 1971), vol. 1, p. 265.

21. Douglas refers to "the great principle of self-government" and adds, "I deny [Congress's] right to force a good thing upon a people who are unwilling to receive it. The great principle is the right of every community to judge and decide for itself, whether a thing is right or wrong, whether it would be good or evil for them to adopt it. . . . It is no answer to this argument to say that slavery is an evil, and hence should not be tolerated. You must allow the people to decide for themselves whether it is a good or an evil" (*The Lincoln-Douglas Debates*, ed. R. W. Johannsen [Oxford: Oxford University Press, 1965], pp. 27–28). Lincoln responds, "Any man

can say that [he doesn't care whether slavery is voted up or down] who does not see any thing wrong in slavery, but no man can logically say it who does see a wrong in it; because no man can logically say he don't care whether a wrong is voted up or voted down. . . . If [slavery] is a wrong, [Douglas] cannot say people have a right to do wrong" (*Debates*, p. 319; cf. p. 225). Douglas can maintain his view only if he treats the slaves as nothing more than property; but for Lincoln that contradicts the teaching of nature. For Douglas, the teaching is open to a vote, and the will of the majority is definitive, that being the essence of liberty and self-determination. Lincoln shows that this interpretation of democracy amounts to the doctrine that might makes right, and he opposes to that doctrine the assertions about natural right in Jefferson's Declaration. That is, as in the case of the abortion issue, there is no "neutral" ground in his debate.

22. John Locke, *A Letter Concerning Toleration*, ed. P. Romanell (Indianapolis: Bobbs-Merrill, 1985), p. 52.

23. My guess is that a number of the American founders did not believe that in their private capacities virtue depended on religious belief. That is, they thought that atheists and nonbelievers could be moral (see Jefferson's letter of 13 June 1814, to Thomas Law, in *Writings*, pp. 1335–39; cf. Plato's *Laws*, 908b). But in Platonic spirit, they tended to couch in religious vocabulary their public utterances about basic moral norms. My question here is whether a reasonably coherent, free, and peaceful community can afford to dispense with *all* "objective norms," whether stated in secular or religious vocabulary. This question has a practical side (the question of motivation to behave morally) and a theoretical side (the question as to the unavoidability of a Platonic "ascent" to first principles). The question just posed is directed to the latter. In recent years, the issue of "neutral" political principles has been discussed with reference to Rawls's *A Theory of Justice*. The issue of liberty or religious belief is a key one for Rawls, and his solution to the problem has been vigorously challenged by Thomas Nagel, Michael Sandel, Ronald Dworkin, Adina Schwartz, and Alasdair MacIntyre, among others. For an interesting defense of Rawls that denies the need for appeal to "objective political principles" to solve the problem of war (including religious war), see R. Rorty's "The Priority of Democracy to Philosophy," in *The Virginia Statute for Religious Freedom*, pp. 257–82.

Chapter Four

1. For the main points (body politic, constitutional consensus, avoidance of state of nature), see Locke's *Second Treatise*, sec. 97; and also secs. 89, 95–96, 98–99. Locke's account of the powers of government (specifically, the legislative, executive, and federative powers) is found in chapters 11 and 12 of that work. Locke's discussion of *express* consent, that is, the permanent or standing consent of citizen-members, occurs in sections 116–18; and his further account of it and contrast with *tacit* consent, that is, the temporary consent of visitors, etc., is found in sections 119–22. The idea of implied consent has been developed by A. J. Simmons in *Moral Principles and Political Obligation* (Princeton: Princeton University Press,

1979), pp. 88–91; and my discussion has drawn on his, with modifications.

2. The argument for this interpretation is developed in my paper "Hobbes and the Doctrine of Natural Rights: The Place of Consent in His Political Philosophy," *Western Political Quarterly* 33 (1980): 380–92. See also section 2 of this essay (which draws, at points verbatim, on this earlier paper). For another discussion that, in general, supports the reading I have given, see Carole Pateman, *The Problem of Political Obligation: A Critique of Liberal Theory* (Cambridge: Polity Press; in association with Basil Blackwell, Oxford, 1985), chap. 3. Hobbes's terms, "standing aside" and "laying down," and his discussion of them can be found in *Leviathan*, chap. 14, p. 85, and chap. 28, p. 203. Where specific page numbers are given in this essay, the reference is to the text edited by M. Oakeshott (Oxford: Basil Blackwell, 1957).

3. See David Hume, "Of the Original Contract," in *Social Contract,* ed. Ernest Barker (New York: Oxford University Press, 1947), pp. 150, 160; see also pp. 151, 161. I should add that the texts of Hobbes and Locke were known to Hume; Rousseau's work, of course, came after Hume's essay.

4. For the obligationist, the establishment of a strict obligation to obey the law is necessary for there to be rule-issuing authority (otherwise the entailment $R \rightarrow O$ fails). Some of the important obligationists in the history of political philosophy may well have regarded it as sufficient as well (as in $O \rightarrow R$). But whether obligation is being conceived as merely necessary or as both necessary and sufficient to rule-issuing authority, the point is that the justification of strict political obligation must be, given the program outlined here, an external one.

5. In this regard, Dalgarno distinguishes, as does Hobbes himself (chap. 14, p. 86), renunciation from transfer. For a transfer, unlike a renunciation, is always *to* someone in particular, intended or designated. (See M. T. Dalgarno, "Analysing Hobbes's Contract," *Proceedings of the Aristotelian Society* 76 [1975–76]: 209–226, esp. pp. 216–17; such transfers he calls "donational" [p. 220].) So far as I can tell, no contemporary writer conceives a renunciation of one's natural rights that is not explicitly, or in effect, a transfer of that which is renounced to the sovereign. See, for one example here, Clifford Orwin, who speaks of "abdicating" one's original or natural right "in favor of the sovereign" ("On the Sovereign Authorization," *Political Theory* 3 [1975]: 27, 29; and for another, T. E. Jessop, who refers to a "surrender" of natural liberty but counts such surrendered liberty as transferred to the ruler (see his *Thomas Hobbes* [London: Longmans, Green, 1960], p. 21).

6. See Morton Kaplan, "How Sovereign Is Hobbes' Sovereign?" *Western Political Quarterly* 9 (1956): 389–405, esp. pp. 397, 398.

7. See S. Beackon and A. Reeve, "The Benefits of Reasonable Conduct: The *Leviathan* Theory of Obligation," *Political Theory* 4 (1976): 425.

8. Here we touch upon a part, at least, of the classic question of the inalienability of natural rights. As I have tried to show, Hobbes holds, despite his talk of renunciation and transfer, that such rights are inalienable. The question of inalienability, as a general one and not just as regards Hobbes, has been the subject of several sophisticated recent studies. Note, in par-

ticular, B. A. Richards, "Inalienable Rights, Recent Criticism, and Old Doctrine," *Philosophy and Phenomenological Research* 29 (1969): 391–404; Marvin Schiller, "Are There Any Inalienable Rights?" *Ethics* 79, (1969): 309–15; Judith J. Thomson, *Self-Defense and Rights,* the 1976 Lindley Lecture (Lawrence: University of Kansas, Department of Philosophy, 1977); and Joel Feinberg, "Voluntary Euthanasia and the Inalienable Right to Life," *Philosophy and Public Affairs* 7 (1978): 93–123. The main issues are summarized in R. Martin and J. W. Nickel, "Recent Work on the Concept of Rights," *American Philosophical Quarterly* 17 (1980), sec. 3.

9. T. H. Green, *Lectures on the Principles of Political Obligation and Other Writings,* ed. Paul Harris and John Morrow. (Cambridge: Cambridge University Press, 1986), sec. 48, p. 44.

10. For a general account of Rawls's theory along these lines, see my book *Rawls and Rights* (Lawrence: University Press of Kansas, 1985). Some of Rawls's most recent papers seem to adhere, quite consciously, to the idea of a program of internal justification; note in particular his "Justice as Fairness: Political not Metaphysical," *Philosophy and Public Affairs,* 14 (1985): 223–51, and his "The Idea of an Overlapping Consensus," *Oxford Journal of Legal Studies* 7, no. 1 (1987): 1–25.

11. See here *Rawls and Rights,* chap. 2, sec. 2.

12. Even some of the more distinguished twentieth-century political philosophers have not grasped the implications of Hobbes's failure; they still hold onto one piece or another of his theory of sovereignty. See, for example, Charles H. McIlwain, *Constitutionalism: Ancient and Modern* rev. ed. (Ithaca: Cornell University Press, 1947), esp. pp. 141–146.

Chapter Five

1. A. V. S. de Reuck, "The Logic of Conflict," in *Conflict in World Society,* ed. M. H. Banks (Brighton: Harvester Press, 1984), pp. 96–111.

2. A. V. S. de Reuck, "A General Theory of International Relations: A Personal Synthesis," in *International Relations: A Handbook of Current Theory,* ed. M. Light and A. J. R. Groom (London, England; Francis Printer Publishers, 1985), pp. 100–10.

3. See P. Ekeh's *Social Exchange Theory* (London: Heinemann, 1974), which expounds the theory and contains an excellent bibliography.

4. W. C. Mitchell, *Sociological Analysis and Politics: The Theories of Talcott Parsons* (Englewood Cliffs, N.J.: Prentice-Hall, 1967). Talcott Parsons, *Politics and Social Structure* (New York: Free Press, 1969).

5. See de Reuck, "A Theory of International Relations."

6. P. M. Blau, *Exchange and Power in Social Life* (New York: John Wiley, 1964).

7. The four subsystems also correspond roughly with those considered by Talcott Parsons as functionally essential for the persistence of any social system (see note 4 above).

8. Strictly speaking, social relations are mapped onto a behavioral-cultural space, a multidimensional manifold whose dimensionality remains to be investigated. It is the map of social relations projected in three di-

mensions, which yields a cone, or on to two dimensions, which forms a set of concentric contours. The behavioral-cultural space might conveniently and comprehensively be described as social space, noting that in other contexts it may also be desirable to distinguish relations similarly mapped in political or economic spaces.

9. P. Bourdieu, *Distinction: A Social Critique of the Judgement of Taste*, trans. R. Nice. (London: Routledge and Kegan Paul, 1984).

10. A. V. S. de Reuck, "International Relations: A Theoretical Synthesis," *International Interactions* 14, no. 4 (1988): 321–41.

11. E. Leach, *Custom, Law, and Terrorist Violence* (Edinburgh: Edinburgh University Press, 1975).

12. Tort is an English legal concept. It defines breach of relations between private persons whereby one acquires a right of private legal action against the other for damages.

13. Mary Douglas, *Purity and Danger* (London: Routledge and Kegan Paul, 1966); *Natural Symbols* (London: Barrie and Rockliff, 1970); *In the Active Voice* (London: Routledge and Kegan Paul, 1982).

14. M. Douglas and A. Wildavsky, *Risk and Culture* (Berkeley: University of California Press, 1985).

Chapter Six

1. Thomas Hobbes, *Leviathan*, chap. 13. Where pages are given, I refer to the 1962 Oakeshott edition published by Collier.

2. According to Hobbes, two or more parties are in the state of nature relative to each other just in case there is no one person or group with sufficient power to "keep them all in awe"—to see to it that they honor their agreements with each other and otherwise conduct themselves in certain specific ways (chap. 13, pp. 98ff.). (For a valuable discussion, see Gregory Kavka, *Hobbesian Moral, and Political Theory* [Princeton: Princeton University Press, 1986], pp. 88 ff.). It is sometimes denied, for example by Charles Beitz, that the nations of the world are actually in (something like) "the state of nature" in this sense (see Beitz's *Political Theory and International Relations* [Princeton: Princeton University Press, 1979], pp. 27–50). However, as I try to show below, this claim rests on a failure to distinguish Hobbes's *definition* of the state of nature—or, rather, of what it is to be in the state of nature relative to another—from his assumptions about the characteristics of the parties he is imagining there and the circumstances he wishes to suppose they would confront.

3. See Jean Hampton, for example, *Hobbes and the Social Contract Tradition* (Cambridge: Cambridge University Press, 1986), pp. 58–79.

4. See, for example, Hobbes's intriguing remarks about the prisoner of war who has covenanted to pay a ransom if freed, and who is then freed (chap. 14, p. 110), as well as his very provocative remarks in his interchange with "the Fool" (chap. 15, pp. 114ff.). For a discussion of the implications of these passages for Hobbes's doctrine as a whole, see my "Reason and Right Conduct in Hobbes's *Leviathan*," *History of Philosophy Quarterly* 1, no. 3 (July 1984): 297–314. But see also, for rather different views about

their implications, Hampton, *Hobbes and the Social Contract Tradition,* pp. 58–79, and Kavka, *Hobbesian Moral, and Political Theory,* pp. 137–56.

5. For the best recent accounts, see the works cited in the preceding note by Hampton (pp. 189–255) and Kavka, (pp. 179–244).

6. I am assuming, of course, that the nations of the world are in fact in the state of nature, relative to each other, in Hobbes's sense (see note 2 above). As I have already indicated, this is because all it takes for two or more parties to be in the state of nature is that it be the case that there is no single person or group with the power to force these parties to do what he or she (or it) tells them to do. Our interest here, obviously, is in whether, given that the nations of the world are in the state of nature relative to each other, it is reasonable to suppose that the characteristics Hobbes attributes to the individuals he imagines in the state of nature are characteristics we can attribute to nations as well. Thus, even if we find reason to believe that certain of these characteristics do not apply to nations, we will have shown, not that nations are not in a Hobbesian state of nature, but, rather, that nations, in the state of nature or not, are in crucial respects different from individuals. Compare, for a very different view, Beitz, *Political Theory,* pp. 35–50.

7. See, for example, David Gauthier, *The Logic of Leviathan* (Oxford: Oxford University Press, 1969), pp. 207–12.

8. Here I follow Gauthier (ibid., p. 207).

9. Two possible objections to our account thus far should be mentioned briefly here. First, it might be said that Hobbes means more by "war," or "the state of war," than a willingness (in the state of nature) to do battle should one's interests appear to require it. Second, it might be said that, Hobbes's conception of war to one side, the prospect of an allegedly inevitable state of war is of interest only if the "war" in question includes both a willingness to do battle, should this be necessary, and a not insignificant probability that battle(s) will occur. (For this second objection I am indebted to Don Hubin.) And in fact I think both of these objections have some merit. As for the first, Hobbes is ambivalent, I believe, about whether to include a significant probability of actual fighting in his definition of the state of war (see especially, in this connection, Kavka, *Hobbesian Moral, and Political Philosophy,* pp. 87–92). And as for the second, it is clear, I think, that if a significant probability of actual battle is not included in our conception of being in a state of war, the evident undesirability of being in such a state is much diminished. Unfortunately, limits of space prevent me from pursuing these points here. It will have to suffice, for now, to note that it seems reasonable to suppose that under most circumstances, nations who are "at war" in Hobbes's (narrow) sense, at least in a Hobbesian state of nature, will in fact almost always be at a high risk of actually going to war, in the ordinary manner of speaking, especially if we suppose that some of these nations are either less than perfectly rational or are less than fully confident of the rationality of other nations.

10. What I assume here, simply, is that given our assumptions, it is unlikely we could bring it about—without some form of international sovereignty—that individual nations will be unwilling to go to war if they

believe their interests will thus be best served. This does not preclude the possibility, which we cannot study here, of attempting to ensure, without the creation of an international sovereign, that it will never be reasonable for a nation to believe that it can in fact best serve its national interests by going to war. Obviously, achieving this latter state of affairs is the principal aim of creating some form of sovereignty (both in the case of individuals and the creation of a state and in the case of nations and the creation of an international "superstate"). Thus, if this could be achieved without the creation of a sovereign, and without the creation of risks even more daunting than those the acceptance of a sovereign seems to entail, it might well be that this way of proceeding would be judged superior, by rational individuals and by rational states, to either acceptance of a suitable form of sovereignty or remaining in the state of nature.

11. Fear of actual warfare is "inevitable," of course, for rational parties in a Hobbesian state of nature, only if there is a non-zero probability of actual warfare occurring. But then, given the problem expressed by the second objection mentioned in note 9, it is conceivable that under certain circumstances a fear of actual warfare will not be rational in the state of nature, even though the parties there are "at war" in Hobbes's sense, since the latter's being true is consistent with its also being true that the relevant parties effectively face a non-zero probability of actual warfare. Obviously, under such (extremely unlikely) circumstances, the preceding point about the desirability of ending the state of war would be considerably less compelling.

12. Obviously, other interesting outcomes are possible. I ignore them here solely for the sake of brevity.

13. Here, of course, it might be argued that a more discriminating analysis would yield the conclusion that at least some of the smaller (or weaker) nations will rationally resist the call to support some form of international sovereignty on very much the same grounds as the larger (or stronger) nations. At least some of the former might plausibly be expected to believe that they are doing well enough, playing the larger nations off each other, to make a risk of accepting an international sovereign a bad bet. If so, then Hobbes's argument is even worse off than is suggested in the text.

14. I am indebted to Don Hubin for a number of extremely penetrating criticisms of an earlier version of this essay.

Chapter Seven

1. Thomas Hobbes, *De Cive*, chap. 1, see 12, p. 11, in *The English Works of Thomas Hobbes*, vol. 2, ed. W. Molesworth (London: John Bonn, 1840). Citations to this work in the text are from this edition.

2. Hobbes, *Leviathan*, chap. 6, par. 19 (pages 26–27 of 1651 edition). All quotations in this essay use the C. B. Macpherson edition (Harmondsworth: Penguin Books, 1968), which contains the 1651 pagination. I include paragraph numbers in the text to aid readers who use different editions.

3. Hobbes, *The Elements of Law*, part 1, chap. 14, sec. 4, p. 54, in the F. Tonnies edition (Cambridge: Cambridge University Press, 1928). All citations in the text are from this edition of the work.

4. Jean-Jacques Rousseau, *The Social Contract*, in *The Social Contract and Other Discourses*, trans. G. D. H. Cole (New York: Dutton, 1950), p. 222.

5. See Immanuel Kant, *Groundwork of the Metaphysics of Morals*, trans. H. Paton (New York: Harper and Row, 1964), chap. 2.

6. Note that the fear (or belief) that one has been degraded in any of these senses presupposes that one is drawn to (or accepts) a profoundly non-Kantian theory of individual worth that grants that human beings can be very unequal in value and status in virtue of some feature, action, or ability.

7. This is not always true; for example, parents can resent harms done to their children, but this is the kind of exception that proves a rule. Resentment only seems possible for the parents because they regard their children as somehow an extension of themselves. Resentment of crimes against others is possible only when one connects oneself in a significant way to these others.

8. Note that this analysis treats resentment as an emotion that is not heavily cognitive in character but that also furthers certain purposes we all have. See a general discussion of this point in note 11 below.

9. I am indebted to Philippa Foot who directed me to the competitive element in hatred and thereby sparked this line of analysis.

10. Robert Adams proposed this idea to me.

11. While rejecting the Sartrean idea that we have emotions for a purpose, William Lyons does endorse the idea that some emotions are useful to (or serve the purposes of) the person who has them (see his *Emotion* [Cambridge: Cambridge University Press, 1980], pp. 187ff.). Nonetheless, he argues that this is not true of the emotion of hatred, which he believes is not in any way useful or conducive to our basic interests. My analysis aims to show that while this may be true, those who hate do not believe it is true. I argue that hatred is regarded as personally useful insofar as it furthers a basic interest in the advancement of our own worth (what Hobbes calls the desire for glory). And surely the very fact that hatred is something we tend to enjoy, even relish on occasion (however much we may be ashamed of our enjoyment) is psychological proof that we take the emotion to be useful to us.

12. See Jeffrie Murphy and Jean Hampton, *Forgiveness and Mercy* (Cambridge: Cambridge University Press, 1988), chap. 2.

Chapter Eight

1. The complete quotation, from which I take snippets in my text, is as follows: "But though there had never been any time, wherein particular men were in a condition of war one against another; yet in all times, kings, and persons of sovereign authority, because of their independency, are in continual jealousies, and in the state and posture of gladiators; having their

weapons pointing, and their eyes fixed upon one another; that is, their forts, garrisons and guns upon the frontiers of their kingdoms; and continual spies upon their neighbours; which is a posture of war" (p. 115). I cite pages in the Molesworth edition, *The English Works of Thomas Hobbes* (London: John Bonn 1839–45). References to the *Leviathan* are all found in volume 3 of that edition. This practice whereby I provide more complete documentation in notes will be used throughout this essay. I add no discussion here of similar passages and their variations in Hobbes's other works.

2. All but the third of these first five axioms (as I call them) I take to be presuppositions governing the discussion of glory in *Leviathan*, chapter 13, especially in the important paragraph just before this deriving the third cause of quarrel, which is—a bit surprisingly—entitled "glory." "Again, men have no pleasure, but on the contrary a great deal of grief, in keeping company, where there is no power able to over-awe them all. For every man looketh that his companion should value him, at the same rate he sets upon himself: and upon all signs of contempt, or undervaluing, naturally endeavors, as far as he dares, (which amongst them that have no common power to keep them in quiet, is far enough to make them destroy each other), to extort a greater value from his contemners, by damage; and from others, by the example" (p. 114). Concerning the added notion of persons, see a later note.

3. Also in chapter 10, we read: "THE POWER *of a Man*, (to take it universally) is his present means, to obtain some future apparent good" (p. 74). "The manifestation of the value we set on another is that which is commonly called honouring, and dishonouring. To value a man at a high rate, is to *honour* him; at a low rate, is to *dishonour* him. But high, and low, in this case, is to be understood by comparison to the rate that each man setteth on himself" (p. 76).

4. In his discussion of the passions, Hobbes derives "glory" and correlate terms thus: "*Joy*, arising from imagination of a man's own power and ability is that exultation of the mind which is called GLORYING: which if grounded upon the experience of his own former actions, is the same with *confidence*: but if grounded on the flattery of others; or only supposed by himself for delight in the consequences of it, is called VAIN-GLORY: which name is properly given; because a well grounded confidence begetteth attempt; whereas the supposing of power does not, and is therefore rightly called *vain*" (p. 45). Note the implied reference to rating in his famous definition of, laughter: "*Sudden glory*, is the passion which maketh those *grimaces* called LAUGHTER; and is caused either by some sudden act of our own, that pleaseth them; or by the apprehension of some deformed thing in another, by comparison whereof they suddenly applaud themselves" (p. 46).

5. I think the contrary, though I shall here only assert it, with little attempt at justification. The other seven sayings I have offered as axiomatic are themselves a logistic representation of units, respective interconnections among them, indices, comparative measures, reduction to commensurable values, and demonstrations showing consequences of attempts to combine them into this or that scheme. Such natural content as conforms

to them derives (as does all natural science for Hobbes) from defining supposed internal or hidden causes and thence showing the appearances resulting on their interaction. Among these topics, many are familiar to us, since we are ourselves human beings. But—as in geometry—they are honed to a shape that can be called "idealized," and they apply only to so much of fact as conforms to them. Thus Hobbes's analysis of the natural condition of mankind demonstrates the impossibility of a figure constructed from units with the assumed propensities.

6. One "has no more to do in learning the laws of nature, but when weighing the actions of other men with his own, they seem too heavy, to put them into the other part of the balance, and his own in their place" (p. 144).

7. "*Equity,* and *laws* [are] an artificial *reason* and *will*" (p. x). This was intended presumably in a sense superlative to our usual meaning, whose more special application is incorporated under the tenth law of nature.

8. This emphasis on the strictly mathematical character of the laws of nature is heterodox and reminiscent of the "Taylor Thesis" in its Kantian tone. As with my quasi-geometrical understanding of the natural condition, I offer no defense here. But see my various papers on Hobbes's geometry, especially "Hobbes: The Art of the Geometricians," *Journal of the History of Philosophy* 18 (1980): 131–46.

9. "The public worth of a man, which is the Value set on him by the commonwealth, is that which men commonly called DIGNITY. And this value of him by the commonwealth, is understood, by offices of command, judicature, public employment; or by names and titles, introduced for distinction of such value" (p. 76).

10. A peculiar *natural* equality among individuals remains, for civil law constrains but does not abrogate the natural right (or liberty) of each to return to the condition of nature so far as he is able and thinks it needful or fit for preservation. Indeed, all alike are so enjoined, when peace fails, by the second part of the first law. However, no one will endeavor this breach without calculation of equal hopes, claims, or chances.

11. "So that in the nature of man, we find three principal causes of quarrel. First, competition; second, diffidence; thirdly, glory. The . . . third, [maketh men invade] for reputation . . . for trifles, as a word, a smile, a different opinion, and any other sign of undervalue, either direct in their persons, or by reflection in their kindred, their friends, their nation, their profession, or their name" (p. 114).

12. The first law of nature is: "*That every man, ought to endeavour peace, as far as he has hope of obtaining it; and when he cannot obtain it, that he may seek, and use all helps, and advantages of war*" (p. 117). I take equality in the broad sense of consent to mutual rating to be explicit in all of the remainder.

Even assemblies or individuals holding sovereign power remain bound by the laws of nature, though only God can bring them to account for their actions, and despite denial of God's existence. Being human, they are liable to the dangers in arousing indignation, and they are obliged by reason to seek peace and conform to equity. For arguments in support of this odd twist, consult chapter 31 of *Leviathan*, "Of the Kingdom of God by Nature."

13. That is, all are bound, *in foro interno:* "The laws of nature oblige *in foro interno;* that is to say, they bind to a desire they should take place: but *in foro externo;* that is, to the putting them in act, not always" (p. 145).

14. I so allow with much hedging, for I disagree. Intermediate federation, pacts, border agreements, treaties, continuing friendships, trade, cultural exchange, common enmities, relatively controlled skirmishes and threats, and specifically limited transactions are usual among nations. They are viable ways to avoid total sorts of warfare or perfected peace, each of which alternatives is barely thinkable. A constitution is no less than a compilation recognizing these; and if it is also more, it is augmented largely by its scope, by the geographical and temporal continuity attributed to it, and by the internal and personal allegiances it invokes. Nonetheless, such reciprocal government of competition and distrust depends in turn, as I think, on glory mutually acceptable. Hence I discuss this norm, along with those counsels and moral obligations that work against its infringement.

15. Such splendid attributions to natural persons are not lacking in Hobbes, although he does not supply as much psychiatric attention to inner quandaries as fascinates us today.

16. Hobbes insists on this title with his usual attention to etymology. In it he foreshadows an incipient theory of political representation. The text and definitions are found in the superb transitional chapter, chapter 16, which concludes part 1 of *Leviathan*. From this I supply the following definitive quotations: "A PERSON, is he *whose words are considered, either as his own, or as representing the words or actions of another man, or of any other thing to whom they are attributed, whether truly or by a fiction.* When they are considered as his own, then is he called a *natural person;* and when they are considered as representing the words and actions of another, then he is a *feigned* or *artificial person*" (p. 147). The word is Latin, "and from the stage hath been translated to any representer of speech and actions, as well in tribunals, as theatres" (p. 148).

17. Cf. the following quotations: "As much experience is *prudence;* so is much science *sapience*" (p. 37)" and "When the thoughts of a man, that has a design in hand, running over a multitude of things, observe how they conduce to that design; or what design they may conduce unto; . . . this wit of his is called PRUDENCE; and depends on much experience, and memory of the like things, and their consequences heretofore" (p. 60).

Chapter Nine

1. Thomas Hobbes, *Leviathan* (Indianapolis: Bobbs-Merrill, 1958), pp. 104–5.

2. For purposes of simplicity, I will assume that the significant consequences of human conduct do not extend across sovereign borders. To the extent that, in reality, such consequences do cross borders, the notion of sovereignty must be adjusted to accommodate that fact.

3. Nancy Rosenblum summarizes Bentham's view this way: "Where states exist and foreign relations are governed by the best interests of states,

the greatest chance for peace exists" (*Bentham's Theory of the Modern State* [Cambridge: Harvard University Press, 1978], p. 117).

4. Kant argued that human history was tending toward the creation of a worldwide federation of republics that would live in perpetual peace with one another. As Kant saw things, it was essential for all nation-states to have a republican form of government for this epoch of peace to emerge. See Immanuel Kant, *Perpetual Peace*, ed. L. W. Beck (Indianapolis: Bobbs-Merrill, 1957).

5. Alexis de Tocqueville, *Democracy in America* (New York: Random House, 1945), vol. 1, pp. 331–33.

6. Michael Doyle, "Kant, Liberal Legacies, and Foreign Affairs, Part 1," *Philosophy and Public Affairs* 12, no. 3 (Summer 1983): 213 (italics in original).

7. One could easily imagine a scenario where one liberal democratic state might rightfully challenge the legitimacy of another, even assuming the Lockean social contract idea that political legitimacy rests on the voluntary consent of the governed. Suppose that a group of persons murders those who rightfully inhabit a certain territory, settles in that territory, and sets up its own liberal democracy to govern over the land. Other liberal democracies should and could consistently declare that such a state has no legitimate authority over the territory that it claims. Although the state would have the consent of its people, it would be ruling a territory over which its people had no right to give it the authority to rule. The voluntary consent of the governed may be a necessary condition for political legitimacy, but it cannot be correctly regarded as a sufficient condition within anything like a Lockean framework. The governed must also have the right to give to their state authority over its particular territorial boundaries.

Hobbes does not run into this complication regarding territoriality because he thinks that in the state of nature everyone has a right to everything. I do no wrong in murdering you and occupying your territory, and so the government that I then establish cannot be tainted by my action.

It is crucial to the current mutual perception of legitimacy among existing liberal democracies that the question of whether their citizens have the right to give to their states authority over the territories which define their boundaries is not pressed too far. The history of coercion and violent aggression that led to the current territorial boundaries of liberal democracies tends to be ignored when discussions of political legitimacy arise. Moreover, when that history is addressed, the Lockean social contract line of argument tends to be displaced by a utilitarian one, to the effect that the territorial boundaries resulting from the coercion and aggression in question are morally justified because they have served the long-range good of humankind. The mutual perception of legitimacy among liberal democracies rests, then, partly on Lockean social contract ideology, partly on historical amnesia, and partly on utilitarian thinking.

8. Arthur Schopenhauer, *The Will to Live*, ed. Richard Taylor (New York: Frederick Ungar, 1962), pp. 284, 286.

9. David Johnston has recently argued that Hobbes's model of the rational egoist is not meant to be a descriptively correct portrait of humans.

Rather, it is intended as an account of what humans could become and of what they must become for states to have a secure foundation. Johnston thus sees the model as part of a prescriptive argument by Hobbes to the effect that cultural conditions ought to be changed so as to make men into rational egoists. Johnston suggests that Hobbes has another model of human beings, one that takes them to be essentially irrational, when he is concerned to portray with descriptive accuracy humans as they have been up to his day and age.

This interpretation of Hobbes is well worth considering, but it does have some problems. One is that it fails to take account of the fact that Hobbes uses the rational egoist model to help explain why humans act in the way they do. Explanations may not demand perfect descriptive accuracy from the models on which they rely. Yet the models must be at least approximations in the relevant respects of the reality to be explained, and there is no reason to think that Hobbes would deny such a connection between explanatory adequacy and descriptive accuracy.

A second, related problem with Johnston's interpretation is that it implies a cultural malleability to human nature that is inconsistent with the psychologism that is fundamental to Hobbes's method. If the fundamental principles of human psychology can change from one culture (or era) to the next—as Johnston's interpretation implies—then such principles cannot provide the basic explanations of human conduct. One would need to go deeper and ask why certain psychological principles hold at certain times or places and others in different times and places. Johnston's interpretation implies that what we now call societal (or sociological) facts are at the bottom of the explanations of human behavior. Hobbes's method, on the other hand, presumes that there are immutable facts of psychology that are the fundamental explanatory variables when it comes to accounting for human conduct. See David Johnston, The Rhetoric of Leviathan (Princeton: Princeton University Press, 1986).

Chapter Ten

1. Thomas Hobbes, Leviathan (Oxford: Clarendon Press, 1909), chap. 6, p. 48. All references in the text to this work are from this edition. Cf. also Hobbes's De Homine in William Molesworth's 1952 edition of the Latin Works, vol. 2, p. 103.

2. See James D. Hunt, Gandhi and the Nonconformists (New Delhi: Promilla and Co., 1986).

3. Gay Wilson Allen, William James: A Biography (New York: Viking Press, 1967), p. 451.

4. Ibid.

5. James's article appeared in the Youth's Companion.

6. Presidential address, American Philosophical Association, Columbia University, 28 Dec. 1906.

7. See Irving Kristol, Reflections of a Neoconservative (New Delhi: Allied Publishers, Indian Reprint, 1986), p. 82.

8. Young India (Ahmedabad), 5 Nov. 1931, p. 341.

9. *Harijan* (Ahmedabad), 5 Sept. 1936, p. 236.

10. For example, the *tamasik* (inert) stands in contrast to the *rajasik* (active) and the *sattvik* (the eternal/true/perfect—an untranslatable ontological category).

Chapter Eleven

1. I quote from C. B. Macpherson's edition of Hobbes's *Leviathan* (Baltimore: Penguin Books, 1985), pp. 239–40. All subsequent references to *Leviathan* are from this edition, and page references are given in the text.

Chapter Twelve

1. Georg Hegel, *Philosophy of Right* (1821), Preface.

2. This is a self-quotation from *Ueber die wissenschaftlichen Behandlungsarten des Naturrechts* (1802–3). In the addition to this paragraph, Hegel calls peace "ein Versumpfen der Menschen."

3. Immanuel Kant, *Critique of Judgment* (1790), Sec. 28.

4. "Ye shall love peace as a means to new wars—and the short peace more than the long. . . . war and courage have done more great things than charity." (Friedrich Nietzsche, *Thus Spake Zarathustra* [1883], chap. 1, "Of War and Warriors").

5. Heraclitus, frag. 53, in *Ancilla to the Pre-Socratic Philosophers*, ed. K. Freeman (Cambridge: Harvard University Press, 1971), p. 28.

6. Kant, *Idea for a Universal History* (1784), no. 9.

7. Kant, *An Old Question Raised Again: Is the Human Race Constantly Progressing?* (1798), no. 8.

8. Ibid., no. 9, note: "It is sweet, however, to imagine constitutions corresponding to the requirements of reason (particularly in a legal sense), but rash to propose them and culpable to incite the populace to abolish what presently exists. . . . However late it may be, to hope someday for the consummation of a political product, as it is envisaged here, is a sweet dream; but that it is being perpetually approached is not only *thinkable*, but so far as it is compatible with the moral law, an *obligation*, not of the citizens, but of the sovereign."

9. Ibid.

10. Ibid.

11. Augustine, *De Civitate Dei* 19, chaps. 10–14.

12. See Thomas Hobbes, *Leviathan* (1651), vol. 2, chap. 17: "And in all places where men have lived by small families, to rob and spoil one another, has been a trade, and so far from being reputed against the law of nature, that the greater spoils they gained, the greater was their honour."

13. Thomas Aquinas, *Summa Theologica* 2a2ae, quar. 29, art. 1, ad 1.

14. See the text quoted above, note 8.

15. This would correspond also to the biblical view, according to which peace is not only an eschatological promise, but "the normal condition of things" (W. Förster, in *Theologisches Wörterbuch Zum Neuen Testament*,

ed. Gerh. Kittel [Stuttgart: W. Kohlhammer, 1935], vol. 2, pp. 410ff., 416].

Chapter Thirteen

1. R. G. Collingwood, *The New Leviathan* (New York: Thomas Y. Crowell, 1971), p. 334.

2. Thomas Hobbes, *Leviathan,* ed. Michael Oakeshott, (Oxford: Basil Blackwell, 1957), p. 82.

3. See, for example, Kenneth Boulding, *Stable Peace* (Austin: University of Texas Press, 1978), p. 6. For other examples, see Juergen Dedring's *Recent Advances in Peace Research* (Beverley Hills: Sage Publications, 1976).

4. Wladyslaw Strozewski, "The Search of the Essence of Peace," *Dialectics and Humanism* 9, no. 4 (1982): 161.

5. George Lakoff and Mark Johnson, *Journal of Philosophy* 77, no. 8 (1980): 455.

6. Walter Isard, *Journal of Peace Science* 4, no. 1 (1979): 4.

7. This analysis is developed in detail, along with a number of concrete examples, in Dietrich Fischer's *Preventing War in the Nuclear Age* (Totowa, N.J.: Rowman and Allanheld, 1984).

8. For descriptions of three traditions of such peacemaking, see Roger Fisher and William Ury's *Getting to Yes* (New York: Penguin Books, 1981); Joan Bondurant's *The Conquest of Violence: The Gandhian Philosophy of Conflict* (Los Angeles: University of California Press, 1965); and Michael Sheeran's *Beyond Majority Rule* (Philadelphia: Yearly Meeting of the Religious Society of Friends, 1983).

Chapter Fourteen

1. Thomas Hobbes, *Leviathan,* ed. C. B. Macpherson (Harmondsworth: Penguin Books, 1968).

2. Alexander Hamilton, with James Madison and John Jay, *The Federalist Papers* (New York: New American Library, Mentor Books, 1961), p. 170.

3. Ibid., p. 171.

4. L. N. Tolstoy, *War and Peace,* trans. Rosemary Edmonds (Harmondsworth: Penguin Books, 1982), p. 920.

5. William Butler Yeats, "An Irish Airman Foresees His Death," in *The Collected Poems of W. B. Yeats* (New York: Macmillan, 1956), p. 133.

6. Hobbes, *Leviathan,* p. 187.

7. Virginia Woolf, *A Room of One's Own* (New York: Harcourt Brace Jovanovich, 1929), p. 110.

8. Alexis de Tocqueville, *Democracy in America,* vol. 1, trans. Henry Reeve, ed. Francis Bowen and Phillips Bradley (New York: Alfred A. Knopf, Vintage Books, 1945), p. 92.

9. George C. Beckwith, *The Peace Manual; or, War and Its Remedies* (Boston: American Peace Society, 1847), p. 123.

10. Tolstoy, *War and Peace,* p. 574.

Chapter Fifteen

1. This quotation is taken from a 1988 pamphlet from the Consortium on Peace Research, Education, and Development concerning their conference entitled "Toward Positive Peace."

2. Ronald Glossop, *Confronting War*, 2d ed. (Jefferson, N.C.: Mc-Farland, 1987), p. 10.

3. Ibid

4. Ibid., p. 11.

5. Ibid., p. 19.

6. This question assumes that war and peace are mutually exhaustive of the universe of states of relations between nations. But denying this assumption would actually make it easier to make a case for adopting a positive concept of peace.

7. Thomas Hobbes, *Leviathan* (Indianapolis: Bobbs-Merrill, 1958), p. 107.

8. Earlier versions of this essay were presented at a conference on "The Causes of Quarrel" at George Washington University in June 1987 and at a conference of Soviet and American philosophers on issues of war and peace in Moscow in August 1988, and I wish to thank the other participants for their comments. While completing this essay, I held a MacArthur Foundation grant, and the original version was written while I held a Rockefeller Fellowship at the Institute for Philosophy and Public Policy at the University of Maryland. For these sources of support, I also express my thanks.

Notes on the Contributors

Andrew Altman is associate professor of philosophy at the George Washington University. He is author of *Law, Politics, Philosophy: A Liberal Critique of Critical Legal Studies* (forthcoming).

Peter Caws is University Professor of Philosophy at the George Washington University. His chief current interests are in continental philosophy and the philosophy of the social sciences, and his most recent books are *Sartre* (1979 and 1984) and *Structuralism: The Art of the Intelligible* (1988).

Margaret Chatterjee is professor of philosophy at Delhi University, India, and currently director of the Indian Institute of Advanced Study at Shimla, India. She is the author of *Gandhi's Religious Thought* (1983) and *The Concept of Spirituality* (forthcoming). She has published widely on Gandhian studies and on the comparative study of religions in the Indian context.

R. Paul Churchill is associate professor of philosophy at the George Washington University. He is the author of *Becoming Logical: An Introduction to Logic* (1986). His articles on social and political philosophy cover such topics as nonviolent resistance, nuclear deterrence and just war theory, human rights, and normative issues in foreign policy.

Gray Cox is a visiting professor at College of the Atlantic and a leader of workshops on peacemaking and envisioning alternative world orders. He is author of *The Will at the Crossroads: A Reconstruction of Kant's Moral Philosophy* (1984) and *The Ways of Peace* (1986).

Anthony de Reuck recently retired as head of international relations at the University of Surrey, England. Among the thirty books he edited for the Ciba Foundation was *Conflict in Society* (1966). He was a founder member of the International Policy Foundation in London and of the Foundation for International Conciliation in Geneva. His current research includes the group dynamics of conflict resolution and the transactional theory of international relations. A recent article, "International Relations: A Theoretical Synthesis," appeared in *International Relations* (1988).

Daniel M. Farrell is professor of philosophy at the Ohio State University. He has published a number of papers on Hobbes's moral and political thought. He has also published a series of recent papers on the nature and

213

justification of deterrent violence, both in the institution of punishment and in international relations. He is currently completing a book on this latter topic, entitled *Deterrent Violence and the Principles of Self-Defense.*

Charles L. Griswold, Jr., is associate professor and acting chair of the philosophy department at Howard University. His book *Self-Knowledge in Plato's Phaedrus* (1986) won the American Philosophical Association's Franklin J. Matchette Prize in 1988. He is editor of *Platonic Writings, Platonic Readings* (1988), and author of numerous articles on ancient philosophy and political theory.

Jean Hampton is associate professor of philosophy at the University of California, Davis, and has taught at UCLA and the University of Pittsburgh. She is the author of *Hobbes and the Social Contract Tradition* (1986) and (with Jeffrie Murphy) *Forgiveness and Mercy* (1988). Her interests range over topics in political philosophy, ethics, and the philosophy of law.

Peter Henrici is University Professor of History of Philosophy at the Pontifical Gregorian University in Rome, and director of its Interdisciplinary Centre on Social Communication. Apart from his books *Hegel und Blondel* (1958) and *Aufbrüche christlichen Denkens* (1978), he has contributed to some thirty volumes and many scholarly journals. He is currently co-editor of the German edition of the international Catholic review *Communio.*

Charles Landesman is professor of philosophy at Hunter College and at the graduate school of the City University of New York. He is the author of *Discourse and Its Presuppositions* (1972) and *Color and Consciousness: An Essay in Metaphysics* (1989).

Steven Lee is associate professor of philosophy at Hobart and William Smith Colleges. His areas of interest are social philosophy, ethics, and philosophy of law. Recently, he has published several articles on the ethics of nuclear deterrence. He has co-edited *Nuclear Weapons and the Future of Humanity* (1986) and is currently writing a book entitled *Morality, Prudence, and Nuclear Weapons.*

Rex Martin is currently professor of philosophy at the University of Kansas in Lawrence. His fields of major interest are political and legal philosophy (in particular, rights) and the philosophy of history. He is the author of *Historical Explanation: Reenactment and Practical Inference* (1977) and *Rawls and Rights* (1985).

William Sacksteder is professor of philosophy at the University of Colorado in Boulder. He is the author of many papers on philosophy and on various topics of humanistic and literary interest. Many of these concern the philosophies of Thomas Hobbes and Benedict de Spinoza. He is also the compiler of *Hobbes Studies (1879–1979): A Bibliography,* and he participated actively in many events associated with the celebration of Hobbes's quatercentenary in 1988.

Index

Index

Determinism, in Hobbes, 19
Deterrence, 9, 21, 178, 191; costs of
war, 166; rejected by advocates of
nonviolence, 135
Diels, Hermann, and Walther Kranz,
Die Fragmente der Vorsokratiker,
193
Diffidence: alternative to, 136; as a
cause of quarrel in Hobbes, 3, 4, 8,
19, 24, 97, 101, 105, 131, 176; compared with distrust in Madison, 133;
etymology of, 3; as learned, 144; rests
on uncertainty, 137; rooted in desire
for power and safety, 24
Division of labor, a condition of *Gesellschaft,* 56
Dogma, meaninglessness of, for
Hobbes, 25
Douglas, Mary: *In the Active Voice,*
200; category of cosmology in, 63; on
individual and social thought, 51; on
microcultural climates, 60; *Natural
Symbols,* 200; on paradoxes of perception of risk, 62; *Purity and Danger,* 200
Douglas, Mary, and A. Wildavsky, *Risk
and Culture,* 200
Douglas, Stephen A., debates with Lin-
coln, 34, 196–97
Doyle, Michael: on absence of war be-
tween liberal democracies, 120;
"Kant, Liberal Legacies, and Foreign
Affairs," 207
Duke of York, grand old, 181
Durkheim, Emile. *See* Comte, Auguste
Dworkin, Ronald: criticism of Rawls,
197; on rights in strong sense, 29;
Taking Rights Seriously, 195

Economics, 18, 55; momentum in, 130;
and structure of human reciprocity,
52
Egoism: collective, acknowledged by
realists, 9; national, 15–16; permits
cooperation in Prisoner's Dilemma,
71–72; psychological, in Hobbes, 19,
64; in Schopenhauer, 123; of states,
15–16
Eichmann, Adolf, 174
Eisenhower, Dwight David, farewell
address, 179
Ekeh, P., *Social Exchange Theory,* 199
Electoral College, 112
Equality: before the law, 101; between
human beings by nature, in Hobbes,
7, 24, 144–45; as legal fiction, 103–
4; Madison's skepticism about, 28;
moral, as basis for separation of
church and state, 34; between na-

tions, 68–70, 109, 116; violation of,
actionable in principle, 102
Equity, in Hobbesian commonwealth,
100–101
Eristic, 165, 168
Eschatology, Christian, 155–56, 160
Evaluation, 83–86, 91, 93–94, 96, 101.
See also Grading; Rating; Value
Evenus, 173

Farrell, Daniel M., "Reason and Right
Conduct in Hobbes's *Leviathan,*"
200
Fear: of death, 24, 27, 34; as Hobbes's
twin, 3, 170; of insult, 88; of nuclear
holocaust, 3; may trigger return to
state of nature, 103
Federation: without sovereign, 4; nonviolence as ground of, 134
Federalism, 49
Federalist, The, 1, 4, 29, 33, 171, 179
Feinberg, Joel, "Voluntary Euthanasia
and the Inalienable Right to Life,"
199
Fischer, Dietrich, *Preventing War in
the Nuclear Age,* 210
Fisher, Roger, and William Ury, *Get-
ting to Yes,* 210
Foot, Philippa, 203
Force: monopoly of, by government, 36,
41–42, 73; settlement of disputes by,
71; threat of, by state, 142
Förster, W., *Theologisches Wörterbuch
zum Neuen Testament,* 209
Founders, American, 23–35 passim;
attitude to glory, 96; on military
appropriations, 171; philosophical
spirit of, 1
Franklin, Benjamin, 1
Frazier, Joe, 122
Freeman, Kathleen, *Ancilla to the Pre-
Socratic Philosophers,* 209
French Revolution, Kant's view of, 154
Freud, Sigmund, Oedipus complex, 164
Friends of the Earth, 62

Galilei, Galileo: chronological relation
to Hobbes, 50; *Dialogue Concerning
the Two Chief World Systems,* 163
Games, theory of, 71, 166
Gandhi, Mahatma (Mohandas Karamchand), 22, 89, 135–36; *An Autobiography,* 194; and James's moral
equivalent of war, 134, 138; *Non-
Violent Resistance,* 194; objection to
secrecy, 135; *satyagraha,* 132, 134;
work in South Africa, 130
Gauthier, David, *The Logic of Leviathan,* 201

217

Index

Gemeinschaft and *Gesellschaft*, 56–60, 135
Geometry, 205
George, Wally, 81, 96
Germany: and causes of World War II, 119; object of youthful hatred, 170
Glaucon, 26
Glory, 78–96 passim, 97–113 passim, 114–127 passim; alternatives to, 136, 146–47; as a cause of quarrel in Hobbes, 4, 8, 19, 24, 131, 144, 176; and pride, 4; and recognition, 24. *See also* Laughter
Glossop, Ronald: *Confronting War*, 211; criticism of positive conception of peace, 187–88
God: belief in, 24; his description of Leviathan, 8; American Founders' views of, 32–33; irresistible power of, 24–25; kingdom of, 25; laws of, 25; neglect of, by priesthood, 30; obedience to, 39; unwilling to cause death of sinner, 172; word of, 31
Grading, 83, 84
Gray, J. Glenn, *The Warriors*, 193
Green, T. H., *Lectures on the Principles of Political Obligation*, 199
Groups: characteristics of, 50–54; Hobbes's neglect of, 95; Mary Douglas's views on, 60–61
Guerilla warfare, 107

Hamilton, Alexander, on standing armies, 171, 179, 182
Hampton, Jean, *Hobbes and the Social Contract Tradition*, 200–201
Hatred, 88–95; in Schopenhauer, 123
Hegel, G.W.F.: cunning of reason, 153; dialectic of history, 164; *Philosophy of Right*, 150, 152; *Über die wissenschaftlichen Behandlungsarten des Naturrechts*, 209; universal history, 155; World Spirit, 152
Helvetius, Madison on, 195
Hempel, C. G., 165
Heraclitus, 14, 20, 150
Hiroshima, 13
Hobbes, Thomas: birth, 3, 139, 170; *De Cive*, 202; *De Homine*, 208; influence on Founders, 4; and image of leviathan, 8. *See also* Comte, Auguste
Hofstader, Richard, "The Founding Fathers: An Age of Realism," 195
Honor, 99; Hobbes's definition of, 204; as kind of power, 24; of nations, 95; titles of, 147
House of Representatives, 112

Hubin, Don, 201–2
Human nature, 139–48 passim, 181; in Aristotle, 173; causes of quarrel as reflections of, 24–25; descriptive and normative, 172–73; Hobbes on, 128–29, 131, 173; need for change in, 26; peace rooted in, 149
Hume, David, 39, 142
Hunt, James D., *Gandhi and the Nonconformists*, 208

Ideology: and philosophy, 1; and glory, 4; of liberal democracy, 120; national, 108–9, 112; as arousing passion, 140–41; and peace, 2–3, 188
Immortality, 27; of the soul, 24
India, conflict in, 23
Indignation, 87
Individualism, 2, 60, 62; Hobbesian, 26–29, 65–67, 95, 130
Injustice, impossible for government, 43–44
International relations, 64–77 passim; domestic analogy, 16–18
Internationals, 5
Iran, cultural exclusion in, 59
Irangate, 62
Ireland, conflict in, 4, 23
Israel, preemptive strike in 1967 war, 166
Isard, Walter, 166
I/T ratio, 178

Jainism, 135
James, Henry, 99
James, William: on moral equivalent of war, 132–35; on San Francisco earthquake, 133
Japan, absence of army in, economic benefits of this, 181
Jefferson, Thomas, 1, 29, 33–34; criticism of slavery, 29, 196; on morality and religion, 197; *Notes on the State of Virginia*, 196; opinion of Plato's *Republic*, 28; "Statute for Establishing Religious Freedom," 30, 32
Jessop, T. E., *Thomas Hobbes*, 198
Jews, in Shakespeare's *Merchant of Venice*, 125
Johnson, Mark. *See* Lakoff, George, and Mark Johnson
Johnson, Samuel, on patrons, 53
Johnston, David, *The Rhetoric of Leviathan*, 207–8
Justice: and contracts, in Hobbes, 27; as culturally relative, 51; and peace, 185; in Plato's *Republic*, 26

218

Index

Just war doctrine, 17, 188; rejected by advocates of nonviolence, 135

Kant, Immanuel, 120, 156; *An Old Question Raised Again: Is the Human Race Continually Progressing?* 209; categorical imperative, 172; *Critique of Judgment*, 150; federation of nations, 152; *Groundwork of the Metaphysics of Morals*, 203; *Idea for a Universal History*, 209; on individual worth, 82–83; "finality of Nature," 160; *Perpetual Peace*, 154–55; philosophy of history, 153; *Religion within the Limits of Reason Alone*, 153

Kaplan, Morton, "How Sovereign Is Hobbes's Sovereign?" 198

Kavka, Gregory, *Hobbesian Moral and Political Theory*, 200–201

Kennan, George, as political realist, 9, 15

Kierkegaard, Søren, on collective agency, 173

King, Martin Luther, Jr., 22, 89, 130; *A Testament of Hope*, 194

Kipling, Rudyard, "lesser breeds without the law," 58

Kissinger, Henry, influenced by Westphalian system, 18

Kristol, Irving, *Reflections of a Neoconservative*, 208

Ku Klux Klan, 35

Kutuzov, Prince Mikhail Illiaronovich, 20

Lakoff, George, and Mark Johnson, argument as war, 165

Latin America, Tocqueville on democracy in, 120

Laughter, as sudden glory, in Hobbes, 204

Law, 52; civil actions at, 58; equality before, 101; international, 13, 129; moral logic of, 103–4; obligation to obey, 37–41, 48; sacred elements in, 57

Law of nature, 100, 103, 109; medieval view, 160

Law, Thomas, letter of Jefferson to, 197

Leach, Edmund, *Custom, Law, and Terrorist Violence*, 59

League of Nations, U.S. discomfort with, 5

Lebanon, conflict in, 23

Legitimation: by consent of the governed, 120, 207; mutually acknowledged, 121; object of *Leviathan*, 131

Leibniz, G. W., 50

Levellers, Hobbes associated with, 95–96

Leviathan, in book of Job, 8–9

Liberty: as absence of external impediments, 27; danger to established religion, 31; not license, 29; moral values as basis for, 35; theological grounding of, in Founders, 33

Light, M., and A.J.R. Groom, *International Relations: A Handbook of Current Theory*, 199

Lincoln, Abraham, debates with Douglas, 34, 196–97

Little, David, "Religion and Civil Virtue in America," 196

Locke, John, 33–34; consent of the governed, 207; contract theory of obligation, 37–39; contrasted with Hobbes, 48–49; influence on Founders, 1, 24; *Letter Concerning Toleration*, 30; *Second Treatise of Government*, 195; on sovereign abuse of power, 27

London, German bombing of, 5

Love: object of human striving, 53; moral, 89

Lutoslawski, Wincenty, correspondence with William James, 133

Lyons, William, *Emotion*, 203

Mace, George, *Locke, Hobbes, and the Federalist Papers*, 193

Machiavelli, Niccolo: influence on realism, 15; *The Prince*, 153, 160

McIlwain, Charles H., *Constitutionalism: Ancient and Modern*, 199

Macintyre, Alasdair, criticism of Rawls, 197

Madison, James, 33–34; criticism of Frances Wright, 28; doctrine derived from Hobbes, 4; *Federalist* no. 51, 29; *Federalist* nos. 55 and 76, 196; on human nature, 133–34, 138; "Memorial and Remonstrance against Religious Assessments," 30, 32; on Robert Owen, 28, 195; on slavery, 195; "Universal Peace," 29

Mafia, meaning of term, 2

Malice, a neglected aspect of human nature, 123–27

Market, 33, 62; as model for structure of social exchange, 52, 54–55, 86

Martin, Rex: "Hobbes and the Doctrine of Natural Rights," 198; *Rawls and Rights*, 199

Martin, Rex, and J. W. Nickel, "Recent Work on the Concept of Rights," 199

219

Index

Rorty, Richard, "The Priority of Democracy to Philosophy," 197
Rosenberg, Jay F., *The Practice of Philosophy*, 193
Rousseau, Jean-Jacques, 6, 39, 137; "Paix perpetuelle," Madison's criticism of, 29; on passions as socially learned, 79–80, 86; *Social Contract*, 203; on social contract as reason itself, 153; thought of, systematized by Kant, 153
Rule(s): issuance of and obedience to, 36, 40–41, 48, 136, 143; moral, 87; under law, 103
Roman Catholicism, and cultural polarization in Belfast, 54–55
Rosenblum, Nancy, *Bentham's Theory of the Modern State*, 206–7
Runciman, W. G., 56

Sacksteder, William, "Hobbes: The Art of the Geometricians," 205
Sampson, R. V., *The Discovery of Peace*, 194
Sandel, Michael, criticism of Rawls, 197
Sartre, Jean-Paul: emotions as purposive, 203; "hell is other people," 164; responsibility of writer, 5
Saul, King, 92–94
Schiller, Marvin, "Are There Any Inalienable Rights?" 199
Schopenhauer, Arthur: on human malice, 123–25; *The Will to Live*, 207
Schwartz, Adina, criticism of Rawls, 197
Science: emergence of, in Hobbes's time, 50; progress in, as amplifying military power, 141
Secrecy, Gandhi's objections to, 135
Self-deception, in pursuit of glory, 86
Self-defense, as justifying use of force, 22
Self-interest, 33; challenged as basis of ethics, 16; disrupted by malice, 126; Hobbesian, 29; inadequate as basis of social structure, 52; Madison on, 30; national, 17, 121; power of, acknowledged by realists, 9; rational regard for, in Hobbes and Hampton, 115
Self-observation, as basis of Hobbes's views, 147
Self-worth, 84, 85, 126
Senate, U.S., 112
Separation of church and state, 30–32, 34
Separation of powers, 49
Shakespeare, William, *The Merchant of Venice*, 124–26

Sharp, Gene, *The Politics of Non-Violent Action*, 21–22
Sheehan, Michael, *Beyond Majority Rule*, 210
Shylock, 124–26
Simmons, A. J., *Moral Principles and Political Obligation*, 197
Slavery: Jefferson on, 29; Madison to Frances Wright on, 28; and moral worth, 83
Smith, Adam: influence on Founders, 24; *Wealth of Nations*, 31
Social contract, 27; as basis of rights of sovereign, 147
Sociology, 13, 50
Socrates, 25, 26
Sovereign: absence of in Constitution, 4; conflict of with religious authorities, 25; Hobbesian, 8, 10, 26, 64–67, 78, 80, 101, 106, 117, 126, 140–42, 189; international, 65–77 passim, 115, 117, 190–91; nuclear weapons as equivalent to, 8–9; rights of, 147; Westphalian concept of, 17
Sovereignty, 36–49 passim; of nation-states, 118–19
Soviet Union, 17, 116, 187, 189; consul's toast to peace, 2
Speech, concept of, in Hobbes, 111, 139
State(s): choice between anarchy and, 143; definition of, 36; international, 73; may cease to be major actors, 22; modern, in Hegel, 151; proliferation of small, 2; Westphalian concept of, 17. *See also* Nation-state; Separation of church and state
State Department, 5
State of nature: characteristics of, 147, 171; Hobbesian, 7, 15–17, 19, 43–47, 64–77, 116, 143–44, 146, 148, 164, 190; international, 64–77, 105, 118, 119, 190; Rousseau on, 79
Strauss, Leo, *The Political Philosophy of Hobbes*, 194–95
Strozewski, Wladyslaw: "The Search for the Essence of Peace," 210; on uncertain value of peace, 163–64
Structural analysis, in Mary Douglas, 62
Structure: microsocial, 60; social, 51–55; sociocultural, 63
Summum bonum: denied by Hobbes, 24; need for, 33
Summum malum. See Death
Superstate, 73, 75–77
Switzerland, defensive strategy in World War II, 166
Systems analysis, 13

Index

Technology: confidence in, 62; of death, 173; Gandhi's critique of, 135; momentum of advances in, 130; nuclear as dominant and limiting case, 178; of power, 117; progress in, as amplifying military power, 141

Terrorism, 174, 178; threat of, 137

Theology: and separation of church and state, 30–31; starting point of philosophy, in Hegel, 152

Third World, 57, 59

Thirty Years' War, its impact on Hobbes, 17

Thomson, Judith J., *Self-Defense and Rights*, 199

Thrasymachus: and foundations of realism, 15; represents Hobbes's standpoint in the *Republic*, 25

Thucydides, on the Athenian generals, 15

Tocqueville, Alexis de: *Democracy in America*, 207; on democracy in South America and Mexico, 120; on instability of power in U.S., 177

Tolerance: and Founders, 33; Locke on, 30; paradox of, 34

Tolstoy, Leo (Count Lev Nikolayevich), 22, 174; on Hobbes, 21; on virtuous idleness of military life, 180; *War and Peace*, 20, 171, 180

Tort, 200; distinguished from crime, 58

Trade, influence on political development, 18

Tyranny: contrasted with monarchy, 139–40; Hobbes's dismissal of as "monarchy misliked" no longer acceptable, 141; international, 75

Ulster, terrorism in, 59

UNESCO, U.S. discomfort with, 5

United States, 17, 35, 179, 187, 189; absence of religious warfare in, 23; and Native American nations, 116; as "number 1," 81, 95–96; discrimination in, 59; as possible exemplar of peaceful society, 181–82; vainglory of, 95; without army on night of 2 June 1784, 181. *See also* Constitution of the United States

Utility, utilitarian, 27, 29–30, 39–40

Utopianism: dangers of, 160; in Plato, 28

Vainglory: defined by Hobbes, 79, 80; as source of conflict, 94–96; as substitute for glory, 99

Value: of individual, in Hobbes, 28; objective knowledge as free from, 165; personal, 82–87, 94. *See also* Evaluation

Versailles, Treaty of, 119

Veterans' Affairs, Department of, 179

Vienna, Congress of, 18

Vietnam War: Memorial, 173; protest against, 179

Violence, 71, 114–127 passim; anomic, 59; Hannah Arendt on, 22; between groups, proportional to sociocultural distance, 57; etymology of, 172; Hobbes on, 19; Hobbesian theory of human worth as conducive to, 86; meaning of, 172; as means of solving conflict, 2, 94–96; prompted by insult, 80; renunciation of, 42–43; restraint of, 8; right to, in sovereign and citizen, 46; Tolstoy on, 21; Simone Weil on, 22; women as targets of, 83. *See also* Nonviolence

Virgil, not enough reason in arms, 182

Waltz, Kenneth, as political realist, 15

War: absence of between liberal democracies, 120; of all against all, not inevitable, 147–48; benefits of, in Hegel, 150; defensive, rarity of, 180; definition of, 171; etymology of, 177; as father of all, in Heraclitus, 150; not possible without peace, in Augustine, 158; "men bent on," in Augustine, 156; religious, 23–25, 180; of some against others, 129; sublimity of, in Kant, 150. *See also* Nuclear war

War Department, 181

Weber, Max, and ethics of responsibility and perfection, 132. *See also* Comte, Auguste

Weil, Simone: study of violence, 22; "The Iliad, or The Poem of Force," 194

Westphalia(n): model, as cause of World War I and influence on Henry Kissinger, 18; Peace of, as foundation of modern state system, 17; system, dominance and decline of, 17–18

White House, 5

Williams, Roger, influence on Jefferson, 32

Women, as targets of violence, 83

Woods, Martin T., and Robert Buckenmeyer, *The Morality of Peace and War*, 194

Woolf, Virginia: on the importance of taking sides, 176; *A Room of One's Own*, 210

World Court, U.S. discomfort with, 5

World federalists, 16

223